FINANCIAL ACCOUNTING BASICS:
Accounting Data Processing Cycle and Accounting for a Merchandising Firm

Ralph E. Smith
Professor of Accounting
School of Accountancy
Arizona State University

Rick Birney
Director of Instructional Technology
College of Business
Arizona State University

McGraw-Hill, Inc.

New York   St. Louis   San Francisco   Auckland   Bogotá
Caracas   Lisbon   Madrid   Mexico City   Milan   Montreal   New Delhi
San Juan   Singapore   Sydney   Tokyo   Toronto

FINANCIAL ACCOUNTING BASICS:
Accounting Data Processing Cycle and
Accounting for a Merchandising Firm

Copyright © 1995 by McGraw-Hill, Inc. All rights reserved.
Printed in the United States of America. Except as permitted
under the United States Copyright Act of 1976, no part of this
publication may be reproduced or distributed in any form or by
any means, or stored in a data base or retrieval system, without
the prior written permission of the publisher.

 This book is printed on recycled paper
containing 10% postconsumer waste.

1 2 3 4 5 6 7 8 9 0 SEM SEM 9 0 9 8 7 6 5 4

ISBN 0-07-059232-2

The editor was Alan Sachs;
the production supervisor was Denise L. Puryear.
Semline, Inc., was printer and binder.

About the Authors

Ralph E. Smith, PhD, CPA, is a Professor of Accountancy at Arizona State University where he has taught graduate and undergraduate courses and seminars in financial accounting. He has also been active in developing and conducting a number of professional development seminars. Professor Smith received his PhD in accounting from the University of Kansas. He is a member of the American Accounting Association and the American Institute of Certified Public Accountants. He has served on several committees of the American Accounting Association and also holds membership in Beta Gamma Sigma and Beta Alpha Psi. He has written a number of articles on financial accounting and related business topics that have been published in *The Accounting Review,* the *Journal of Accountancy,* the *Journal of Financial and Quantitative Analysis,* and other professional and academic journals.

Rick Birney is the Director of Instructional Technology for the College of Business at Arizona State University. His primary responsibilities include the integration of technology into the business curriculum. Mr. Birney teaches upper-division courses in Instructional Courseware Design, Computer Based Training and Accounting Authoring Software. In addition, he holds faculty and staff workshops on classroom presentation and multi-media development techniques. He worked over 20 years in engineering management, systems applications and training for Hughes Aircraft, Pioneer Corporation of America and Kaiser Aerospace and Electronics. Mr. Birney has published articles in various publications, including the *IEEE Journal.* He has been a featured presenter at numerous American Accounting Association and American Institute of Certified Public Accountants workshops and conferences. He serves on the board of directors for the new Center for Educational Technology in Accounting at the University of North Texas.

FINANCIAL ACCOUNTING BASICS:
ACCOUNTING DATA PROCESSING CYCLE AND ACCOUNTING FOR A MERCHANDISING FIRM

CONTENTS

PREFACE

The objective of this manual is to introduce you to the procedural aspects of accounting. It is designed to accompany *The Introductory Accounting Lab: An Interactive Tutorial* which is available from McGraw-Hill, Inc. The contents of this manual introduces the accounting procedures that are considered generally accepted accounting practices in this country. As you perform your assignments you must keep this in mind. Although the manual and companion courseware focus on accounting rules and procedures, you must understand, apply, and be able to explain the rules and procedures. As you read this manual and do the computer assignments, you should strive to understand each procedure and its relationship to accounting information.

The computer courseware is used to simulate a manual accounting system. When performing your computer assignments you will be maintaining accounting records for fictional clients. Using the computer software allows you to practice accounting procedures and receive immediate feedback. However, the accounting topics are introduced in this manual. You should read and study the related chapter in this accounting manual first, then complete the computer assignments. To test your understanding of the topics covered in the manual, a practice activity is provided after each major section. Answers to these activities are provided at the end of the chapter.

The topics covered in this manual and the interactive software will introduce you to the accounting cycle and accounting for a merchandising firm. There are 12 chapters:

Chapter	1	The Accounting Equation
Chapter	2	Analyzing Business Transactions
Chapter	3	Transaction Analysis: Debit and Credit Rules
Chapter	4	Recording Transactions in the General Journal and Posting to the General Ledger
Chapter	5	Accrual Basis and Cash Basis Methods of Accounting
Chapter	6	Preparing Adjusting Entries
Chapter	7	Preparation of a Worksheet and Completion of the Accounting Data Processing Cycle-Service Firm
Chapter	8	An Alternative Method of Recording Deferrals and Preparing Reversing Entries
Chapter	9	Accounting for Merchandising Operations-Perpetual Inventory System
Chapter	10	Accounting for Merchandising Operations-Periodic Inventory System
Chapter	11	Subsidiary Ledgers and Special Journals
Chapter	12	Inventory Cost Flow Methods

We are indebted to a number of individuals for their contributions to the development of this manual. In particular, Jack Helmkamp, Indiana University, and Roy Imdieke, Arizona State University, were instrumental in the writing of a textbook from which this material was adapted.

Ralph E. Smith
Rick Birney

CHAPTER 1

The Accounting Equation

Contents

- Chapter Overview and Objectives
- The Accounting Process
- Entity Assumption
- Assets
- Liabilities
- Owners' Equity
- Accounting Equation
- Communicating Accounting Information through Financial Statements
- External Financial Statements -- An Overview

CHAPTER OVERVIEW AND OBJECTIVES

This chapter presents an overview of the purpose of accounting and a review of the financial statements. When you have completed this chapter, you will be able to:

1. Explain the accounting process.
2. Recognize typical transactions entered into by a business.
3. Describe the relevance of the entity assumption.
4. Define what the accountant means by the terms assets, liabilities, and owners' equity.
5. Identify two forms of the accounting equation and its basic components.
6. Describe the functions and the content of the balance sheet, income statement, and retained earnings statement.
7. Define each of the following terms:

Accounting	Owners' equity	Revenues
Entity assumption	Capital stock	Expenses
Asset	External statements	Gains
Cost principle	Fiscal year	Losses
Liability	Interim reports	Retained earnings statement
Creditors	Income statement	Balance sheet

Accounting is often thought of as an information processing system because it is a means of communication that involves a flow of information about a business. The accounting information is intended to be useful in making economic decisions. In this chapter, you will see that accounting information is accumulated in terms of an accounting model called the accounting equation. It will be shown that the accounting model consists of three elements: assets, liabilities, and owners' equity. As we develop the procedural aspects of accounting, you will see that there are subelements of owners' equity. Financial statements are then reviewed in the context of the accounting model.

THE ACCOUNTING PROCESS

Accounting has developed to at least partially satisfy the need for information by various user groups. It is an information system that is designed to collect and report particular kinds of financial information about an organization to interested parties. Thus, accounting is a service activity producing information. The accounting process does not result in the production and sale of a tangible product such as a desk or computer.

Accounting can be defined as the process of recording and communicating financial information that is intended to be useful in making economic decisions. The accounting process consists of the following:

1. Recording financial information: A business engages in a continuous series of economic activity. Accountants observe this activity and identify those events that can be measured in monetary terms and that meet the criteria for being entered in the accounting records. Money serves as a common measurement for expressing each transaction. Events that are measured in money and recorded in the accounting records are called transactions. The purchase of equipment for $10,000 cash is an example of a transaction. Borrowing money from a bank is another example. The recording phase consists of: (1) observing business activity, (2) identifying recordable information, (3) measuring the transaction in monetary terms, and (4) entering the information in the accounting records.

2. Communicating financial data: The effects of the recorded transactions on the reporting entity are communicated to statement users through financial statements and special reports. To make the accounting data more useful in making decisions, the effects of possibly thousands of transactions are classified and summarized. For example, all transactions involving the sale of merchandise can be grouped into one total sales figure, all transactions involving cash can be grouped into one single net cash figure, and a total amount is reported for amounts due from customers rather than listing the amount due from each individual customer. This information is then classified into useful groups or categories. For example, debts of a service or retailing firm are usually classified into two categories: those due within one year and those due beyond a one-year period. The financial statements and special reports usually

summarize the effects of all business transactions occurring during some period of time such as a month, a quarter, or a year.

In summary, the function of the accounting process is to record and communicate economic data about an organization to interested parties for decision making.

An *accounting system* consists of the business forms, records, procedures, management policies and controls, and data-processing methods used to transform economic data into useful information. The accounting system may take the form of a simple manual system or a sophisticated computerized system. Regardless of its form, the dual purpose of any accounting system is to keep track of a firm's business transactions and report their effects on its operating performance and financial position.

In this course you will be exposed to accounting procedures used in a manual accounting system. In even relatively small businesses, much of the routine accounting work has become highly automated. An accountant, however, must have a thorough understanding of the underlying accounting framework. Such knowledge is more easily acquired by studying and actually performing the procedures.

ENTITY ASSUMPTION

If the transactions of a business are to be recorded, summarized, and reported in the financial statements, the accountant must be able to identify clearly the boundaries of the unit for which accounting records are maintained. Under the **entity assumption**, a business is considered a separate entity distinguishable from its owners, creditors, employees, and all other entities. For example, a retail clothing store is a separate accounting entity from the owners of the business. If the clothing store borrows money from a bank, the bank is another accounting entity. The clothing store is considered an entity separate and apart from its employees. A separate set of accounting records is maintained for each business, and the prepared financial statements represent the financial position and results of operations of that business only.

ASSETS

A business needs resources such as money, supplies, equipment, and furniture to start and to operate. In accounting, resources owned by a business that have money value are called **assets**. Assets may take different forms, and the type owned by a business depends on the nature of the business. They may be tangible or intangible in form. A tangible asset has a physical existence (e.g., land, buildings, furniture, and equipment). An intangible asset is characterized by legal claims or rights (e.g., accounts receivable, patent rights, or rights to use leased assets). Assets have economic value because they contain service benefits that can be used in future operations or sold to another entity.

Under the **cost principle** in accounting, business transactions are entered in the accounting system at cost. Cost assigned to an asset includes its purchase price, sales tax, freight, and any other cost needed to prepare the asset for sale or for its intended use. Subsequent increases in value are not recorded until that item is involved in a transaction with another entity. In other words, accountants do not enter increases in value in the accounting records until there is a transaction to confirm, or provide evidence of, the increase in value.

A business obtains its assets to operate from two sources: investment by individuals in the business or from other entities. The investment by the owners is called owners' equity. A company may also acquire assets from a variety of financing sources such as a bank or from buying goods or services on credit. Debts owed by the business are called liabilities.

The first transaction entered in the accounting records is the investment by the owners. Although investments may take various forms (such as cash, land, or equipment), the initial investment is frequently cash. Individuals invest in a business in anticipation of eventually being able to withdraw assets in excess of those invested. In other words, they expect that the firm will operate at a profit and that they will receive a return on their investment. The mere holding of cash invested by the owners will not provide a return. Cash is useful as a medium of exchange or as a measure of value, but essentially it is a nonproductive asset. One of the primary reasons for making a cash investment is to use the cash to purchase productive assets, such as equipment, buildings, and inventory for sale to its customers. These assets may be purchased with cash or financed on credit. The noncash assets are used to provide goods or services for customers in exchange for cash or the customer's promise to pay cash in the future. The cash received is then used to pay expenses, or to pay debts owed, retained in the business for expansion, or distributed to the owners as a return on their investment.

PRACTICE ACTIVITY 1-1

1. The owner of Bill's Towing Service purchased a tow truck. The truck had an invoice price of $28,600, but the dealer and Bill agree to a purchase price of $27,400 plus freight cost of $780. Bill would have been willing to pay $28,400 including the freight. In addition, Bill must pay a sales tax of $1,680. Compute the cost of the tow truck to be recorded on the books of Bill's Towing Service. $_____

2. A firm was offered $120,000 for land that it had purchased for $70,000 ten years ago. What amount should the land be recorded at on the firm's records? $_____
    This is an example of applying the _____ _____.

3. A company that includes the personal assets of a stockholder in its records is violating the _____ _____.

LIABILITIES

Liabilities are the debts owed by a business. The person or entity to whom the debt is owed is called a **creditor**. Liabilities include amounts owed to suppliers for goods or services purchased on credit (accounts payable), amounts borrowed from banks or other lenders (notes payable), amounts owed to employees for salaries and wages, and amounts owed to tax agencies for taxes incurred but not yet paid. Liabilities may also be thought of as creditors' claims against the assets of the business.

Liabilities also include amounts received in advance from customers for goods or services to be provided by the firm. Such an advance is reported as a liability, called unearned revenue, because the cash has been received and the firm has an obligation to provide the goods or services. Examples include the collection of the current month's rent at the beginning of the month from a tenant and cash received for an airline ticket for a flight to be flown next month. The liability is satisfied as the tenant uses the building and when the traveler takes the flight. Such liabilities do not represent monetary debt, but the firm is liable to provide goods or perform services. Thus, cancellation of a liability requires either an outlay of assets (generally cash) or the performance of future services.

PRACTICE ACTIVITY 1-2

Listed below are items normally found in the accounting records of a business. Indicate whether the item is an asset or a liability by placing a check mark in the proper box.

Item	Asset	Liability
Accounts Payable	___	___
Office Supplies	___	___
Building	___	___
Notes Payable	___	___
Land	___	___
Salaries Payable	___	___
Patent	___	___
Cash received by a publisher for a three-year magazine subscription	___	___

OWNERS' EQUITY

Owners' equity is the owners' interest in the assets of the business. Owners' equity for a corporation is often referred to as stockholders' equity. Owners' equity may be thought of as the owners' claims against the assets. Creditors' claims take legal precedence over owners' claims; if the assets are sold, creditors must be paid before the claims of the owners are recognized. Thus, owners have a claim to the assets remaining after creditors are satisfied, called a residual claim. The claims of the owners are subdivided into two parts: paid-in capital and retained earnings.

1. Paid-in capital (direct investment by the owners)-- Owners' equity is increased when the owners of the business invest cash or other assets in the entity. This may be either the initial investment made at the time of formation to start the business or additional investments made at a later date. When stockholders invest in a corporation, they are given shares of the corporation's stock as evidence of their ownership. A corporation may be authorized to issue two basic types of stock, *preferred and common*. The term **capital stock** refers to all classes of ownership shares, both preferred and common, issued by a corporation. In this course, we will assume that one type of stock is issued, *common stock. S*ince common stock is the only class of stock purchased by the stockholders from the company, we may also use the term capital stock.

2. Retained earnings--Retained earnings represent the interest of the stockholders in the accumulated earnings that have not yet been distributed to them. This claim of the owners can be explained as follows. Revenues are the inflows of assets to an entity resulting from the sale and delivery of goods or the rendering of services. That is, when a business either sells goods or provides services, it receives an asset from its customers, usually cash or the customer's promise to pay in the future (an account receivable). Revenues are measured by the amount of cash or other assets received. Expenses are the cost of assets used in the operations of the business to sell the goods or render the services. (An expense may result in an increase in a liability, but for simplicity, this possibility is ignored for now.)

Net income, which is sometimes referred to as *earnings* or *profit*, for the period is the excess of revenues over expenses. (Gains and losses are also included in net income but are defined in a later section of this chapter.) Since revenues increase assets and expenses decrease assets, assets are increased if the business operates at a net income. Since the owners have the residual interest in the firm, net income also represents an increase in owners' equity. That is, the increase in assets that result from profitable operations belongs to the company's owners. Conversely, a net loss decreases assets and owners' equity. Owners' equity is also decreased by paying dividends to the owners. A dividend is a distribution of assets, usually cash, to the stockholders. Such a distribution is based on the increase in assets generated from previously earned profit. The accumulated business earnings that have not been distributed to its owners are called retained earnings.

The owners' interest in the assets of the firm is equal to the sum of these two elements. The owners' equity in the business, however, is an aggregate or a general claim against the total assets. That is, the owners do not have claims against a specific asset.

PRACTICE ACTIVITY 1-3

1. Retained earnings are increased if the business operates at a net _____ and are decreased if it operates at a net _____ or pays a _____ to its stockholders.

2. Net assets are increased if the business operates at a net _____.

3. Indicate in the space provided whether the type of change increases or decreases the owners' interest in the business.

Type of Change	Effect on Owners' Equity
Owners' investment	_____
Revenues	_____
Expenses	_____
Net loss	_____
Dividend payment	_____

ACCOUNTING EQUATION

Assets of a firm must be equal to the sources of the assets, or stated another way, the total assets of the business must be equal to the claims against the assets. The relationship may be shown mathematically as:

$$Assets = Sources\ of\ assets$$

or

$$Assets = Claims\ against\ the\ assets$$

Assets are obtained from two sources: creditors and owners. Thus the equation can be restated to:

$$Assets = Liabilities + Owners'\ equity$$

The two sides of the equation are always equal because they simply reflect two views of the same thing. The sum of the assets shows the resources owned by the business. The right side shows the amounts of resources provided to the business by the creditors and the owners, respectively. This equation is known as the accounting equation, sometimes referred to as the balance sheet equation.

As noted earlier, creditors' claims have priority over claims of the owners. The owners have a claim against the remaining assets, called a residual interest. Because the owners have a residual interest in the assets, the equation is sometimes stated as:

$$\text{Assets - Liabilities = Owners' equity}$$

The owners' equity component of the accounting equation may be expanded as follows:

$$\text{Owners' equity = Paid-in capital + Retained earnings}$$

$$\text{Retained earnings = Beginning balance + Revenues}$$

$$\text{- Expenses - Dividends}$$

PRACTICE ACTIVITY 1-4

Compute the missing element for each independent case.

Case	Assets	Liabilities	Paid-in Capital	Retained Earnings
1.	$142,000	$48,000	$60,000	?
2.	?	$16,000	$30,000	$12,000
3.	$88,000	?	$35,000	$15,000

Case	Beginning Retained Earnings	Revenue	Expense	Dividends	Ending Retained Earnings
4.	$30,000	$60,000	$40,000	$10,000	?
5.	$30,000	$60,000	?	$10,000	$15,000
6.	?	$60,000	$28,000	$12,000	$40,000

COMMUNICATING ACCOUNTING INFORMATION THROUGH FINANCIAL STATEMENTS

Accounting is an information system designed to provide financial data to interested parties for decision-making purposes. The final result of the accounting process is the preparation of various financial statements that serve as important communication devices. The financial statements are generally classified into two types: internal statements and external statements. Internal statements are prepared at the request of management for the sole use of managers within the firm. Consequently, they are *not* intended for use by external users.

External statements, however, are designed and prepared specifically for use by outside parties such as creditors and stockholders. Because these outside parties are unable to specify the content and procedures to be followed in the preparation of the statements, generally accepted accounting procedures (GAAP) serve as guides in the preparation of the statements. External financial statements must be prepared in accordance with GAAP.

The life of a firm is divided into a series of time periods of equal length called accounting periods. Accounting periods of approximately equal length are established to enable the users of the financial statements to make meaningful comparisons of operating results of the current period with those of prior periods. A complete set of financial statements is issued to interested parties at least once a year as part of a firm's annual report.

A firm may select any 12 consecutive months for reporting. This period is called a **fiscal year**. If a firm's annual period begins on January 1 and ends on December 31, it is referred to as a calendar year firm. Many firms select a *natural business year* as a reporting period. A natural business year is a 12-month period that ends when business activities are at their lowest level during the year. For example, a retail firm's inventory is usually lowest after the post-Christmas sales. Thus, retail firms often select a fiscal year of February 1 to January 31 because the employees generally have more time to complete the year-end accounting and there is less inventory to count. An added plus is that accounting cost is reduced.

Annual reports are used by creditors, investors, and other interested parties to assess the firm's progress from year to year. Although the basic accounting period for which financial statements are presented is one year, quarterly statements are commonly issued to external parties to provide timely information on the operations of the firm. Generally, quarterly statements are not as detailed as annual reports. Many firms also prepare monthly or weekly statements for internal use by management. Statements prepared before the end of the annual period are called **interim reports**.

The emphasis in this course is on the processing of information for the preparation of external financial statements.

PRACTICE ACTIVITY 1-5

A firm's _____ year is any 12 consecutive month period selected for reporting.

A firm whose annual period ends on December 31 is called a _____ year firm.

A _____ _____ year is a 12-month period that ends when business activities are at their lowest level during the year.

Accounting reports prepared for shorter time intervals than the fiscal period are called

_____ _____ .

EXTERNAL FINANCIAL STATEMENTS -- AN OVERVIEW

Some knowledge of the content of external financial statements (hereafter simply called financial statements) and the types of information they are designed to communicate will help you better understand the underlying concepts and measurement process followed in accounting. The twofold purpose of such financial statements is to communicate to users (1) the results of operating activities during a specified time period and (2) the business's financial position at the end of the period. The four main financial statements prepared for use by external decision makers are:

1. Income statement

2. Retained earnings statement

3. Balance sheet

4. Statement of cash flow

These statements are often called general-purpose financial statements because they provide general information for use by all external users. To facilitate the analysis and interpretation of financial data, relatively standard classification schemes have evolved over time. If the structure and content of the financial statements are based on the general needs of users, and if that structure is followed consistently, then the information most user groups want should be available.

Preparation of the statement of cash flows is not covered in this course. The accounting system is not designed to prepare a statement of cash flows directly from the accounting records as is the case with the other statements. Thus, the preparation is rather complex and coverage is deferred to more advanced accounting courses. However, do not infer from this that the statement is unimportant.

USE OF DOLLAR SYMBOL, COMMAS, AND PERIODS

Before we review a set of financial statements, we need to examine the procedures followed by accountants in the use of the dollar symbol, commas, and periods. A common practice in formal reports, such as financial statements, is to place a dollar sign before the first amount in a column of figures, and also before the total amount. (Some accountants place a dollar symbol before a subtotal amount as well as the total amount.) Also, a single ruled line is placed under a column of figures to indicate that the amounts above the line are added or subtracted. A double line is placed after a total.

When dollar amounts are entered in ruled columns, commas and periods are not necessary. For the convenience of the statement reader, commas and periods should be used if the paper is not ruled. When amounts are in even dollars, accountants often place a dash in the cents column rather than writing out the two zeros.

In practice, transactions are in fact recorded in cents. However, when the data are aggregated in the financial statements, the dollar amounts are rounded, often to the nearest thousand. Very large companies round amounts to the nearest million. In this course, we will follow the practice of rounding computations to the nearest dollar in most cases. Thus, the cents column is usually omitted because the transaction and computations are in whole amounts.

CLASSIFICATION WITHIN EXTERNAL FINANCIAL STATEMENTS

We will now use the financial statements of Mesa Software City, a retailer of computer software, as a basis for reviewing the contents of the income statement, retained earnings statement, and balance sheet. Our emphasis is on the content of and classification within the various statements rather than on the determination of dollar amounts. You are not expected to learn and understand all facets of financial statements in this chapter, but you should understand main features so that you can understand better the content of later chapters where many of the items presented in financial statements, including the determination of dollar amounts, are discussed in detail. Our order of presentation will be (1) the income statement, (2) the retained earnings statement, and (3) the balance sheet.

INCOME STATEMENT

The **income statement** is designed to report the results of earning activities for a specific time period—such as a month, quarter, or year. Net income for the period is the excess of revenues and gains over expenses and losses. If expenses and losses for the period exceed revenues and gains, a net loss is incurred. Thus, the income statement equation might be expressed as:

Net income or Net loss = (Revenues + gains) - (Expenses + losses)

The period covered by the statement is indicated in the heading along with the name of the business and the name of the statement. Identification of the period covered is particularly important because it indicates the length of time it took to earn the reported net income. Without a clear indication of the period, the data in the income statement would have little, if any, meaning to a user.

An income statement for Mesa Software City for the fiscal year ended December 31, 19X1, is presented in Figure 1-1. The format shown in Figure 1-1 is called a multiple-step income statement because it is divided into several sections. As a result, several subtotals are shown to highlight significant relationships such as gross profit on sales. Note that there are four main sections in this income statement: revenues, expenses, other revenue and expense, and income taxes.

1. **Revenues** are defined as inflows of assets resulting from either the sale and delivery of goods or the rendering of services. Some additional descriptive term is often used to identify the type of revenue. For example, revenue of a business performing a service is generally called service revenue, and revenue of a business that sells a product is called sales revenue.

   Most businesses permit dissatisfied customers to either return unsatisfactory goods or keep the goods but pay a reduced price. These returns and allowances are treated as a reduction in sales revenue. Note in Figure 1-1 that gross sales revenue is reduced directly for sales returns and allowances to produce net sales revenue.

2. **Expenses** are defined as outflows or other uses of assets to earn revenues during an accounting period. On the income statement, expenses are generally classified into several groups that vary somewhat depending upon the type of business. For a merchandising company that purchases goods ready for sale to customers, the normal classifications are:

   Cost of goods sold. Cost of goods sold shows the total cost of the merchandise that was sold during the period. Cost of goods sold is subtracted from sales to arrive at an intermediate income amount called either gross profit or gross margin on sales.

   Operating expenses. Operating expenses are those expenses normally incurred while operating the business during the period. Operating expenses are often subclassified by function into selling expenses and administrative expenses. Selling expenses are those expenses, other than cost of goods sold, incurred to perform the sales activity. Administrative expenses are those expenses incurred for operating activities other than sales activity, including such items as administrative salaries and the cost of maintaining an accounting department.

Operating activities that are related to the primary (i.e., ongoing major or central) business activities of the firm, such as selling a product or providing services to customers, are reported in the revenues or expenses categories. For example, a sales commission received by a real estate office for selling a house is revenue resulting from its primary business activity. Advertising the firm's services, supplies used in the office, telephone expense, and property taxes on the office are examples of expenses directly related to its primary business activity. What is the primary operations of a business is obviously dependent on the nature of the business.

FIGURE 1-1
INCOME STATEMENT

MESA SOFTWARE CITY
Income Statement
For the Year Ended December 31, 19X1

Gross sales revenue		$524,900
Less: Sales returns and allowances		29,420
Net sales revenue		495,480
Less: Cost of goods sold		257,650
Gross profit		237,830
Operating expenses:		
Selling expenses:		
Advertising expense	$ 35,230	
Delivery expense	3,820	
Depreciation expense — Store equipment	18,000	
Repairs and maintenance	8,800	
Sales salaries	62,250	
Total selling expense	128,100	
Administrative expenses:		
Administrative salaries	42,400	
Bad debts	4,280	
Depreciation expense	7,200	
Repairs and maintenance	4,320	
Total administrative expenses	58,200	
Total operating expenses		186,300
Income from operations		51,530
Other revenue and expense:		
Interest expense	(6,400)	
Rent revenue	1,400	
Loss on sale of equipment	(800)	
Net other revenue and expense		5,800
Income before income taxes		45,730
Income taxes expense		13,700
Net income		$ 32,030

3. Other revenues and expenses: A firm may also engage in other activities that affect income but are not directly associated with the primary operations of the company. Two common types of transactions are reported in the other revenue and expense category. First are recurring revenue and expense transactions that are not directly related to the primary operations of a firm. Examples are interest expense related to the financing of asset purchases, dividends received from an investment in the stock of another company, rent revenue earned by a retail store renting excess space, and interest received on loans made to outside parties. Interest expense is included in this category on the basis that it is a financing expense, not an operating expense.

   The second type of transaction is related to an increase or decrease in an asset that is not typical of the firm's routine or day-to-day activities. The sale of an asset not acquired for resale is an example of this type of transaction. The difference between the selling price and the asset's value on the books of the company is referred to as a gain or loss on the sale. Gains and losses are increases or decreases in net assets, resulting from peripheral or incidental transactions. More specifically these terms are defined as:

   Gains are net inflows of assets from incidental transactions that are not revenue or owner investment transactions.

   Losses are net outflows of assets from incidental transactions that are not expenses or dividend distributions.

   For example, if a company sells, for $10,000, equipment used in the business that is recorded on its books for $6,000, a $4,000 gain is reported in the income statement. (As you will see in more advanced accounting courses, a gain or loss that is both of an unusual nature and infrequent in occurrence is separately reported as an extraordinary item.)

4. Income tax expense is the amount owed to the federal and other governmental units that levy a tax on business income. Income taxes are reported as a separate item because they are usually significant. The business corporation is the only form of business organization that is subject to income taxes. Note that this category is the tax based on income. Other forms of taxes, such as property taxes and employment taxes (such as social security), are reported as expenses in other sections of the income statement.

PRACTICE ACTIVITY 1-6

Refer to the income statement in Figure 1-1, and answer the following questions.

1. What information is contained in the heading of the statement?

2. What is the period of time covered by the statement?

3. What is the purpose of the income statement?

4. What are the primary activities of the company?

5. What is the net income or net loss for the period?

6. Why is there a net income or net loss?

RETAINED EARNINGS STATEMENT

The **retained earnings statement** shows the changes taking place in retained earnings for the period being reported on. The most common changes in retained earnings come from net income (or net loss) for the period and dividend distributions. The statement is constructed as follows:

> Retained earnings at beginning of the period
> + Net income (or minus net loss)
> − Dividends declared during the period
> = Retained earnings at the end of the accounting period

A retained earnings statement for Mesa Software City for the year ended December 31, 19X1, is presented in Figure 1-2. The heading shows the name of the company, the name of the statement, and the time period covered. The beginning retained earnings balance was $49,760. Note that the December 31 balance of retained earnings ($61,790) is reported as part of stockholders' equity in the balance sheet.

FIGURE 1-2
RETAINED EARNINGS STATEMENT

MESA SOFTWARE CITY
Retained Earnings Statement
For the Year Ended December 31, 19X1

Retained earnings, January 1, 19X1	$49,760	
Add: Net income for 19X1		32,030
Total		81,790
Less: Dividends distributed to stockholders		20,000
Retained earnings, December 31, 19X1		$61,790

Also observe that dividends were not subtracted from revenues in the income statement. Dividends are not directly related to earning revenue and, thus, are not an expense. Dividends are a distribution of assets to the stockholders that reduces retained earnings.

PRACTICE ACTIVITY 1-7

Refer to the retained earnings statement in Figure 1-2, and answer the following questions.

1. What is the period of time covered by the statement?

2. How much did retained earnings increase or decrease during the period?

3. Why did the retained earnings increase or decrease?

4. Why is there a single ruled line above the $61,790?

5. Why is there a double line below the $61,790?

BALANCE SHEET

The **balance sheet** reports the financial position of a business at a specific point in time. Consequently, it is often called the "*statement of financial position*." Financial position is reflected by the amount of the business's assets (resources), the amount of its liabilities (debts owed), and the amount of its owners' equity (assets minus liabilities).

Figure 1-3 shows a balance sheet for Mesa Software City on December 31, 19X1, the last day of its fiscal year. The balance sheet heading indicates the name of the business, the name of the statement, and the statement's date. The balance sheet is divided into three main sections: assets, liabilities, and owners' equity. The basic accounting model (accounting equation) for the balance sheet is as follows:

$$\text{Assets} = \text{Liabilities} + \text{Owners' equity}$$

In the balance sheet format illustrated in Figure 1-3, called the *report form*, assets, liabilities, and owners' equity amounts are listed in vertical columns. This format is commonly used when the balance sheet is reported on one sheet. In another format, called the *account form*, assets of the business are listed on the left side and the liabilities and owners' equity are listed on the right side. A balance sheet is an expanded expression of the accounting equation. It is an itemized list of a company's assets, liabilities, and owners' equity on a specific date. Note that the totals ($242,500) on each side of the balance sheet are equal. This equality must exist because the left side lists the assets of the business and the right side shows the sources of the assets.

The three major categories of the balance sheet with their subclassifications are:

Assets	Liabilities	Stockholders' Equity
Current assets	Current liabilities	Paid-in capital
Long-term investments	Long-term liabilities	Retained earnings
Property, plant, and equipment		
Intangible assets		
Other assets		

FIGURE 1-3
BALANCE SHEET

MESA SOFTWARE CITY
Balance Sheet
December 31, 19X1

Assets
Current assets:

Cash		$19,400
Marketable securities		2,000
Notes receivable		1,600
Accounts receivable	$23,100	
Less: Allowance for bad debts	2,780	20,320
Merchandise inventory		32,200
Prepaid expenses		1,980
Total current assets		$ 77,500
Long-term investments:		
Investment in stock of other companies		7,300
Property, plant, and equipment:		
Land	45,000	
Buildings	$80,000	
Less: Accumulated depreciation	16,000	64,000
Store and office equipment	60,000	
Less: Accumulated depreciation	25,300	34,700
Total property, plant, and equipment		143,700
Intangible assets:		
Trademarks and trade names		4,000
Other assets:		
Land held for expansion		10,000
Total assets		$242,500

Liabilities
Current liabilities:

Accounts payable	$ 19,800
Short-term notes payable	12,000
Wages payable	2,620
Income taxes payable	5,200
Unearned revenue	800
Total current liabilities	$ 40,420
Long-term liabilities:	
Mortgage note payable	64,000
Total liabilities	104,420

Stockholders' Equity
Paid-in capital:

Common stock (60,000 shares, $1 par value)	60,000
Paid-in capital in excess of par value	16,290
Retained earnings	61,790
Total stockholders' equity	138,080
Total liabilities and stockholders' equity	$242,500

These subclassifications facilitate the evaluation of financial data. They are arranged in the balance sheet so that important relationships between two subcategories are shown. For example, the *liquidity* of a firm—that is, its ability to satisfy short-term obligations as they become due—is of primary concern to most statement users. To facilitate the evaluation of a firm's liquidity, assets and liabilities are subclassified as current (or short-term) and long-term (or noncurrent).

Note that each asset in the balance sheet has an assigned dollar amount. Recall that under the cost principle in accounting, assets are initially recorded at cost. The cost of asset is subsequently allocated to the periods that benefit from their use. Thus, the income statement shows the cost of resources used as expenses, and the balance sheet reports the unallocated cost of the resources. The balance sheet does not show market value (except in those cases where it is acceptable to use the lower-of-cost-or-market rule) even though the current value of an asset may be greater than its cost. Thus, it is important to remember that the dollar amounts reported do not show the amounts that would be received if the assets were sold, but rather they show the unallocated cost of the assets.

Classification of Assets

Current assets are cash and other types of assets, such as marketable securities and accounts receivable, that are reasonably expected to be converted into cash, sold, or used up during the normal operating cycle or within one year after the balance sheet date, whichever is longer. The normal operating cycle varies for different types of businesses. For a merchandising concern it is the average length of time that it takes to acquire inventory, sell that inventory to customers, and collect cash for the sale.

The length of the operating cycle tends to vary for different businesses and is dependent on factors such as the length of the credit period extended to customers. The type of inventory involved and the nature of the firm's operations also affect the length of the cycle. For example, a grocery store should have a shorter cycle than a jewelry store because it sells its inventory faster. The cash collected from customers is used to pay for the inventory purchased and for other operating activities of the firm. The cycle keeps repeating itself. The normal operating cycle is depicted graphically in Figure 1-4.

The operating cycle for a service company involves using cash to acquire supplies and services, using these supplies and services to perform services for customers, and then collecting cash from the customers. For many merchandising and service firms, the operating cycle is one year or less. For others, such as firms involved in long-term construction projects, distilling products, and lumbering operations, the cycle is longer. The specific operating cycle of such firms, rather than the one-year criterion, is used to classify assets between current and long-term.

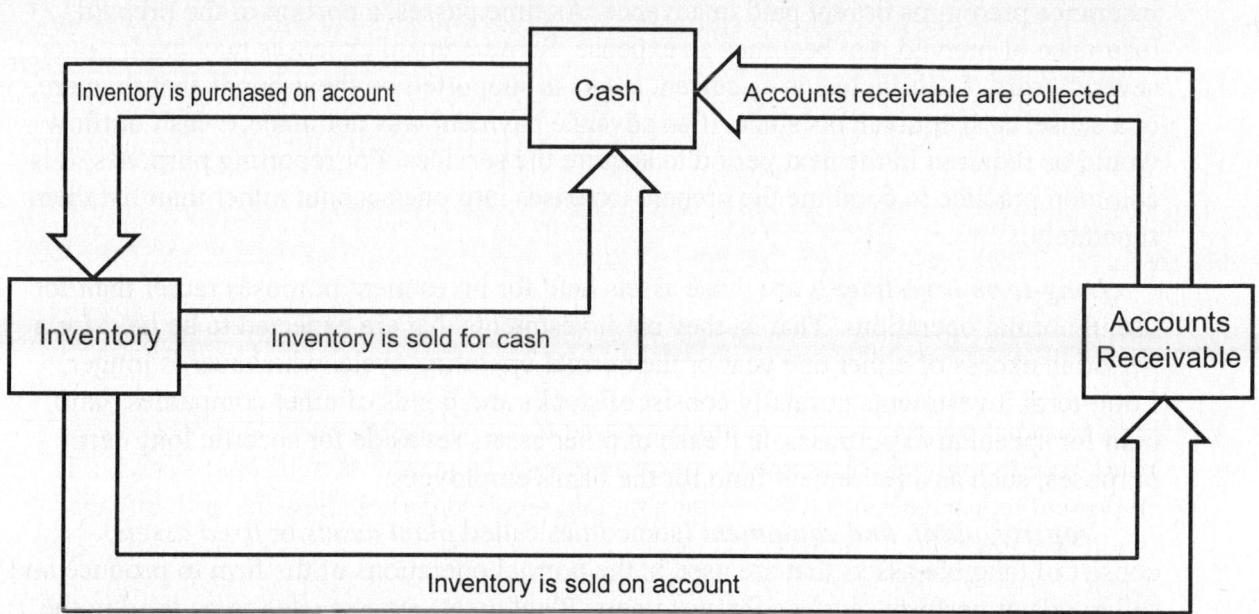

FIGURE 1-4
NORMAL OPERATING CYCLE FOR A MERCHANDISING FIRM

Current assets are normally listed in order of their liquidity. The term *liquidity* as it is used here refers to the average period of time it takes to convert a noncash asset into cash. In addition to cash, current assets include marketable securities, accounts and notes receivable, merchandise inventory, and prepaid expenses.

Marketable securities are current assets representing temporary investments of excess cash. They are expected to be sold for cash within the next year or operating cycle.

Notes receivable are claims against another party that are evidenced by a signed legal document, called a promissory note. A promissory note is signed by the maker and contains, among other things, a promise to pay a definite sum of money at a specified time. It is normally interest bearing.

Accounts receivable are amounts due from customers who have been extended short-term credit. Therefore, they are expected to be collected within the near future. An estimated amount of bad debts (uncollectible accounts) is deducted as a contra to accounts receivable. The amount of uncollectible accounts is estimated, based on an analysis of the company's past experience.

Merchandise inventory is a current asset because it is expected to be sold within the near future. When the inventory is sold, its cost is transferred to cost of goods sold and deducted from sales revenue on the income statement.

Prepaid expenses represent payment for services to be received in the future, such as insurance premiums or rent paid in advance. As time passes, a portion of the prepaid insurance or prepaid rent becomes an expense. Some prepaid expenses may expire over several years. Their inclusion as current assets is supported on the grounds that they are, in a sense, cash equivalents since, if an advance payment was not made, a cash outflow would be required in the next period to acquire the services. For reporting purposes, it is common practice to combine the prepaid expenses into one account rather than list them separately.

Long-term investments are those assets held for investment purposes rather than for use in normal operations. That is, they are investments that are expected to be held for a period in excess of either one year or the normal operating cycle, whichever is longer. Long-term investments normally consist of stocks and bonds of other companies, land held for speculative purposes, and cash or other assets set aside for specific long-term purposes, such as a retirement fund for the firm's employees.

Property, plant, and equipment (sometimes called *plant assets* or *fixed assets)* consist of tangible assets that are used in the normal operations of the firm to produce and sell goods or perform services for customers. Plant assets are expected to be used in the business for a number of years and are not, therefore, held for resale. Examples include land, buildings, equipment, furniture, fixtures, and patterns and dies used in operating the business.

Plant assets (except for land) have limited useful lives. Their cost is assigned to expense over their estimated useful lives. This assignment of cost is called *depreciation,* and the depreciation recorded to date is shown as *accumulated depreciation.* Accumulated depreciation is deducted from the cost of the related asset in the balance sheet to derive the asset's *book value.*

Intangible assets are those assets that have no physical substance but that are expected to provide benefits to the firm for several years. Intangible assets derive their value from the rights that possession and use confer to their owners. Like plant assets, the cost of intangibles is assigned to future periods over their estimated useful lives. Examples of intangibles are patents, trademarks, copyrights, franchise fees, secret processes, and trade names.

Other assets is a category used to report those assets that do not fit readily into one of the categories described earlier. Some examples are plant and equipment items being held for future sale and land being held for future expansion.

Classification of Liabilities

Current liabilities are obligations of the firm that are reasonably expected to be paid or settled in the next year or the normal operating cycle, whichever is longer. Most current liabilities require the payment of cash in the near future. Examples include the following:

Short-term notes payable is a liability evidenced by a promissory note. A note payable is a written promise to pay a specified amount to another party, the creditor, at a specified time. Promissory notes are often issued when a business borrows money from a bank or finance company. Notes are also commonly issued when relatively high-cost items of equipment are purchased on credit. Notes are normally interest bearing.

Accounts payable are amounts owed to creditors for the purchase of merchandise, supplies, and services on account in the normal course of operating a business.

Unearned revenue are advances received from customers for the payment of goods to be delivered or services to be performed in the future. Such advances are liabilities to the firm receiving the advance until the goods are delivered or the services performed.

Other short-term liabilities include amounts owed by the firm for services that have been received but have not been paid. This may include amounts owed to employees, various taxing authorities for payroll, income and property taxes, and utility companies.

Within the current liabilities section, there is no general agreement or uniform order of presenting accounts. One approach is to list the accounts from the largest amount due to the smallest. Another approach commonly used is to list the notes payable first, followed by accounts payable, other short-term liabilities, unearned revenue, and then the current portion of the long-term debt (see discussion below).

Generally, current liabilities are those that are expected to be paid out of the current assets listed on the balance sheet. The excess of current assets over current liabilities is called *working capital*. In Figure 1-3, Mesa Software City has current assets of $77,500 and current liabilities of $40,420; consequently, the dollar amount of working capital is $37,080 ($77,500 − $40,420). Expressed in the form of a ratio, Mesa's ratio of current assets to current liabilities is 1.92 ($77,500/ $40,420). This means that the company is in a relatively good position to settle its short-term debts.

Long-term liabilities are those obligations that do not require payment within the next year or the normal operating cycle, whichever is longer. In other words, liabilities not classified as current are reported in the long-term liability section of the balance sheet. Thus, if a firm's normal operating cycle is one year or less, obligations that mature more than one year beyond the balance sheet date are reported as long-term. Mesa Software City has one liability classified as long-term, a mortgage note payable. A *mortgage note payable* is a note for which the creditor has a secured claim against one or more of the firm's assets. A *secured claim* means that if the firm is unable to pay the obligation when due, the creditor may force the sale of the asset(s) pledged as security to recover the debt.

The portion of long-term debt due within the next year or operating cycle, if longer than one year, is reported as a current liability. For example, the portion of a mortgage note due next year is a current liability.

Stockholders' Equity

Stockholders' equity represents the owners' interest in the assets of the company. There are two main sources of stockholders' equity: (1) amounts invested in the business by the owners (paid-in capital) and (2) amounts earned by the company but not yet distributed to the owners (retained earnings). Paid-in capital is subclassified into amounts representing par value and amounts paid in excess of par value. Par value is a designated dollar amount per share that is established by the corporation. The paid-in capital in excess of par value is the excess amount paid for the stock over par value. Mesa Software City has stockholders' equity of $138,080, consisting of paid-in capital of $76,290 and retained earnings of $61,790.

PRACTICE ACTIVITY 1-8

I. Refer to the balance sheet in Figure 1-3, and answer the following questions.

1. When was the balance sheet prepared?

2. Does the balance sheet report on a specific point in time or for a specific time period?

3. What is the purpose of the balance sheet? By what other name is it frequently called?

4. What are the total assets?

5. How much is the total claim of the creditors?

6. What is the amount of the current liabilities?

7. What is the owners' interest in the assets of the firm?

II. From the following list of accounts, prepare the current asset and current liability sections of a balance sheet, and compute the working capital and current ratio.

Prepaid insurance	$ 3,700	Land	$10,000
Salaries payable	2,100	Bonds held for speculation	22,500
Cash used for operations	14,000	Accounts payable	8,200
Unearned revenue	1,200	Accounts receivable	9,400
Utilities payable	250	Short-term notes payable	2,800

SOLUTIONS TO PRACTICE ACTIVITIES

PRACTICE ACTIVITY 1-1

1. $27,400 + $780 + $1,680 = $29,860
2. $70,000; cost principle
3. entity assumption

PRACTICE ACTIVITY 1-2

Item	Asset	Liability
Accounts Payable	—	√
Office Supplies	√	—
Building	√	—
Notes Payable	—	√
Land	√	—
Salaries Payable	—	√
Patent	√	—
Cash received by a publisher for a three-year magazine subscription	—	√

PRACTICE ACTIVITY 1-3

1. income; loss; dividends
2. income
3. Owners' investment — Increase
   Revenues — Increase
   Expenses — Decrease
   Net loss — Decrease
   Dividend payment — Decrease

PRACTICE ACTIVITY 1-4

1. $34,000
2. $58,000
3. $38,000
4. $40,000
5. $65,000
6. $20,000

PRACTICE ACTIVITY 1-5

1. fiscal
2. calendar
3. natural business
4. interim reports

PRACTICE ACTIVITY 1-6

1. name of the business, name of the statement, and the date covered by the statement
2. The fiscal year ended December 31, 19X1. That is, the twelve-month period beginning January 1, 19X1, and ending December 31, 19X1.
3. The income statement is designed to report the results of earnings activities (operations) for a specific time period.
4. Selling software
5. Net income, $32,030
6. Net income results because revenues exceeded expenses for the period.

PRACTICE ACTIVITY 1-7

1. The fiscal year ended December 31, 19X1.
2. $12,030
3. $32,030 net income exceeded $20,000 dividends distributed to stockholders.
4. A single rule indicates that the amounts above the rule have been totaled.
5. A double rule indicates that the $61,790 is a total of a column of figures.

PRACTICE ACTIVITY 1-8

I. 1. December 31, 19X1
    2. specific point in time
    3. The balance sheet reports the financial position of a business in terms of its assets, liabilities, and owners' equity.   Statement of financial position
    4. $242,500
    5. $104,420
    6. $40,420
    7. $138,080

II.

Current assets:		Current liabilities:	
Cash	$14,000	Notes payable	$ 2,800
Accounts receivable	9,400	Accounts payable	8,200
Prepaid insurance	3,700	Salaries payable	2,100
		Utilities payable	250
		Unearned revenue	1,200
Total current assets	$27,100	Total current liabilities	$14,550

Working capital = $27,100 – $14,550 = $12,550
Current ratio = $27,100 ÷ $14,550 = 1.9

CHAPTER 2

Analyzing Business Transactions

Contents

CHAPTER OVERVIEW AND OBJECTIVES

Chapter 1 introduced the accounting equation and the basic elements of the income statement, balance sheet, and retained earnings statement. It was noted that transactions constitute the inputs of the accounting process and that the financial statements are the final result of the accounting process. In this chapter, we will begin our discussion of the procedures used to accumulate the information presented in the financial statements. The various steps that relate to the processing of accounting data, that is, from the occurrence of a transaction to the preparation of financial statements, are often called the *accounting data processing cycle* (or simply the *accounting cycle*).

This chapter introduces a simple accounting system that can be used for recording the effects of transactions on a firm's financial position. In this chapter you will learn how accounting transactions affect the elements of the accounting equation. When you have completed this chapter, you will be able to:

1. Identify transactions recorded in the accounting records.
2. Explain the need for and the use of source documents.
3. Describe the purpose of an account.
4. Analyze transactions in terms of their effect on the accounting equation.

5. Define each of the following terms:

Transaction

External transaction

Internal transaction

Source document

Objectivity

Account

Double-entry accounting

General ledger

The first eight chapters of this manual focus on a business that performs a service for its customers. Accounting for a firm that buys and sells inventory will be covered in later chapters.

CHARACTERISTICS OF ACCOUNTING INFORMATION

Accounting is the process of recording and communicating financial information that is used in making economic decisions. Financial information reported in the general-purpose financial statements is the result of economic activities of a business expressible in monetary terms. Accountants often use the term **transaction** to refer to all events that affect a firm's assets, liabilities, and owners' equity that can be measured in terms of money. Accountants classify these business transactions into external transactions and internal transactions.

External transactions are exchange events between two independent entities. When a business purchases merchandise from a supplier, borrows money from a bank, or sells merchandise to customers, it participates in an external transaction. In an external transaction there is an exchange of economic resources and/or obligations between the firm and one or more outside parties. For example, when a business purchases merchandise for cash, it gives up one resource (cash) in exchange for another resource (inventory). When it buys equipment on credit, it receives the equipment in exchange for an obligation to pay for it in the future.

Internal transactions are those events that take place entirely within one firm. The conversion of wheat into flour, the use of supplies by an employee, and the use over time of machinery and equipment are internal transactions. Such business activities do not involve any transactions with outside parties, but are recorded in the accounting system because they affect the relationships among the firm's assets, liabilities, and owners' equity.

A firm may carry on many business activities that are not business transactions. Such activities are of importance to the firm but are not recorded because there has not been an exchange of goods or services--for example, receiving an order from a customer, entering into a commitment to purchase an asset in the future, the hiring or the retirement of an employee, or changes in market interest rates. In other words, such events do not initially affect the firm's recorded assets, liabilities, and owners' equity. Such activities may eventually be given accounting recognition if an exchange takes place. For example, when goods are delivered to customers, an asset is received that was ordered; an employee is paid for services performed; or money is borrowed at the market rate of interest. Other events that do not involve an exchange of resources, such as the destruction of an office building by fire or the city's donation of land to a company, are given accounting recognition because assets and owners' equity are decreased or increased.

Financial accounting is based on a framework of rules for determining which events constitute accounting transactions. Two difficulties encountered in the study of accounting are determining which events to record and deciding when to give an event accounting recognition. Unfortunately, there are no simple rules to follow.

PRACTICE ACTIVITY 2-1

Business activity completed by a firm is given below. Indicate in the space provided whether each of the activities is an internal transaction (internal), an external transaction (external), or not a recordable business event (not recorded).

	Business Activity	Type of Event
1.	Stockholders invested cash in the business.	_____
2.	Purchased equipment on credit.	_____
3.	Office supplies were purchased for cash.	_____
4.	The company hired a new employee at a weekly salary of $600.	_____
5.	At the end of the first week the employee was paid $600.	_____
6.	A client placed an order for services the company is to perform next month.	_____
7.	Raw materials are used by employees to manufacture a product to be sold in the future.	_____
8.	The State in which the company operates gave the company land for the construction of a warehouse.	_____

PREPARATION OF SOURCE DOCUMENTS

Transactions are entered in the accounting records in order to keep track of a firm's financial position and results of operations. Before a transaction can be entered, data about the transaction must be collected. These data are usually obtained from a business record called a source document. A **source document** provides written evidence (documents) that a transaction has occurred and contains information about the nature of the transaction and the dollar amounts involved. A source document is generally prepared at the "source" or time a transaction occurs. Source documents prepared for external transactions take the form of sales invoices (credit sales), purchases invoices (purchase of merchandise), and cash register tapes (cash sales). Figure 2-1 gives an example of a sales invoice. Other examples will be presented throughout this material. The recording of internal transactions–such as the annual depreciation expense entry to record the cost allocation of equipment used, supplies used by employees, and the conversion of raw materials into a finished product–is based on special schedules or other supporting documentation prepared internally. Figure 2-2 is an example of a source document used to support wages paid to a particular employee.

Before a transaction can be recorded, the accountant must be made aware that one has taken place. The arrival of a source document in the accounting department generally initiates the recording process. Once received, the source document is analyzed to determine the amount and the effect of the transaction on the firm's financial position. Thus, it is important that a firm establish procedures to ensure that the effects of all transactions are recorded.

Source documents are also important during an audit. For example, when a firm's financial statements are audited by an independent certified public accountant (CPA), the source documents provide evidence of the underlying transaction that was processed by the accounting department. Accounting data that are verifiable (sometimes called **objectivity**) are considered to be more useful for external statement users. Verifiable means that essentially similar measures and results would be produced if two or more qualified persons examined the same data. For example, the price agreed upon in an exchange transaction is verifiable because it is based upon negotiations between independent parties. The amounts entered in the accounting records should be supported by adequate evidence–such as an actual invoice, contract, canceled check, physical count, or other document.

**FIGURE 2-1
SOURCE DOCUMENT
SALES INVOICE**

NORTON OFFICE EQUIPMENT		SALES INVOICE NO. 3476		
17662 Southwest Highway 50				
Austin, Texas 84567		Date: January 4, 19X1		
(817) 322-6789				
		Terms: Cash		
SOLD TO: Bird Towing				
1879 University Drive				
Austin, Texas 84570				
Quan	Description		Unit Price	Amount
2	Executive teak desk		$ 890	$1,780
1	Notebook computer		$2,230	2,230
	Total			$4,010
	Sales tax			180
				$4,190

**FIGURE 2-2
SOURCE DOCUMENT
TIME CARD**

Time Card			
Employee Name	Clint Black		
Date	For the Week Ended		July 16, 19X1
Date	Time Started	Time Ended	Hours
7/10	8:00	3:00	7
7/11	9:00	12:00	3
7/12	8:00	4:00	8
7/13	12:00	6:00	6
7/14	8:00	4:00	8
7/15			0
7/16			0
	Total Hours		32
Approved by:	RES		

PRACTICE ACTIVITY 2-2

Complete the following statements by entering a word in the blank space that will make the statement a valid statement.

1. A _____ _____ is a business form that provides evidence that a transaction has occurred.

2. A transaction is _____ if two accountants reviewed the information and agreed that the amount recorded was proper.

True-False

___1. A bill received from a utility company is an example of a source document.

___2. Source documents are usually ignored when a CPA performs an audit of the company's books.

___3. Verifiable accounting data are considered to be more useful by external statement users.

ENTERING TRANSACTIONS--THE USE OF ACCOUNTS

Transactions are the recordable activities engaged in by a firm and that provide the inputs to the accounting system. The occurrence of a transaction causes a measurable change in the amounts reported for a firm's individual assets, liabilities, and the various components of owners' equity. Part of the accounting function is classifying the effects of transactions into meaningful categories and summarizing the results in the firm's financial statements. To facilitate the accumulation of the information needed to prepare the financial statements, a record of each transaction and its effect on each element contained in the financial statements is needed.

Because a business may engage in numerous transactions during a given period, a practical approach is needed to summarize the effects of the transactions. Fortunately, many transactions for a given business are repetitive in nature and cause a change in the same items. For example, a company may complete hundreds of cash sales that each individually increase its cash balance and the amount of revenue.   An accounting record, called an **account**, is used to provide a detailed record of increases and decreases and the resulting balance in each type of asset, liability, and owners' equity. For example, a firm will maintain a separate account to record increases and decreases in cash, a separate account to record increases and decreases in equipment, a separate account for each type of liability, and still another account for capital investment. Each account has a name, called the account title, that should be descriptive of the nature of the item being recorded in the account.

TRANSACTION ANALYSIS

The total of a firm's assets is always equal to the creditors' claims and owners' claims. The relationship is expressed in the accounting equation as:

Assets = Liabilities + Owners' Equity

Accounting transactions affect the elements of the accounting equation. Therefore, each transaction must be analyzed to determine its effects on the account balances. Although the individual account balances change as a result of each transaction, the two sides of the accounting equation must always be equal. In order for the accounting equation to remain in balance, each recorded transaction must affect at least two accounts. An increase in one side of the equation must equal an increase to the other side. Or a decrease to one side of the equation must be equal to a decrease on the other side. This dual recording process is known as **double-entry accounting**. Note, however, that double-entry does not mean that a transaction must affect each side of the equation. A transaction could result in an increase in one account and an equal decrease in another account that are on the same side of the equation. For example, the purchase of equipment for cash affects two asset accounts with an increase in one asset account and an equal decrease in another asset account.

The evidence that a transaction has occurred is usually provided by a written source document. Once the source document is received in the accounting department, it must be analyzed to determine the following:

1. What are the individual accounts (at least two) affected by the transactions?

2. Is each account affected to be increased or decreased as a result of the transaction?

3. By what amount is each account to be changed?

You should practice analyzing transactions in the steps outlined above.

After each transaction is entered in the accounting records, the accounting equation must be in balance. That is, the total of the account balances on the left side of the equation must equal the total of the account balances on the right side of the equation. This equality should be verified periodically.

EFFECTS OF TRANSACTION ON ACCOUNTING EQUATION ILLUSTRATED

Several transactions for International Travel Agency will now be used to illustrate transaction analysis and their effects on the accounting equation. Each transaction is described, followed by an illustration of its effect on the accounting equation. The type of transaction, external or internal, is identified in the list below in parentheses. The company used the following accounts to keep a record of its transactions.

<u>Assets</u>   =   <u>Liabilities</u>   +   <u>Owners' Equity</u>
Cash   Liabilities   Stockholders' Equity
Accounts Receivable
Office Supplies
Office Equipment

As will be discussed in more detail in a later chapter, a collection of the complete set of accounts established by a specific firm is called a **general ledger**.

In this illustration, transactions are first analyzed and then entered in a columnar worksheet as shown below. Such a worksheet will be referred to as a transaction analysis worksheet.

Transaction Analysis Worksheet
International Travel Agency

	Assets				=	Liabilities	+	Owners' Equity	
Cash +	Accounts Receivable +	Office Supplies +	Office Equipment =		=	Liabilities	+	Stockholders' Equity	Explanation

In this illustration, a separate column is established for each asset. Because of space limitations, however, all liabilities are entered in a single column and changes in owners' equity are entered in a single column. The types of changes to owners' equity are identified as to capital investment, withdrawal, revenue, or expense. In subsequent chapters a separate account will be established for each type of liability and owners' equity.

Transaction 1: Mary West and Jane Tuttle decided to open International Travel Agency. The company is organized as a corporation. Each investor purchased 1,000 shares of $10 par value common stock for $10 per share. (This is an external transaction, because under the entity assumption, the business is a separate entity distinguishable from its owners.)

A check similar to the one shown in Figure 2-3 was received from each of the investors. A deposit ticket was prepared, and the checks were deposited in the bank account opened for International Travel Agency. A copy of the deposit ticket was sent to the firm's accountant for analysis and for entering the transactions in the transaction analysis worksheet.

FIGURE 2-3
CHECK FROM INVESTOR

Mary West
444 West Maple
Salt Lake City, UT 34588

Jan. 2 19 *X1*

Pay to the order of *International Travel Agency* $ *10,000*

Ten-Thousand and no/100------------------------------ Dollars.

For *Investment* *Mary West*

UTAH STATE BANK 00234 56378 2212 00012

Analysis

The business is receiving cash in exchange for an ownership interest in the business.

*Cash is an asset. It is increased by $20,000 (2 investors X 1,000 shares X $10 par value = $20,000).

*The investment by the owners increases their interest in the business. Owners' equity is increased $20,000. Following the entity assumption, personal assets and debts of the owners are not part of the business endeavor and therefore are excluded from the equation.

Accounts Involved

Accounts	Increased or Decreased	Amount
Cash	Increased	$20,000
Owners' Equity	Increased	$20,000

	Assets				=	Liabilities	+	Owners' Equity	
Cash	+	Accounts Receivable	+	Office Supplies	+ Office Equipment =	Liabilities	+	Stockholders' Equity	Explanation
1) +20,000					=			+20,000	Capital investment

Verification that accounting equation is still in balance.

Assets	=	Liabilities	+	Owners' Equity
$20,000	=	-0-	+	$20,000

Transaction 2: After making the initial investment, the business purchased office equipment for $18,000 cash. The list price of the equipment was $19,000, but after some hard negotiations, the supplier agreed to sell the equipment for $17,050 plus sales tax. (This is an external transaction.)

A sales invoice (see Figure 2-4) was received from AAA Office Equipment. After verifying that the purchase was made and the equipment was received, the document is analyzed to determine the effects on the accounts.

FIGURE 2-4
SOURCE DOCUMENT--SALES INVOICE

	AAA OFFICE EQUIPMENT	SALES INVOICE NO. 285
	1515 S. 48th Street	
	Salt Lake City, Utah 34587	Date: January 2, 19X1
	(543) 678-9000	Terms: Cash

SOLD TO: International Travel Agency
           1653 State Street
           Salt Lake City, Utah 34589

Quan	Description	Unit Price	Amount
3	Office desk and chairs	$1,200	$3,600
3	ICA 486 computers	$3,500	10,500
1	Model 236 office copier	$2,950	2,950
	Total		$17,050
	Sales tax		950
			$18,000

Analysis

The business is receiving office equipment in exchange for cash.

*The equipment will be used in future operations of the business. Therefore, the equipment is an asset. Each item is recorded at its cost for a total of $18,000 in accordance with the cost principle. Note that the tax paid is a part of the cost of the equipment.

*Since the acquisition was paid for in cash, cash is decreased by $18,000.

Accounts Involved

Accounts	Increased or Decreased	Amount
Office Equipment	Increased	$18,000
Cash	Decreased	$18,000

		Assets						=	Liabilities	+	Owners' Equity		
	Cash	+	Accounts Receivable	+	Office Supplies	+	Office Equipment	=	Liabilities	+	Stockholders' Equity		Explanation
1)	+20,000							=			+20,000		Capital investment
2)	-18,000						+18,000	=					
	2,000	+		+		+	18,000	=		+	20,000		

Verification of accounting equation:

Assets	=	Liabilities	+	Owners' Equity
$2,000 + $18,000	=	-0-	+	$20,000

Transaction 3: The company purchased $1,200 in office supplies from Fiesta Office Supply Co., agreeing to pay this bill in 45 days. The company expects to consume the supplies over several months as it performs services for its customers. (This is an external transaction.)

An invoice is not shown here as a source document, but one would have been received to verify the supplies acquisition.

Analysis

The business is acquiring office supplies in exchange for the promise to pay cash in the future. This type of transaction, where money is owed, is referred to as a purchase on account or credit purchase.

*The office supplies will be used in future operations of business (an asset). An asset account is increased because the supplies are expected to benefit the current and future periods as the supplies are used. (Before financial statements are prepared, the company will determine the amount of supplies used this accounting period, and that portion will be entered as an expense.)

*Acquiring the supplies on credit increases a liability by $1,200, because the company now owes the money to Fiesta Office Supply Co.

Accounts Involved

Accounts	Increased or Decreased	Amount
Office Supplies	Increased	$1,200
Liabilities	Increased	$1,200

	Assets							=	Liabilities	+	Owners' Equity		
	Cash	+	Accounts Receivable	+	Office Supplies	+	Office Equipment	=	Liabilities	+	Stockholders' Equity		Explanation
1)	+20,000							=			+20,000		Capital investment
2)	-18,000						+18,000	=					
	2,000	+		+		+	18,000	=		+	20,000		
3)					+1,200			=	+1,200				
	2,000	+		+	1,200	+	18,000	=	1,200	+	20,000		

Owners' equity in the business did not change, because assets and liabilities increased by equal amounts. The accounting equation is still in balance with $21,200 in total assets and $21,200 of liabilities and stockholders' equity.

PRACTICE ACTIVITY 2-3

Analyze the following transaction, and enter it in the columnar transaction analysis worksheet.

Transaction 4: The company performed services for customers and received $1,280 in cash.
Analysis

_____

_____

_____

_____

_____

_____

_____

Accounts Involved

Accounts	Increased or Decreased	Amount
_____	_____	$_____
_____	_____	$_____

	Assets							=	Liabilities	+	Owners' Equity		
	Cash	+	Accounts Receivable	+	Office Supplies	+	Office Equipment	=	Liabilities	+	Stockholders' Equity		Explanation
1)	+20,000							=			+20,000		Capital investment
2)	-18,000						+18,000	=					
	2,000	+		+		+	18,000	=		+	20,000		
3)					+1,200			=	+1,200				
	2,000	+		+	1,200	+	18,000	=	1,200	+	20,000		
4)													
		+		+		+		=		+			

Verify that accounting equation is in balance.

Assets	=	Liabilities + Owners' equity

$\$\underline{\hspace{3em}} + \$\underline{\hspace{3em}} + \$\underline{\hspace{3em}} + \$\underline{\hspace{3em}} = \$\underline{\hspace{3em}} + \$\underline{\hspace{3em}}$

$\$\underline{\hspace{3em}} = \$\underline{\hspace{3em}}$

The transactions entered into by International Travel Agency for the remainder of the month are entered in the transaction analysis worksheet in Figure 2-5. Several of these transactions are discussed in more detail in the next section. Study this illustration carefully. You will be working on these skills in your next computer lab. As you study this illustration, observe two important facts.

1. Every transaction recorded affected at least two items in the equation (double-entry accounting).

2. After the effects of each transaction were recorded, the accounting equation remained in balance.

The additional transactions are as follows:

5. Paid $700 of the amount due on the office supplies purchased on credit in transaction 3.

6. Paid $950 to employees for work performed to date.

7. Billed clients $720 for services performed.

8. Received a utility bill for the month of January in the amount of $180. The bill will be paid next month.

9. On the last day of the period, borrowed $5,000 cash from the Valley City State Bank, giving a note in exchange.

10. Received $250 from clients in payment on their account receivable.

11. Determined that $400 in office supplies was used this period.

12. Estimated depreciation from using equipment this month to be $300.

13. Received $550 in advance from clients for services to be performed next month.

14. Paid a cash dividend of $100 to the stockholders.

Several of these transactions will now be discussed in detail because they serve to illustrate two important concepts in accounting: the revenue principle and the recognition of expenses.

DIVIDEND PAYMENT

As noted in Chapter 1, a cash dividend is a distribution of income from the corporation to its stockholders. The effect of a cash dividend distribution is to reduce owners' equity and cash by the amount of the dividend. Although a dividend has the same effect as the payment for an expense, it is not an expense incurred for the purpose of producing revenue and, accordingly, is not reported on a firm's income statement.

A large corporation may have thousands of individual stockholders. The stockholders may sell their shares at any time. To ensure that dividends are paid to the rightful owner of the shares, a large corporation will normally declare on one date and pay on some future date to the stockholders of record on some date between the declaration date and the payment date. A dividend liability is created on the declaration date that will not be settled until the payment date. However, for simplicity in this course, it will be assumed that dividends are declared and paid on the same date. Thus, in transaction (14) the $100 dividend payment is entered as a reduction in cash and owners' equity. A more detailed discussion of accounting for a corporation is contained in more advanced accounting courses.

REVENUE PRINCIPLE

The revenue principle states that revenue should be recognized when it is earned rather than when it is collected. When a business sells a service, it obtains an asset, usually cash [transaction (4)] or an account receivable [transaction (7)], which represents the right to collect cash in the future. In such cases, there is an equal increase in assets on the left side of the equation, and since liabilities are unaffected by a revenue transaction, owners' equity is increased on the right side of the equation. Thus, in transaction (10) the effect of the collection of an account receivable is to increase one asset, cash, and decrease another asset, accounts receivable. This transaction does not change total assets, but rather it changes the composition of the assets. The collection of an account receivable is not revenue; the revenue was recorded as an increase in owners' equity when the services were performed and billed to the customers. In contrast, customers often pay in advance for goods to be delivered or for services to be performed in the future. In transaction (13), International Travel received a $550 advance from clients. Such an advance is a liability to the firm receiving the advance until the services are performed. When the services are performed, revenue will be recognized. Since the revenue is not earned until the service is performed, an advance receipt of cash is often referred to as "Unearned Revenue."

FIGURE 2-5
EFFECTS OF TRANSACTIONS ON THE ACCOUNTING EQUATION

	Cash	+	Accounts Receivable	+	Office Supplies	+	Office Equipment	=	Liabilities	+	Stockholders' Equity	Explanation
1.	+20,000	+		+		+		=		+	+20,000	Cap. investment
2.	-18,000	+		+		+	+18,000	=		+		
	2,000	+		+		+	18,000	=		+	+20,000	
3.		+		+	+1,200	+		=	+1,200	+		
	2,000	+		+	1,200	+	18,000	=	1,200	+	20,000	
4.	+1,280	+		+		+		=		+	+1,280	Revenue
	3,280	+		+	1,200	+	18,000	=	1,200	+	21,280	
5.	-700	+		+		+		=	-700	+		
	2,580	+		+	1,200	+	18,000	=	500	+	21,280	
6.	-950	+		+		+		=		+	-950	Salary expense
	1,630	+		+	1,200	+	18,000	=	500	+	20,330	
7.		+	+720	+		+		=		+	+720	Revenue
	1,630	+	720	+	1,200	+	18,000	=	500	+	21,050	
8.		+		+		+		=	+180	+	-180	Utility expense
	1,630	+	720	+	1,200	+	18,000	=	680	+	20,870	
9.	+5,000	+		+		+		=	+5,000	+		
	6,630	+	720	+	1,200	+	18,000	=	5,680	+	20,870	
10.	+250	+	-250	+		+		=		+		
	6,880	+	470	+	1,200	+	18,000	=	5,680	+	20,870	
11.		+		+	-400	+		=		+	-400	Supplies expense
	6,880	+	470	+	800	+	18,000	=	5,680	+	20,470	
12.		+		+		+	-300	=		+	-300	Depr. expense
	6,880	+	470	+	800	+	17,700	=	5,680	+	20,170	
13.	+550	+		+		+		=	+550	+		
	7,430	+	470	+	800	+	17,700	=	6,230	+	20,170	
14.	-100	+		+		+		=		+	-100	Dividend payment
	7,330	+	470	+	800	+	17,700	=	6,230	+	20,070	

Verification that accounting equation is in balance:

$7,330 + $470 + $800 + $17,700 = $6,230 + $20,070
$26,300 = $26,300

EXPENSE RECOGNITION

Expenses are incurred when assets are used or services are received in the process of earning revenue rather than when they are paid for by the firm. When an expense is incurred, either an asset is decreased (expense is paid in cash or another type of asset such as supplies is used) or in some cases a liability is increased (the service received has not been paid for), thus causing a decrease in owners' equity. Transactions (2), (3), (6), (8), (11), and (12) illustrate this concept. In transactions (2) and (3), office equipment and supplies were acquired in advance of their use in the earnings process. It does not matter whether cash is paid at the time of purchase [transaction (2)] or is to be paid at a later date [transaction (3)]. The equipment and supplies are entered in the accounting records at cost and are accounted for initially as assets until each is used to produce revenue, at which time their cost is allocated to expense [see transactions (11) and (12)]. In other cases, services are received before they are paid for by the firm. In transaction (6), employees performed services prior to the time payment was made. Because the services received are related to earning revenue, they are accounted for as an expense. In these examples, an asset is decreased (cash, office supplies, or office equipment) and owners' equity is decreased because the business has incurred an expense. In transaction (8), services in the form of utilities were received but will not be paid for until the next accounting period, which creates a liability for the firm. Thus, a liability is increased and owners' equity is decreased. When payment is made to the utility company, cash and the liability will be decreased.

The difference between the revenues earned and expenses incurred is net income or net loss. In this case revenues of $2,000 ($1,280 + $720) exceeded expenses incurred of $1,830 ($950 + $180 + $400 + $300). Recall that the dividends of $100 are not an expense related to the earning of revenue.

When Is an Expenditure Recorded as an Expense versus an Asset

A business often acquires resources before they are utilized or consumed in operations. You will observe that sometimes an asset account is increased, as in transaction (3), when an item is purchased for future use in the business operations. The cost of goods and services paid for in advance that are expected to benefit several periods–such as the purchase of office supplies, a 24-month insurance policy, or equipment–is *normally* recorded as assets at the time of acquisition. (An alternative to this approach is discussed in Chapter 8.) At the end of the accounting period the cost of the portion used is computed and the appropriate asset account and owners' equity (expense) are reduced for the cost of the portion used [see transaction (11) in Figure 2-5]. The unused portion of each cost is reported as an asset on the balance sheet. Thus, before the financial statements are prepared, the balance in each asset account is analyzed and allocated between an asset and an expense.

In other cases, however, the acquisition and expiration of the asset occur in the same accounting period. While the costs of such goods and services are considered assets at the time of acquisition, it is common practice to enter such purchases as a reduction in cash and owners' equity if the items are routinely consumed in the current period only. For example, the payment of one month's rent in advance on the first of the month is normally recorded initially as an expense and owners' equity is decreased. Similarly, a payment to employees for salaries they have earned during the period is entered as a decrease in cash and owners' equity.

To illustrate the effects of the two approaches, assume that on March 1 a company paid $2,000 for rent for the month of March.

A. Record prepayment as an asset.

	Cash	Prepaid Rent	=	Owners' Equity
Acquisition	-2,000	+2,000	=	-0-
Record expense		-2,000	=	-2,000
Effect on equation	-2,000	--0--	=	-2,000

B. Record prepayment as an expense.

Acquisition	-$2,000	- -0-	=	-$2,000

Note that the end results are the same; both assets and owners' equity are decreased by an equal amount ($2,000). However, recording the expense at the time of acquisition eliminates the need for an additional entry to adjust the asset account.

As demonstrated above, the initial acquisition of a resource for use in the business can be entered as either an asset or an expense. Although both approaches are acceptable, *in completing lab assignments, the software accepts one answer as correct*. As a convention, you should enter the cost of a resource used within the current period as an expense, whereas the cost of a resource that will be used over several periods should be entered initially as an asset. This requires that you review the length of the accounting period for each problem. For example, when analyzing transactions for a company that has a December 31 year-end, the payment of $600 on June 1 for three months' rent should be recorded as an expense since the rent will expire within this period; the payment should be recorded as a prepaid expense (an asset) if payment is made on December 1 since both this and the next period are affected. As another example, the payment of $600 on June 1 for three months' rent should be entered as a prepaid expense if monthly statements are being prepared because the $600 will be expensed $200 in three different monthly periods.

SUMMARY OF THE EFFECTS OF TRANSACTIONS

A firm may enter into many transactions. However, a limited number of types exist when they are classified as to their effect on the firm's total assets, total liabilities, and owners' equity. The types of transactions are summarized in Figure 2-6.

FIGURE 2-6
SUMMARY OF TYPES OF TRANSACTIONS

Type of Transaction	Assets	= Liabilities	+ Owners' Equity
1. Investment by the owners.	Increase		Increase
2. Acquire an asset for cash.	Increase and Decrease		
3. Acquire an asset on credit.	Increase	Increase	
4. Receive an asset in exchange for services performed.	Increase		Increase
5. Receive an asset in advance of service being performed.	Increase	Increase	
6. Earn advance payment by performing service.		Decrease	Increase
7. Collect an account receivable.	Increase and Decrease		
8. Use an asset in earnings process.	Decrease		Decrease
9. Expense incurred but not paid.		Increase	Decrease
10. Distribute assets to stockholders.	Decrease		Decrease
11. Use an asset to settle a liability.	Decrease	Decrease	

Another type of transaction that is not illustrated in this course is one that increases one liability and decreases another by the same amount. For example, a firm and a creditor may agree to convert an account payable to a note payable.

USING THE TRANSACTION ANALYSIS WORKSHEET TO PREPARE FINANCIAL STATEMENTS

The information collected in the accounts is used to prepare financial statements. An income statement and retained earnings statement are prepared in Figure 2-7. The information needed to do so is taken from the stockholders' equity column in Figure 2-5. A balance sheet is prepared in Figure 2-8.

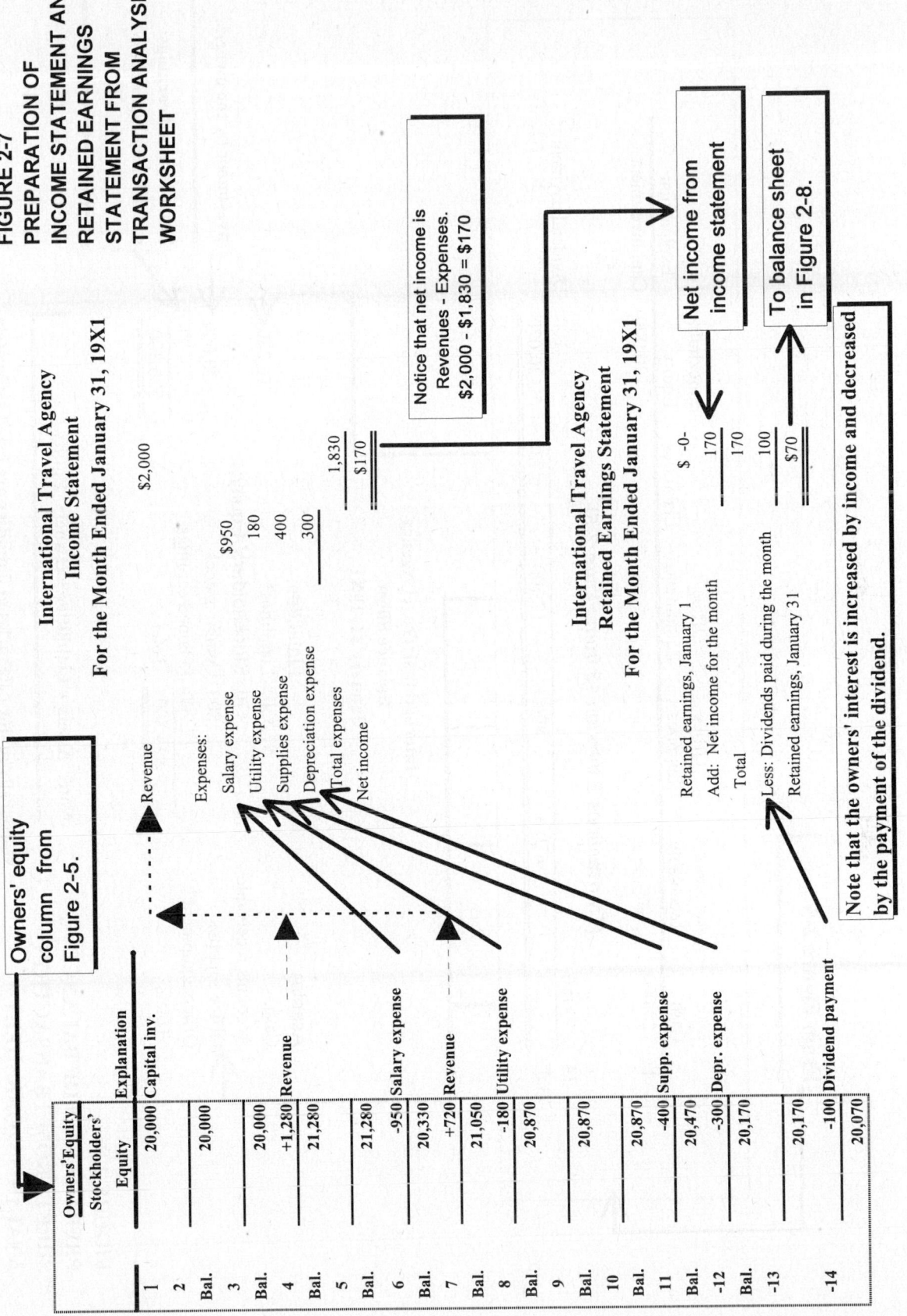

FIGURE 2-7
PREPARATION OF INCOME STATEMENT AND RETAINED EARNINGS STATEMENT FROM TRANSACTION ANALYSIS WORKSHEET

International Travel Agency
Income Statement
For the Month Ended January 31, 19X1

Revenue	$2,000
Expenses:	
Salary expense	$950
Utility expense	180
Supplies expense	400
Depreciation expense	300
Total expenses	1,830
Net income	$170

Notice that net income is Revenues - Expenses. $2,000 - $1,830 = $170

International Travel Agency
Retained Earnings Statement
For the Month Ended January 31, 19X1

Retained earnings, January 1	$ -0-
Add: Net income for the month	170
Total	170
Less: Dividends paid during the month	100
Retained earnings, January 31	$70

Net income from income statement

To balance sheet in Figure 2-8.

Note that the owners' interest is increased by income and decreased by the payment of the dividend.

Owners' equity column from Figure 2-5.

Owners'Equity

Stockholders' Equity	Explanation	
1	20,000	Capital inv.
2		
Bal.	20,000	
3		
Bal.	20,000	
4	+1,280	Revenue
Bal.	21,280	
5		
Bal.	21,280	
6	-950	Salary expense
Bal.	20,330	
7	+720	Revenue
Bal.	21,050	
8	-180	Utility expense
Bal.	20,870	
9		
Bal.	20,870	
10		
Bal.	20,870	
11	-400	Supp. expense
Bal.	20,470	
-12	-300	Depr. expense
Bal.	20,170	
-13		
Bal.	20,170	
-14	-100	Dividend payment
	20,070	

From Figure 2-5

	Cash	+	Accounts Receivable	+	Office Supplies	+	Office Equipment	=	Liabilities	+	Stockholders' Equity	Explanation
1	20,000							=			20,000	Cap. investment

(Transactions 2 through 13 from Figure 2-5)

	Cash	+	Accounts Receivable	+	Office Supplies	+	Office Equipment	=	Liabilities	+	Stockholders' Equity	Explanation
14	-100							=			-100	Dividend payment
Bal.	7,330	+	470	+	800	+	17,700	=	6,230	+	20,070	

International Travel Agency
Balance Sheet
January 31, 19X1

Assets:

Cash	$7,330
Accounts receivable	470
Office supplies	800
Office equipment	17,700
Totals	$26,300

Liabilities:

Liabilities*	$6,230

Stockholders' Equity:

Common stock	20,000
Retained earnings	70
Total	$26,300

Investment by the owners.

From retained earnings statement in Figure 2-7.

Note: Assets = Liabilities + Owners' Equity

*Generally major categories of liabilities are listed separately.

FIGURE 2-8
PREPARATION OF BALANCE SHEET FROM TRANSACTION ANALYSIS WORKSHEET

INTRODUCTION TO THE ACCOUNTING CYCLE

In this chapter, the nature of transactions was discussed. Then, a basic accounting system that summarizes the effects of transactions on the financial position of a business entity was introduced. The International Travel Agency illustration provides an overview of the accounting data processing cycle (accounting cycle). The accounting cycle is a series of steps that begins with a transaction and ends with financial statement preparation. The same sequence of steps is followed period after period. Although there are additional steps that will be covered in subsequent chapters, the steps illustrated here were:

1. Recordable transactions occur, and a source document is prepared to capture the essence of the transaction on paper.

2. Transactions are analyzed to determine the (a) accounts affected by the transaction, (b) the change in the accounts involved, and (c) the dollar amount involved. The effects are then entered in the accounts.

   Every transaction recorded affects at least two accounts. This dual recording process is known as *double-entry accounting*. Also, after the effects of each transaction are entered in the accounts, the accounting equation must remain in balance, with the sum of assets equal to the sum of liabilities plus owners' equity.

3. Account balances are analyzed to determine if there have been changes that have not been recorded (e.g., supplies used and depreciation). Unrecorded changes are entered in the accounts.

4. After the effects of the transactions for the period are taken into account, the financial statements are prepared to report on the financial position as of a certain date and the results of operations for the period.

These steps and others added to the cycle to increase the efficiency of the accounting system are elaborated upon in subsequent chapters.

SOLUTIONS TO PRACTICE ACTIVITIES

PRACTICE ACTIVITY 2-1

	Business Activity	Type of Event
1.	Stockholders invested cash in the business.	External
2.	Purchased equipment on credit.	External
3.	Office supplies were purchased for cash.	External
4.	The company hired a new employee at a weekly salary of $600.	Not recorded
5.	At the end of the first week the employee was paid $600.	External
6.	A client placed an order for services the company is to perform next month.	Not recorded
7.	Raw materials are used by employees to manufacture a product to be sold in the future.	Internal
8.	The State in which the company operates gave the company land for the construction of a warehouse.	External

PRACTICE ACTIVITY 2-2

1. source document
2. objective or verifiable

True/False

1. T
2. F
3. T

PRACTICE ACTIVITY 2-3

Transaction 4: The company performed services for customers and received $1,280 in cash.

Analysis

*One of the prime objectives of a business is to engage in operating activities that will result in net income to the owners. Net income is the excess of revenues (and gains) over expenses (and losses) for a specific time period. Revenues for International Travel are earned by charging a fee for services performed. Because the assets received as revenues belong to the owners, revenues increase owners' equity.

*Since cash was received, the asset Cash is also increased.

Accounts Involved

Accounts	Increased or Decreased	Amount
Cash	Increased	$1,280
Stockholders' Equity	Increased	$1,280

	Cash	+	Accounts Receivable	+	Office Supplies	+	Office Equipment	=	Liabilities	+	Stockholders' Equity	Explanation
1)	+20,000							=			+20,000	Capital investment
2)	-18,000						+18,000	=				
	2,000	+		+		+	18,000	=		+	20,000	
3)					+1,200			=	+1,200			
	2,000	+		+	1,200	+	18,000	=	1,200	+	20,000	
4)	+1,280							=			+1,280	Revenue
	3,280	+		+	1,200	+	18,000	=	1,200	+	21,280	

Verify that accounting equation is in balance.

	Assets		=	Liabilities	+	Owners' Equity
$3,280	+$1,200	+$18,000 =		$1,200	+	$21,280
	$22,480		=			$22,480

CHAPTER 3

Transaction Analysis: Debit and Credit Rules

CONTENTS

- Chapter Overview and Objectives
- The Use of Accounts as a Record
- Debit and Credit Rules
- Normal Account Balances
- Debit and Credit Rules in Transaction Analysis

CHAPTER OVERVIEW AND OBJECTIVES

In Chapter 2, transactions were analyzed and then recorded in columnar form in terms of the accounting equation. Although the columnar accounting system is useful for illustrating double-entry accounting and the fact that the accounting equation must always remain in balance, it is not a practical system for most firms that engage in a large number of transactions. Such firms need a more efficient accounting system that is capable of processing a large number of transactions. We begin our study of a more efficient system in this chapter. When you have completed this chapter, you will be able to:

1. Explain how an account is used in the recording process.
2. Define the three major parts of an account, and compute the balance of an account.
3. State the debit and credit rules for the various classifications of accounts.
4. Analyze transactions in terms of the rules of debit and credit, and enter the effects of the transactions in a T account.
5. Define each of the following terms:

T account	Account balance
Debit	Footing
Credit	Normal account balance
Charge	Chart of accounts

THE USE OF ACCOUNTS AS A RECORD

As defined in Chapter 2, an account is a device used to provide a record of increases and decreases in each item that appears in a firm's financial statements. Accountants, however, do not refer to the changes in the accounts as increases or decreases. Instead, the terms "debit" and "credit" are used. We must be careful to note, however, that a debit does not mean an increase in an account balance, nor does a credit necessarily mean that an account is decreased. To show you how accountants use these terms, it is helpful at this point to examine accounts that are designed for a more efficient processing of large amounts of accounting data.

Although an account may take various forms, each form contains three parts:

1. A title that is brief but descriptive of the nature of the items being recorded in the account. The account title is written at the top of the account.
2. A place for recording increases.
3. A place for recording decreases.

Also, accounts typically provide space for recording an account number, the date of the transaction, an explanation of the transaction, and a posting reference. (The purpose of the posting reference is discussed in the next chapter.) One simplified format, called a **T account**, because of its similarity to the letter T, is shown below.

Account Title

Left side or **debit** side (Abbreviation - Dr.)	Right side or **credit** side (Abbreviation - Cr.)

A T account has a left side and a right side, respectively called the **debit** side and the **credit** side. The terms are frequently abbreviated as "Dr" for debit and "Cr" for credit. An account is debited when an amount is entered on the left side, and the amounts shown on the left side are called debits. Making an entry on the right side is crediting the account, and the amounts shown on the right side of an account are called credits. A debit is also called a **charge** to the account.

A common misconception is that a debit is good and that a credit is bad. You must be careful not to imply any positive or negative connotation to the terms. Debit simply means the left side of an account, and credit means the right side. Whether a debit or a credit is an increase to the account balance depends on whether the account is an asset, a liability, or an owners' equity account.

To illustrate the mechanics involved, assume that the transactions affecting the Cash account of a firm were recorded in a T account as follows: Cash receipts (increases) are recorded on the debit side of the account, and cash payments (decreases) are entered on the credit side.

Cash			
Debit (Dr.)		Credit (Cr.)	
(1)	60,000	(2)	30,000
(4)	6,000	(6)	3,700
(7)	1,100	(8)	5,700
		(9)	600
	67,100		40,000
Balance	27,100		

In practice, amounts entered in an account are usually identified by the date the transaction occurred. As in the Cash account shown above, dates are often omitted when the T account format is used. When dates are not provided, transactions are usually identified by letters or numbers. Since every transaction causes a change in two or more accounts, such identification permits an interested party to review the other accounts to match the other side of an entry. For example, if someone wanted to determine what caused cash to increase by $60,000 [transaction (1)], the remaining accounts would be reviewed to find an entry identified with a (1).

Recording the receipts and payments on different sides of the account facilitates the determination of the account balance. The **account balance** is the difference between the sum of its debits and the sum of its credits. If the sum of the debits exceeds the sum of the credits, the account has a debit balance. A credit balance results when the sum of the credits is greater than the sum of the debits. An account has a zero balance if the sum of the debits equals the sum of the credits. In the Cash account above, the cash receipts of $67,100 exceeded the payments of $40,000, resulting in a debit balance of $27,100.

In a T account format, the totals, called **footings**, are sometimes written smaller or in a different color than the postings so that the totals will not be interpreted as additional debits and credits. The footings are often omitted with just the balance entered after a single rule. The debit balance of $27,100 in the Cash account is inserted on the debit side of the account. A balance sheet prepared at this time would report $27,100 in cash as an asset.

PRACTICE ACTIVITY 3-1

I. Complete the following statements by entering a word in the blank space that will make the statement a valid statement.

1. The left side of an account is called the _____ side; the right side of an account is called the _____ side.
2. An account is _____ when an amount is entered on the left side of the account.
3. Amounts entered on the right side of an account are called _____,

II. A cash account is shown below:

	Cash		
(1)	12,000	(3)	4,000
(2)	7,200	(4)	6,800
		(5)	450

    a. Compute the footing for the debit side of the account.
    b. Compute the footing for the credit side of the account.
    c. Compute the account balance.

DEBIT AND CREDIT RULES

In the analysis of transactions in Chapter 2, we had to determine which items (accounts) were affected by a transaction and the amount by which each item was to be increased or decreased. Each transaction affected at least two financial statement items, a system called *double-entry accounting*. We emphasized that after every transaction, the accounting equation had to be in balance. As discussed earlier, accountants do not refer to the changes in the accounts as increases or decreases, but they use terms with special meaning called "debit" and "credit." Now with the introduction of these terms, each transaction must be analyzed to determine:

1. Which accounts are affected.
2. Whether each account affected is to be increased or decreased.
3. Whether, given the account classification, the account should be debited or credited to record the change.
4. By what amount each account is changed.

We will now examine the rules of debit and credit for each classification of accounts.

RECORDING CHANGES IN ASSETS, LIABILITIES, AND OWNERS' EQUITY

Increases and decreases are recorded in the three categories of balance sheet accounts in the T account format as follows:

Assets		=	**Liabilities**		+	**Owners' Equity**	
Assets			Liabilities			Owners' Equity	
Debit to	Credit to		Debit to	Credit to		Debit to	Credit to
increase	decrease		decrease	increase		decrease	increase
+	−		−	, +		−	+

An increase to an asset account is recorded as a debit; an increase to a liability or owners' equity account is recorded as a credit. The fundamental logic behind these rules lies in the fact that external transactions or exchanges involve two components: that which is received (the debit) and that which is given (the credit). In other words, a receipt of an asset increases that asset, and giving up or consuming an asset, correspondingly, decreases it. With respect to liabilities, a promise to pay later increases the debt and the payment of the debt decreases it. In the case of owners' equity, the credit to increase it shows the entity's acknowledgment to the owners of their increased interest in the firm. The debit to owners' equity shows that the entity has received a release from further accountability to owners for their interest because the owners' interest has been reduced or eliminated by unprofitable operations and/or dividends.

Note the relationship of the debit/credit rules to the accounting equation. Assets are on the left side of the equation and are increased on the left side of the T account (the debit side); liabilities and owners' equity accounts are on the right side of the equation and are increased on the right side of the T account (the credit side). Decreases are recorded opposite of increases. Thus, a decrease in an asset is recorded as a credit; a decrease in a liability or an owners' equity account is recorded as a debit.

The recording of increases to asset accounts on the debit side and increases to liability and owners' equity accounts on the credit side permits an additional check for accuracy. Not only must the accounting equation be in balance but the dollar amounts of the debits must also equal the dollar amounts of the credits for each transaction. Therefore, since each transaction must balance, the sum of the accounts with debit balances must equal the sum of the accounts with credit balances. As will be discussed in Chapter 4, this check does not mean, however, that there are no errors in the accounts. For example, in analyzing a transaction, the wrong amount may be entered in both accounts or the balance in the wrong accounts may be changed. The fact that the sum of the debit balances is equal to the sum of the credit balances simply assures you that, for each transaction, an equal debit and credit were made to the accounts and, given this, the account balances were computed properly.

A DETAILED LOOK AT THE COMPONENTS OF OWNERS' EQUITY

In Chapter 2, all changes in owners' equity were entered in a single column. It was noted that owners' equity is affected by the investment by the owners, distribution of assets to the owners, revenues, and expenses. Because of the volume of transactions, in particular revenues and expenses, a separate account is established for each major type of change in owners' equity.

The owners' equity component of the accounting equation can be classified into paid-in capital and retained earnings. Paid-in capital is increased by the amount invested by the owners. Retained earnings represents the amount of assets earned by the business and not yet distributed.

Paid-in Capital: An investment of cash or other assets in the business by an owner increases the owners' interest in the business and is recorded as a credit in a paid-in capital account. For example, when cash is invested in a corporation, Cash is debited (increased) and Common Stock, a paid-in capital account, is credited (increased). A reduction in the Common Stock account is made as debit. In practice a company may establish several different paid-in capital accounts.

Retained Earnings: As a component of owners' equity, the Retained earnings account is increased by a credit and decreased by a debit. The retained earnings of a firm is computed as follows:

Retained earnings = Beginning balance + Revenues − Expenses − Dividends

Thus, revenues, expenses, and dividends declared accounts are subclassifications of the retained earnings account.

Dividends Declared − Dividends are distributions of assets to the owners that reduce their interest in the business. Since dividend distributions decrease the owners' interest in the business, they are recorded as a debit to an owners' equity account and a credit to an asset account. Although dividends could be debited directly to the Retained Earnings account, a separate account, called Dividends Declared, is often established to provide an individual record of the total dividend distributions made during the period. Thus, Dividends Declared is a subclassification of the Retained Earnings account. A dividend paid to the owners is a distribution of income, not an expense related to the production of revenue. Therefore, dividend distributions are not reported in the income statement.

Revenues and Expenses − Revenues and expenses are changes in the owners' equity that are recorded in separate accounts and are subclassifications of the Retained Earnings account. A separate account is established to account for each major source of revenue and each major expense to facilitate the preparation of the income statement. The debit and credit rules for revenues and expenses are:

Revenues increase owners' equity. An increase in a revenue account is recorded as a credit, which is consistent with the recording of an increase in owners' equity. A decrease is recorded on the debit side.

Expenses decrease owners' equity. An increase in an expense account is entered on the debit side, and a decrease is recorded on the credit side. Note that a debit increases the balance in the expense account, but a debit made to an owners' equity account reduces owners' equity.

Debit and credit rules for owners' equity accounts are shown in Figure 3-1 in T account format.

PRACTICE ACTIVITY 3-2

1. Place a check mark in the appropriate column to indicate the effects of a debit to each of the following account classifications.

	Effects of debit	
	Increase	Decrease
Assets	____	____
Liabilities	____	____
Paid-in capital	____	____
Revenue	____	____
Expenses	____	____

2. A list of events with two columns headed debit and credit is given below. For each event listed, indicate whether the account should be debited or credited by placing a check mark in the correct column.

	Debit	Credit
a. Cash is increased.	____	____
b. A liability is decreased.	____	____
c. Common stock is increased.	____	____
d. Service revenue is increased.	____	____
e. Salary expense is increased.	____	____

Figure 3-1
Debit and Credit Rules for Owners' Equity Accounts

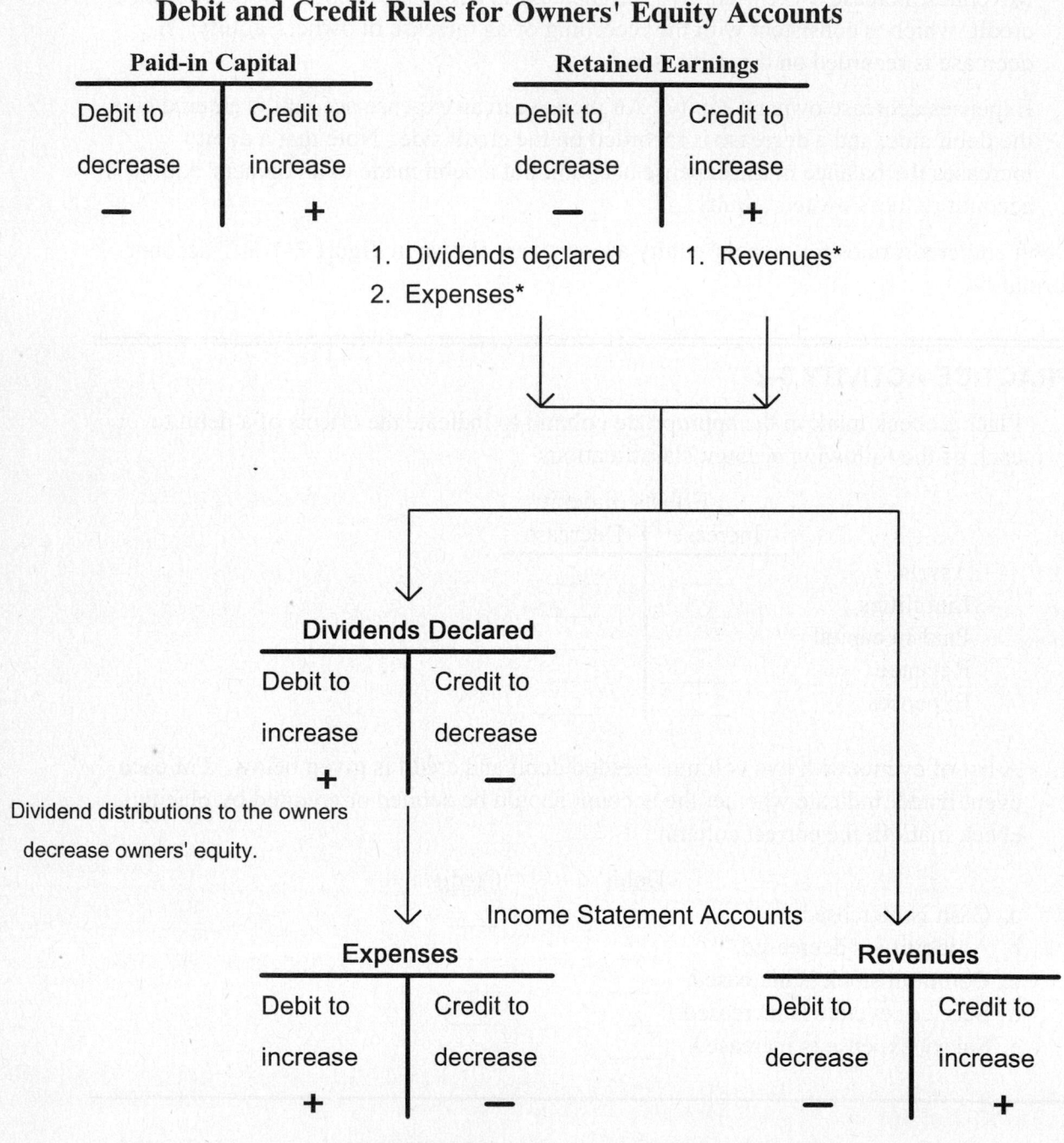

*Revenues minus expenses = net income or net loss. As shown in Chapter 7,
the net effect of revenues and expenses is transferred to retained earnings.

NORMAL ACCOUNT BALANCES

The **normal account balance** of an account is the side on which increases to the account are recorded. Knowing the normal account balance for an account can help find errors.

Type of Account	Side Increases Recorded on	Side Decreases Recorded on	Normal Balance
Assets	**Debit**	Credit	**Debit**
Liabilities	**Credit**	Debit	**Credit**
Owners' Equity			
Paid-in Capital	**Credit**	Debit	**Credit**
Dividends	**Debit**	Credit	**Debit**
Revenues	**Credit**	Debit	**Credit**
Expenses	**Debit**	Credit	**Debit**

If an account has a balance different from its normal balance, it is likely that an error has been made. For example, a credit balance should not be found in the Land account, nor should a debit balance be found in a revenue account. However, if a bank account has been overdrawn, the Cash account will have a credit balance.

Understanding the rules of debit and credit is fundamental to understanding the material in the rest of this book. Thus, these rules should be mastered now. Here are some easy rules to help:

- Remember that to debit an account simply means to enter an amount on the left side of the account.

- To credit an account simply means to enter an amount on the right side of the account.

- A debit may increase or decrease the account balance, depending on whether the account is on the left or right side of the accounting equation. The same is true for a credit.

- Do not think of a debit or credit as an increase or decrease but simply as an entry on the left or right side.

When analyzing a transaction, think in terms of which accounts are affected by the transaction: Given the type of account, should it be debited or credited to properly reflect the change in the account?

PRACTICE ACTIVITY 3-3

For each account listed below, indicate whether it is increased with a debit or a credit entry, and indicate what each account's normal balance should be by placing a check mark in the appropriate column.

	Increase		Normal Balance	
Account	Debit	Credit	Debit	Credit
a. Cash	_____	_____	_____	_____
b. Accounts Payable	_____	_____	_____	_____
c. Service Revenue	_____	_____	_____	_____
d. Salary Expense	_____	_____	_____	_____
e. Common Stock	_____	_____	_____	_____
f. Land	_____	_____	_____	_____

DEBIT AND CREDIT RULES IN TRANSACTION ANALYSIS

We will now illustrate how the debit and credit rules and double-entry accounting are applied in an analysis of transactions entered into by Ace Security Service. After each transaction is analyzed, the information is entered in T accounts. The accountant for the firm established the following accounts to record transactions of the firm. Each account is normally assigned a number that is useful for reference.

100	Cash	200	Accounts Payable	300	Common Stock
110	Accounts Receivable	210	Utilities Payable	320	Retained Earnings
130	Prepaid Rent	230	Unearned Revenue	350	Dividends Declared
140	Office Supplies on Hand			400	Service Revenue
				500	Rent Expense
				510	Salary Expense
				520	Utilities Expense

Such a listing of all account titles used by a firm and their related numbers is called a **chart of accounts.**

Transaction: Common stock is issued for cash.

June 1   Investors purchased 5,000 shares of $5 par value common stock for $25,000.

Analysis: The transaction increases an asset, Cash, which is recorded on the left (debit) side of the Cash account, and increases owners' equity, which is recorded as a credit in the Common Stock account.

Accounts Affected	Type of Account	+ or −	Debit or Credit	Amount
Cash	Asset	+	Debit	$25,000
Common Stock	Owners' Equity	+	Credit	$25,000

Cash	100	Common Stock	300
6/1 25,000			6/1 25,000

Transaction: Paid six months' rent for use of building.

June 1 Rented an office building for $2,000 a month. Paid six months' rent in advance for a total of $12,000.

Analysis: The rent paid in advance is initially recorded as an asset, Prepaid Rent. An asset account is debited to increase its balance. The asset acquired is the right to use the building for six months, which will be expensed as the building is used. The payment of cash decreases the Cash account, a credit.

Accounts Affected	Type of Account	+ or −	Debit or Credit	Amount
Prepaid Rent	Asset	+	Debit	$12,000
Cash	Asset	−	Credit	$12,000

```
              Cash          100           Prepaid Rent       130
   6/1    25,000  | 6/1    12,000     6/1     12,000 |
                  |                                  |
                  |                                  |
```

Transaction: Hired two employees.

Analysis: The hiring of employees is an important event but is not given accounting recognition since there are no effects at this time on the firm's accounting equation.

Transaction: Purchased office supplies on account.

June 1 Purchased office supplies in the amount of $450 on account.

Analysis: This transaction increases both an asset and a liability by the same amount. Increases in assets are recorded by debits, and increases in liabilities are recorded by credits. As the supplies are consumed, their cost will be transferred to an expense account as discussed in Chapter 6.

Accounts Affected	Type of Account	+ or −	Debit or Credit	Amount
Office Supplies on Hand	Asset	+	Debit	$450
Accounts Payable	Liability	+	Credit	$450

```
      Office Supplies
         On Hand       140        Accounts Payable     200
   6/1      450  |                        | 6/1      450
                 |                        |
                 |                        |
```

Transaction: Performed security service for cash and on account.

June 3 Performed a service for a client and charged a fee of $6,000. The agreement
provided for a cash payment of $1,000, and the remainder is due within 24 days.

Analysis: This is a revenue transaction. The company has performed a service in
exchange for cash and the right to receive cash in the future (Accounts Receivable). The
asset accounts Cash and Accounts Receivable are both debited to increase their balances.
Revenue increases owners' equity (a credit). A separate account, Service Revenue, is
established to facilitate preparation of the income statement.

Accounts Affected	Type of Account	+ or –	Debit or Credit	Amount
Cash	Asset	+	Debit	$1,000
Accounts Receivable	Asset	+	Debit	$5,000
Service Revenue	Revenue	+	Credit	$6,000

All transactions illustrated thus far have involved one debit and one credit. Business
transactions may, however, require that more than one debit and/or credit be made to
properly adjust the accounts. The transaction analyzed above involves a change in three
accounts; two are debited and one is credited. Note, however, that the rules of double-
entry accounting are still observed. First, the sum of the debit amount(s) ($1,000+
$5,000) for this transaction equals the sum of the credit amount(s) ($6,000); and second,
the equality of the accounting equation is maintained with assets increasing $6,000 and
owners' equity increasing $6,000.

```
            Cash          100        Accounts Receivable 110
   6/1   25,000 | 6/1   12,000       6/3      5,000 |
   6/3    1,000 |


                     Service Revenue      400
                               | 6/3      6,000
```

Transaction: Paid an expense.

June 20 Paid salaries of $2,500 to the receptionist and part-time employees for services
they rendered during the last two weeks. Withholdings from the employees'
salaries for taxes are ignored for now.

Analysis: The cost of services performed by employees is an expense to the business.
The benefits were considered received when the work was performed. An expense is
increased by a debit. Expenses decrease owners' equity (a debit), but a separate expense
account is created for each major type of expense to facilitate preparation of the income
statement. Cash is decreased by a credit.

Accounts Affected	Type of Account	+ or –	Debit or Credit	Amount
Salary Expense	Expense	+	Debit	$2,500
Cash	Asset	–	Credit	$2,500

Cash			100	Salary Expense	510
6/1	25,000	6/1	12,000	6/20 2,500	
6/3	1,000	6/20	2,500		

The analysis of transactions and entering them in the T accounts for the remainder of this illustration will be shown in summary format.

Transaction: Received cash as payment on account.

June 26 A check for $5,000 was received for services performed on June 3.

Accounts Affected	Type of Account	+ or –	Debit or Credit	Amount
Cash	Asset	+	Debit	$5,000
Accounts Receivable	Asset	–	Credit	$5,000

Cash			100	Accounts Receivable		110
6/1	25,000	6/1	12,000	6/3 5,000	6/26	5,000
6/3	1,000	6/20	2,500			
6/26	5,000					

Transaction: Paid a cash dividend to stockholders.

June 30 Declared and paid a cash dividend of $600 to the stockholders.

Accounts Affected	Type of Account	+ or –	Debit or Credit	Amount
Dividends Declared	Owners' Equity	+*	Debit	$600
Cash	Asset	–	Credit	$600

*The payment of a dividend is a distribution of assets to the owners; it is not an expense related to the production of revenue. A distribution to the owners is recorded as a decrease in assets and a decrease in owners' equity. A Dividends Declared account is used to keep a separate record of dividend payments made to stockholders. A debit to the Dividends Declared account increases the account balance, but it is a decrease in owners' equity.

```
          Cash          100      Dividends Declared   350
 6/1    25,000  6/1    12,000     6/30        600
 6/3     1,000  6/20    2,500
 6/26    5,000  6/30      600
```

Transaction: Received cash for services to be performed in the future.

June 30 Received $500 from a client for security services to be provided in 45 days.

Accounts Affected	Type of Account	+ or −	Debit or Credit	Amount
Cash	Asset	+	Debit	$500
Unearned Revenue	Liability	+	Credit	$500

```
          Cash          100      Unearned Revenue    230
 6/1    25,000  6/1    12,000                  6/30    500
 6/3     1,000  6/20    2,500
 6/26    5,000  6/30      600
 6/30      500
```

Transaction: Paid cash on accounts payable.

June 30 Paid $380 to creditors for office supplies purchased on credit.

Accounts Affected	Type of Account	+ or −	Debit or Credit	Amount
Accounts Payable	Liability	−	Debit	$380
Cash	Asset	−	Credit	$380

```
          Cash          100      Accounts Payable    200
 6/1    25,000  6/1    12,000     6/30    380  6/1     450
 6/3     1,000  6/20    2,500
 6/26    5,000  6/30      600
 6/30      500  6/30      380
```

Transaction: Received a bill for utilities for the month.

June 30 Received, but did not pay, bill for June utilities in the amount of $200.

Accounts Affected	Type of Account	+ or −	Debit or Credit	Amount
Utilities Expense	Expense	+	Debit	$200
Utilities Payable	Liability	+	Credit	$200

Utilities Payable	210	Utilities Expense	520
	6/30 200	6/30 200	

A general ledger in T account format, after the effects of the above transactions have been entered and the balance of each account computed, is presented in Figure 3-2. (Recall that the general ledger is a collection of the complete set of accounts established by a specific firm.) In an actual accounting system, each account would be a separate page in the ledger.

PRACTICE ACTIVITY 3-4

Enter the following transactions in the T accounts given below.

July 1   An individual invested $10,000 in a business and received $10,000 in common stock.

July 9   The company billed clients $2,200 for services completed on July 9.

July 18 Received $1,800 cash from the clients billed on July 9.

July 22 Received $700 cash from clients for services performed. The clients had not been billed previously.

July 24 Paid employees' salaries totaling $1,450.

Cash   Common Stock

Accounts Receivable   Revenue

                                  Salary Expense

FIGURE 3-2

LEDGER FOR ACE SECURITY SERVICE

	Assets	=	Liabilities	+	Owners' Equity

Cash   100

6/1	25,000	6/1	12,000
6/3	1,000	6/20	2,500
6/26	5,000	6/30	600
6/30	500	6/30	380
Bal.	16,020		

Accounts Receivable   110

6/3	5,000	6/26	5,000

Prepaid Rent   130

6/1	12,000		

Office Supplies on Hand 140

6/1	450		

Accounts Payable   200

6/30	380	6/1	450

Utilities Payable   210

		6/30	200

Unearned Revenue   230

		6/30	500

Common Stock   300

		6/1	25,000

Retained Earnings   320

Dividends Declared 350

6/30	600		

Service Revenue   400

		6/3	6,000

Rent Expense   500

Salary Expense   510

6/20	2,500		

Utilities Expense 520

6/30	200		

SOLUTIONS TO PRACTICE ACTIVITIES

PRACTICE ACTIVITY 3-1

I. 1. debit, credit
    2. debited
    3. credits
II. a. $19,200 b. $11,250   c. $7,950

PRACTICE ACTIVITY 3-2

1.

	Effects of debit	
	Increase	Decrease
Assets	√	___
Liabilities	___	√
Paid-in capital	___	√
Revenue	___	√
Expenses	√	___

2.

	Debit	Credit
a. Cash is increased.	√	___
b. A liability is decreased.	√	___
c. Common stock is increased.	___	√
d. Service revenue is increased.	___	√
e. Salary expense is increased.	√	___

PRACTICE ACTIVITY 3-3

		Increase		Normal Balance	
	Account	Debit	Credit	Debit	Credit
a.	Cash	√	___	√	___
b.	Accounts Payable	___	√	___	√
c.	Service Revenue	___	√	___	√
d.	Salary Expense	√	___	√	___
e.	Common Stock	___	√	___	√
f.	Land	√	___	√	___

PRACTICE ACTIVITY 3-4

```
           Cash                              Common Stock
 7/1   10,000  | 7/24   1,450                      | 7/1    10,000
 7/18   1,800  |                                   |
 7/22     700  |                                   |
               |                                   |
               |                                   |


      Accounts Receivable                     Revenue
 7/9    2,200  | 7/18   1,800                      | 7/9    2,200
               |                                   | 7/22     700
               |                                   |
               |                                   |


                        Salary Expense
                   7/24   1,450  |
                                 |
                                 |
```

CHAPTER 4

Recording Transactions
in the General Journal and
Posting to the General Ledger

CONTENTS

- Chapter Overview and Objectives
- The Accounting Data Processing Cycle
- Step 1: Transactions Occur and Source Documents Are Prepared
- Step 2: Transactions Are Analyzed and Recorded in a Journal
- Step 3: Journal Entries Are Posted to the Ledger
- Step 4: Preparation of a Trial Balance
- Illustrative Problem
- Discovery and Correction of Errors

CHAPTER OVERVIEW AND OBJECTIVES

When you have completed this chapter, you will be able to:

1. List the steps in the accounting data processing cycle.
2. Record transactions in the general journal.
3. Post journal entries from the general journal to the general ledger.
4. Prepare a trial balance.
5. Locate and correct errors.

Until this point we have been emphasizing the analysis of transactions in the framework of the double-entry accounting system. Transactions occur and are analyzed continuously during an accounting period. Financial statements and reports can be generated as often as needed, but they are issued to interested parties at least once a year (the firm's fiscal year) as part of a firm's annual report. This cycle, called the *accounting data processing cycle,* is completed at least once each fiscal year. Part of the cycle is completed during the period, and part is performed at the end of the period. In this chapter we will go into greater detail about the accounting procedures carried out during the period in accounting for the operations of a business. The remaining part of the cycle, completed at the end of the accounting period, is discussed in Chapters 6 and 7. The complete cycle is discussed and diagrammed in the first section of this chapter.

THE ACCOUNTING DATA PROCESSING CYCLE

During each fiscal year, a sequence of accounting procedures called the **accounting data processing cycle** (or simply the **accounting cycle**) is completed. The steps in the cycle are diagrammed in Figure 4-1 and are as follows:

Steps Performed during the Period

Step 1   **Transactions occur.** Transactions occur, and source documents are prepared to collect information related to the transactions.

Step 2   **Journalize transactions.** Source documents are analyzed to determine accounts affected and the dollar amounts involved. The transactions are recorded in the general journal (or special journals as discussed in Chapter 11).

Step 3   **Post journal entries to ledger accounts.** Debits and credits are transferred to the proper accounts in the ledger.

Performed at the End of the Period

Step 4   **Prepare a worksheet.** An unadjusted trial balance is prepared as part of the worksheet, and the worksheet is completed.

Step 5   **Journalize and post adjusting entries.** Using the information in the worksheet, adjusting entries are journalized and posted to the ledger.

Step 6   **Prepare financial statements.** Using the information in the worksheet, the following financial statements are prepared.

1. Income statement.
2. Retained earnings statement.
3. Balance sheet.
4. A statement of cash flows is also prepared, the preparation of which is not covered in this course.

Step 7   **Journalize and post closing entries.** Using the information in the worksheet, closing entries are journalized and posted to the ledger.

Step 8   **Prepare post-closing trial balance.** A post-closing trial balance is prepared to verify that accounts are in balance after the adjusting and closing entries have been posted.

Optional Step   **Journalize and post reversing entries.** Reversing entries are dated the first day of the next accounting period. Reversing entries are made to facilitate the recording of routine transactions in the next period.

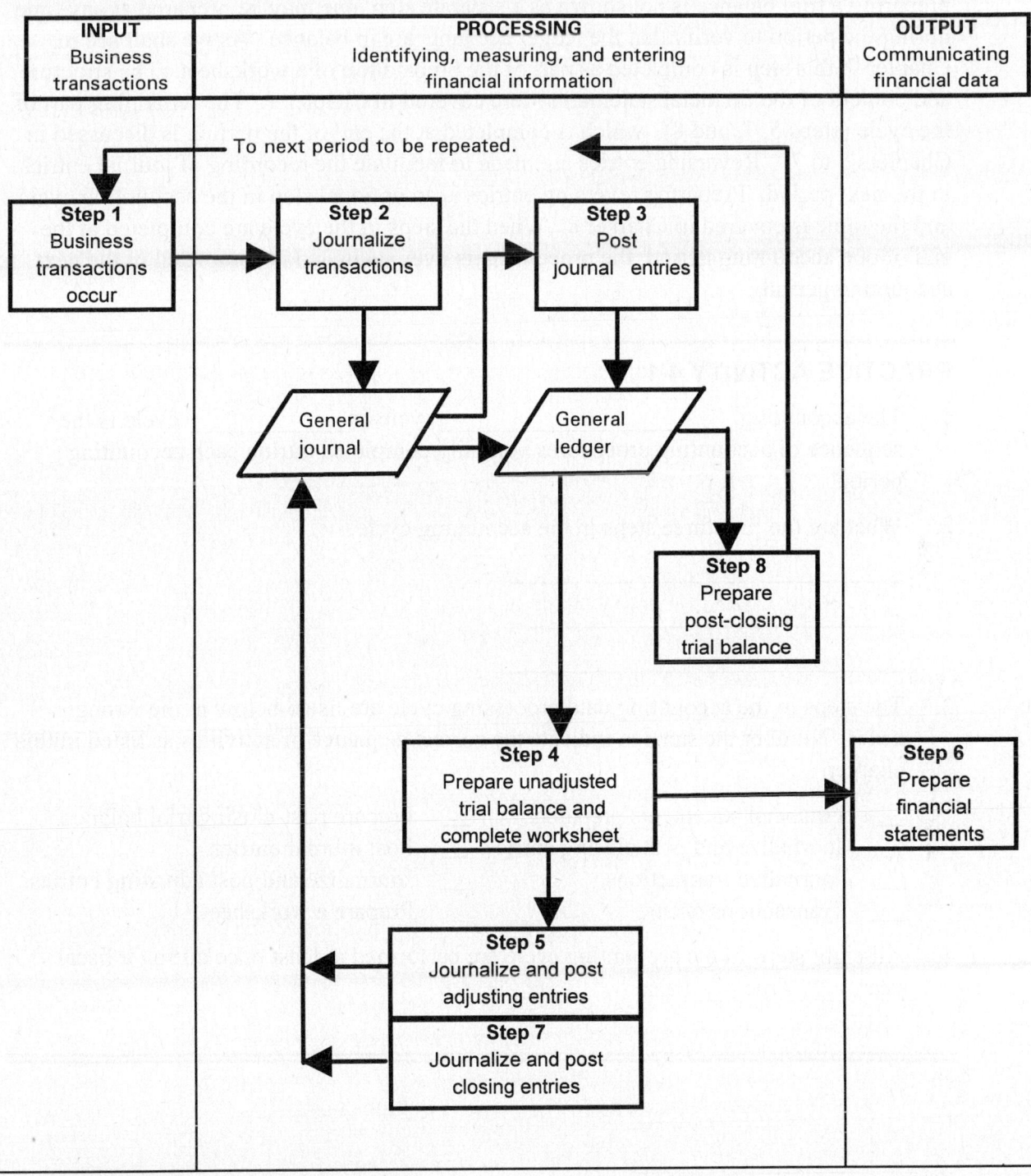

FIGURE 4-1
STEPS IN THE ACCOUNTING CYCLE

The first three steps in the accounting cycle are carried out during an accounting period as transactions occur. These three steps are described in detail in this chapter. Although preparing a trial balance is not shown as a separate step, one may be prepared at any time during the period to verify that the ledger accounts are in balance. As we shall see in Chapter 7, this step is completed as part of the preparation of a worksheet. The structure and content of the financial statements were covered in Chapter 1. The remaining part of the cycle (steps 5, 7, and 8), which is completed at the end of the period, is discussed in Chapters 5 to 7.[1] Reversing entries are made to facilitate the recording of journal entries in the next period. Preparing reversing entries is an optional step in the accounting cycle, and the topic is covered in Chapter 8. When the steps in the cycle are completed at the end of one accounting period, the process starts over again and is completed in the next accounting period.

PRACTICE ACTIVITY 4-1

1. The accounting _____ _____ cycle or _____ cycle is the sequence of accounting procedures normally completed during each accounting period.

2. What are the first three steps in the accounting cycle.

    _____

    _____

    _____

3. The steps in the accounting data processing cycle are listed below in the wrong order. Number the steps to indicate the correct sequence of activities as listed in this chapter.

    ___ Financial statements prepared.   ___ Prepare post-closing trial balance.
    ___ Journalize and post closing entries. ___ Post journal entries.
    ___ Journalize transactions.   ___ Journalize and post adjusting entries.
    ___ Transactions occur.   ___ Prepare a worksheet.

4. All eight steps in the accounting cycle are performed at least once during a fiscal year. ___ True ___ False

---

[1]In practice and in other textbooks, you will find that the sequence in the accounting cycle in which financial statements are prepared varies. Since the end of period part of the cycle is prepared directly from the worksheet, financial statements may be prepared before, after, or in between journalizing and posting of adjusting entries and journalizing and posting closing entries.

STEP 1: TRANSACTIONS OCCUR AND SOURCE DOCUMENTS ARE PREPARED

As discussed in previous chapters, the accounting process begins when a transaction occurs. A source document is prepared that contains information about the nature of the transaction and the dollar amount involved. The identification, measurement, and recording of the economic effects of each transaction are based on an analysis of the source document.

STEP 2: TRANSACTIONS ARE ANALYZED AND RECORDED IN A JOURNAL

Applying the rules of debit and credit in the analysis of transactions was illustrated in the last chapter. In doing so, transaction data were entered directly into the accounts in the general ledger. As a result, each account shows only the increases or decreases in that account. Since each transaction is recorded in two or more accounts in the ledger, no single account will contain a complete record of a transaction. There are times, however, when an interested party may want to examine a complete transaction or all transactions for a certain time period may need to be retrieved. To provide a complete record of all transactions in one place as they occur in chronological order, transactions are first entered in a business record called a journal. In other words, in the typical manual accounting system, the first record of a transaction is in a book called a **journal.** Since this is the initial recording of a transaction, journals are referred to as **books of original entry**.

The journal contains the title and dollar amount of each account (or accounts) to be debited or credited for each transaction. The transactions are then entered in the individual accounts in the general ledger as discussed in a later section of this chapter.

Recording Transactions in a Journal

The number of journals used and the design of each journal vary from firm to firm, depending on the nature of the firm's operations and the frequency of a particular type of transaction. This chapter is concerned with the **general** or **two-column journal**, so called because it contains two columns for entering dollar amounts. Often, when large numbers of transactions of the same type occur, a firm establishes special journals to reduce the clerical work involved in recording and posting the transactions. Special journals are discussed in Chapter 11.

The standard form of a general journal and the conventional format used to enter transactions in the journal are shown in Figure 4-2. Recording transactions in a journal is called **journalizing**. Each transaction recorded is a separate **journal entry**. Two journal entries are illustrated in Figure 4-2. Before a journal entry is prepared, it is necessary to analyze the transaction to determine which accounts are affected and the amount by

**FIGURE 4-2
EXAMPLE OF A GENERAL
JOURNAL**

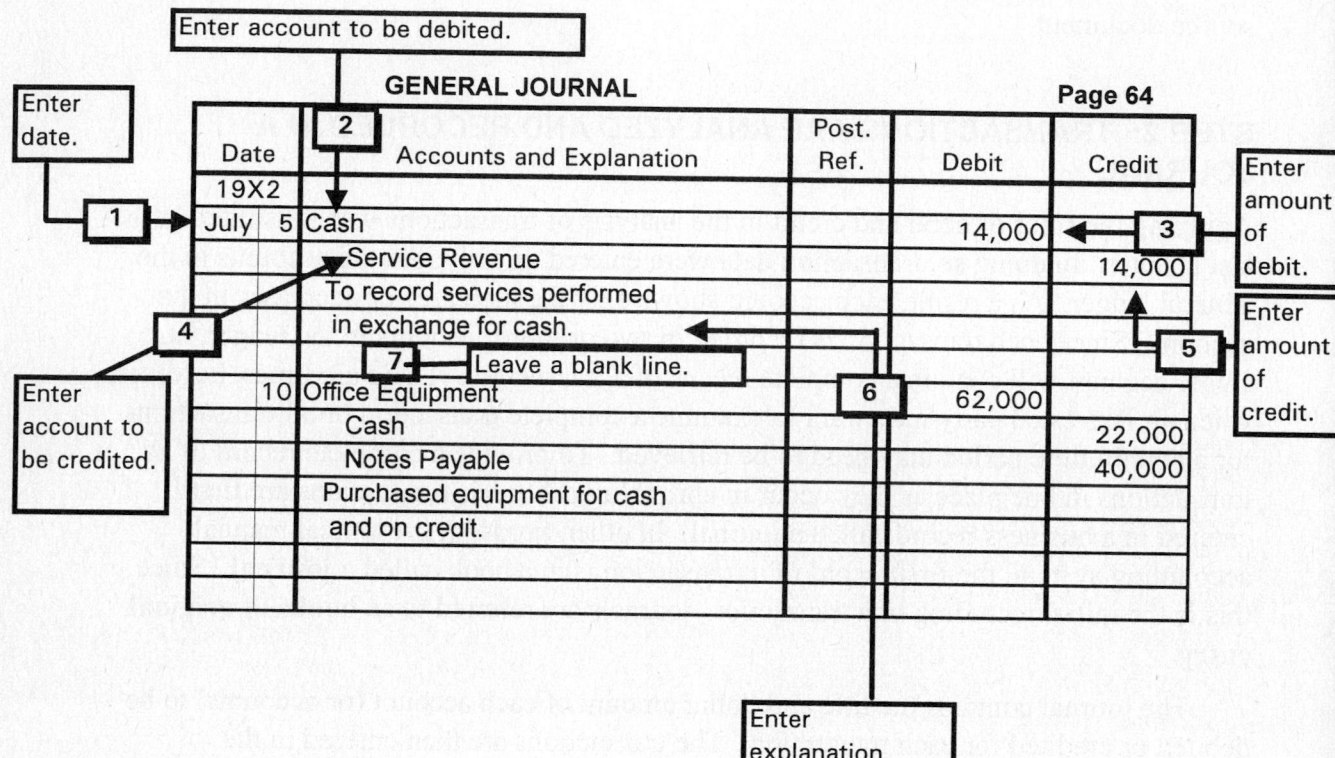

Enter account to be debited.

Enter date.

Enter amount of debit.

Enter account to be credited.

Leave a blank line.

Enter amount of credit.

Enter explanation.

GENERAL JOURNAL   Page 64

Date		Accounts and Explanation	Post. Ref.	Debit	Credit
19X2					
July	5	Cash		14,000	
		Service Revenue			14,000
		To record services performed			
		in exchange for cash.			
	10	Office Equipment		62,000	
		Cash			22,000
		Notes Payable			40,000
		Purchased equipment for cash			
		and on credit.			

which each account is to be changed. The first entry shows that the Cash account is to be debited for $14,000 and a revenue account (Service Revenue) is to be credited for the same amount. The second entry records the purchase of office equipment (debit, $62,000) with a partial payment in cash (credit, $22,000) and the balance financed on credit, called a note payable (credit, $40,000). The second entry is called a *compound journal entry* because it involves more than two accounts. Note that the rules of double-entry accounting are observed for each transaction.

Every page in the journal is numbered for easy reference (page 64 in Figure 4-2). Before an entry is made in the journal, the year and month are written at the top of the first column. They are not repeated until the start of a new page or a new month. The process for journalizing transactions is described below. The steps in the process are keyed to the first entry in Figure 4-2.

1. The date that each transaction occurs is entered in the Date column.

2. The title of the account or accounts to be debited is entered against the left margin of the Accounts and Explanation column.

3. The amount to be debited to each account is entered in the Debit column on the same line as the account title.

4. The title of the account or accounts to be credited is entered on the line immediately below the account debited. A credit is indented to set it apart from the account debited.

5. The amount to be credited to the account identified is entered in the Credit column on the same line as the account title.

6. An explanation of the transaction may be entered on the line immediately below the journal entry. The explanation is also indented as shown in Figure 4-2. Unless a transaction is unusual, this step is often omitted because the nature of the transaction is obvious.

7. A single line is usually skipped between each transaction.

At the time that the journal entry is made, the Posting Reference column (discussed later) is left blank.

PRACTICE ACTIVITY 4-2

I. Complete the following statements by entering a word in the blank space that will make the statement a valid statement.

1. A journal is often called the book of _____ entry.
2. The _____ _____ is a book containing a chronological listing of transactions.
3. Entering transactions in the journal is called _____.

4. The posting reference column of the general journal is left blank when an entry is first entered in the journal. _____ True _____ False

5. When recording a transaction in the general journal, account titles of accounts to be _____ are indented.

6. _____ amounts are placed in the left money column, and _____ amounts are placed in the right money column in the general journal.

II. The following transactions were entered into by Kachina Service Bureau:

Nov. 5   Billed customers for services performed in the amount of $11,400.

10   Purchased office equipment for $8,000. Paid $2,000 in cash and signed a note payable for the balance.

Required:

Enter each of the transactions in the general journal.

General Journal				Page 1
Date	Explanation	Post. Ref.	Debit	Credit

STEP 3: JOURNAL ENTRIES ARE POSTED TO THE LEDGER

The **general ledger** (or *ledger*) is a collection of the complete set of accounts established by a specific firm. In a manual system, each account is usually maintained on a separate card or a separate sheet in a loose-leaf binder. The card file or the loose-leaf binder with all of its pages is, collectively, the general ledger.

Sequence and Numbering of Accounts in the Ledger

Accounts are normally contained in the ledger in the order they appear in the balance sheet and the income statement, making them easier to find when looking for a specific account. Each account has an identification number that is useful for reference and as a means for cross-referencing the transactions entered in a specific account. A **chart of accounts** is a listing of the complete account titles and their related numbers.

When analyzing transactions, one refers to the chart of accounts to identify specific accounts to be increased or decreased. If an appropriate account title is not listed in the chart of accounts, an additional account may be added. A flexible numbering system permits the addition of accounts as necessary. For example:

Type of Account	Account Numbers
Assets	100-199
Liabilities	200-299
Owners' equity	300-399
Revenues	400-499
Expenses	500-599

Some numbers would not be assigned within each classification of accounts to permit the insertion of new accounts as they are needed.

A chart of accounts used in this and later chapters to illustrate the accounting for the Quality Real Estate Office, Inc., is shown in Figure 4-3.

TRANSFERRING DATA FROM THE JOURNAL TO THE LEDGER ACCOUNTS – STANDARD ACCOUNT FORMATS

The T account format described in Chapter 3 is a convenient way to show the effects of transactions on individual accounts and is used primarily in accounting textbooks and in classroom illustrations. In practice, however, companies often use an alternative format called the three-column or running balance format. An example of this format is shown in Figure 4-4. This format includes the parts of an account discussed in Chapter 3. An account title and account number are shown at the top of the account. This format is called the three-column format because there are three columns for entering dollar amounts: a debit column, a credit column, and a balance column. The convention of entering debits on the left and credits on the right is followed in this form. The balance column is added and is used to show the balance in the account after each entry is entered, hence, the name running balance format. There is a place for recording the date that the transaction occurred, an explanation, and a posting reference (discussed in the next section). Accountants generally omit the explanation because the particular entry can be traced back to the general journal for an explanation. This format will be used in the remainder of this chapter.

In computing an account balance, you must determine whether the existing balance is a debit or a credit. To do so, identify the type of account and its normal balance, and then review the previous amounts recorded to ensure that the exiting account balance is normal for that account. You must then adjust the balance for the debit or credit entry currently being made to the account. The Cash account in Figure 4-4 has a normal debit balance. The $22,000 credit entry on July 10 reduces the existing debit balance of $64,000 to $42,000, whereas the $3,500 debit entry increases the current debit balance of $42,000 to $45,500. You must take care in computing new account balances because it is easy to make mistakes.

FIGURE 4-3
CHART OF ACCOUNTS

QUALITY REAL ESTATE OFFICE, INC.

Chart of Accounts

Balance Sheet Accounts		Income Statement Accounts	
Account Title	Acct. No.	Account Title	Acct. No.
Assets		**Revenues**	
Cash	100	Commissions Revenue	400
Accounts Receivable	104	Management Fees Revenue	402
Prepaid Insurance	110	**Expenses**	
Office Supplies on Hand	111	Salaries Expense	500
Land	150	Commissions Expense	505
Building	160	Utilities Expense	510
Accumulated Depreciation—	161	Advertising Expense	520
Building		Insurance Expense	521
Office Equipment	170	Office Supplies Expense	530
Accumulated Depreciation—	171	Depreciation Expense	540
Equipment		Income Tax Expense	560
Liabilities		Interest Expense	590
Accounts Payable	200		
Salaries Payable	210		
Commissions Payable	211		
Interest Payable	215		
Utilities Payable	216		
Unearned Management Fees	220		
Income Taxes Payable	225		
Mortgage Note Payable	230		
Owners' Equity			
Capital Stock	300		
Retained Earnings	310		
Dividends Declared	320		
Income Summary	350		

FIGURE 4-4
EXAMPLE OF THREE-COLUMN ACCOUNT FORMAT

Account: Cash					Account No. 100
Date	Explanation	Post. Ref.	Debit	Credit	Balance
19X2					
July 1	Beginning balance				50,000
5		GJ64	14,000		64,000
10		GJ64		22,000	42,000
14		GJ65	3,500		45,500

Posting Illustrated

The process of transferring amounts entered in the journal to the proper ledger accounts is called **posting**. The objective of posting is to classify the effects of all transactions on each individual asset, liability, owners' equity, revenue, and expense account. Posting is done periodically, for example, at the end of each day or each week.

The posting of one journal entry from Figure 4-2 with one debit and one credit is shown in Figure 4-5. The three-column account format is illustrated here. The debit is posted in the top half of the figure, and the credit is posted in the bottom half. The steps involved in the posting process are:

1. Locate the account to be debited in the ledger .

2. Enter the date that the transaction occurred, as shown in the journal.

3. Enter the debit amount in the Debit column of the ledger account, and compute the account balance.

4. Enter, in the Posting Reference column of the ledger account, the journal and page number from which the entry is being posted.

5. Enter, in the Posting Reference column of the journal, the account number to which the debit amount was posted.

6-10. Repeat steps 1 through 5 for the credit part of the entry.

A new account balance is computed after each posting when the three-column format is used. The explanation column in ledger accounts is often left blank because the nature of each transaction can be traced back to the general journal.

In Figure 4-5, the posting reference (GJ64) in the general ledger account indicates that the entry was posted from page 64 of the general journal. This provides a convenient

FIGURE 4-5
POSTING FROM THE GENERAL JOURNAL
TO THE GENERAL LEDGER

Posting the Debit

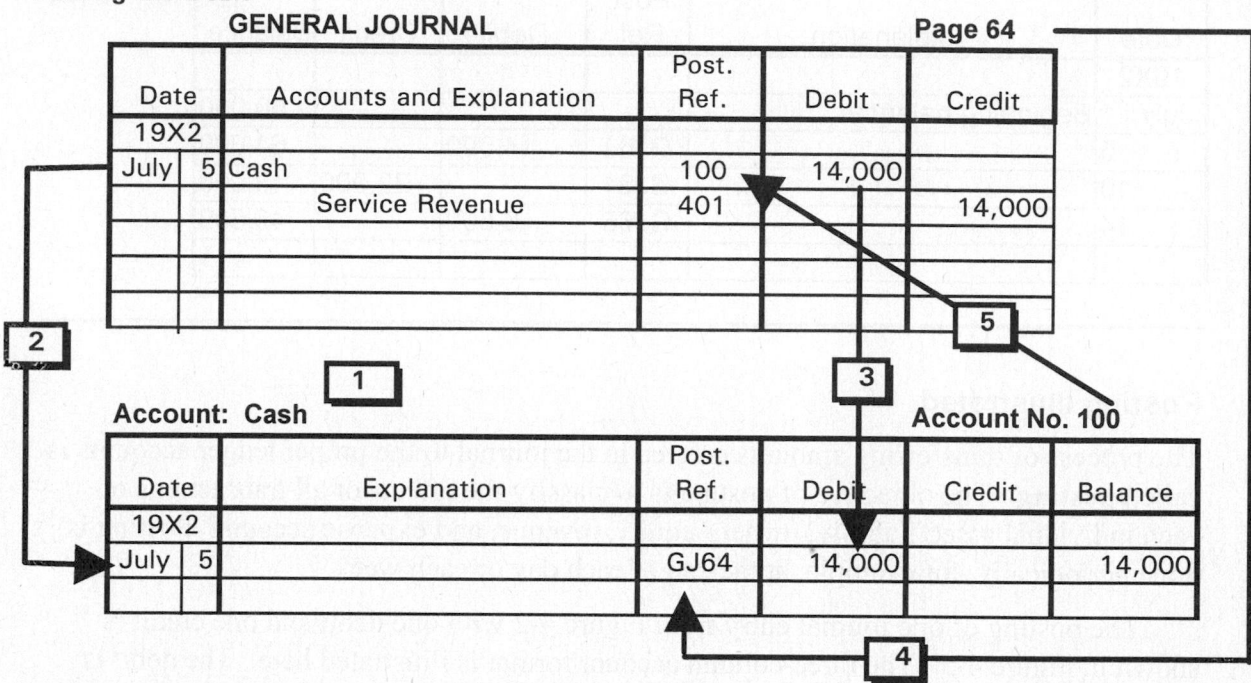

Posting the Credit

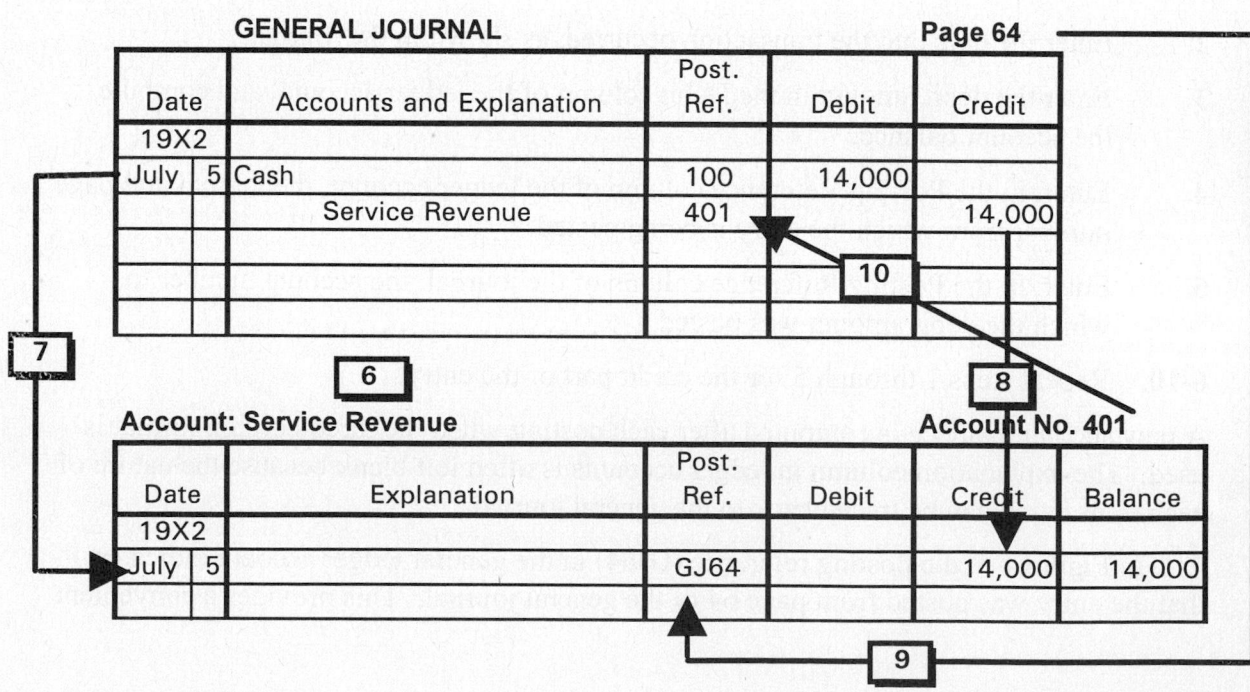

means for tracing an amount recorded in an individual account back to the general journal when additional information is needed about the posting. The account number, entered in the Posting Reference column of the general journal in Step 5, gives the account number to which the amount was posted in the general ledger. A number in this column indicates that the amount has been posted. Thus, the use of posting references allows one to trace any recorded transaction either from the ledger account to the journal or from the journal to the ledger accounts.

When the ledger is kept in T account format, the date (Step 2) and the debit (Step 3) are entered on the left side of the account; the credit part of the transaction is entered in a similar manner on the credit side of the account. The posting reference in the ledger may be inserted as shown here:

	Cash		100
19X2			
7/5	GJ64	14,000	

Often, however, the posting reference is omitted from T accounts when they are for illustration purposes and in preparing solutions to exercises and problems.

PRACTICE ACTIVITY 4-3

Part I.

1. In computing an account balance, is a debit entry added to or subtracted from a debit balance?_____ From a credit balance? _____

2. The _____ _____ has a different account for each asset, liability, and element of owners' equity.

3. The balance in the Accounts Payable account is $5,360. An $800 debit is made to the account. The new balance in the account is $_____.

4. What does the number 100 in the Posting Reference column of the general journal indicate? _____

5. Entering transactions in a journal is called _____, whereas the process of transferring the debits and credits to the appropriate accounts in the general ledger is called _____.

Part II.   The following journal entry was made by the accountant of Bobbie's Bakery.

General Journal				Page 4
Date	Explanation	Post. Ref.	Debit	Credit
19X2				
Oct. 6	Cash		2,000	
	Accounts Receivable			2,000
	Received cash as payment on account.			

Required:

Post the journal entry to the two accounts given below.

Account: Cash   **Account No. 100**

Date	Explanation	Post. Ref.	Debit	Credit	Balance
19X2					
Oct. 1	Beginning balance				20,000

Account: Accounts Receivable   **Account No. 110**

Date	Explanation	Post. Ref.	Debit	Credit	Balance
19X2					
Oct. 1	Beginning balance				8,200

STEP 4: PREPARATION OF A TRIAL BALANCE

One aspect of a double-entry accounting system is that for every transaction there must be equal dollar amounts of debits and credits recorded in the accounts. The equality of debits and credits posted to the ledger accounts is verified by preparing a trial balance. A **trial balance** is a listing of each account in the general ledger along with the balance in each account. The dollar amounts of accounts with debit balances are listed in one column, and the dollar amounts of accounts with credit balances are listed in a second column. The sum of the two columns should be equal. When this occurs, the ledger is said to be "in balance." A trial balance may be prepared at any time during the accounting period to test the equality of debits and credits.

ILLUSTRATIVE PROBLEM

The June transactions analyzed in the last chapter for the Ace Security Service are entered in a general journal in Figure 4-6. These transactions were:

June 1   Investors purchased 5,000 shares of $5 par value stock for $25,000.

June 1   Paid six months' rent in the amount of $12,000 in advance.

June 1   Purchased $450 in office supplies on account.

June 3   Performed services for a client for $6,000 receiving $1,000 in cash with the balance to be paid within 30 days.

June 20   Paid employees $2,500 for work performed to date.

June 26   Received $5,000 as payment on account receivable.

June 30   Declared and paid a $600 cash dividend to stockholders.

June 30   Received $500 cash for services to be performed in the future.

June 30   Made a payment of $380 on account for supplies purchased on credit.

June 30   Received but did not pay a utility bill for the month of June in the amount of $200.

Recall that in transaction analysis each transaction is analyzed to determine:

1. Which accounts are affected.

2. Whether each account affected is to be increased or decreased.

3. Whether, given the nature of each account affected, the account should be debited or credited to record the change.

4. By what amount each account is changed.

Note that each transaction affects two or more accounts with equal debits and credits recorded. Also, although it is not shown here, the accounting equation must be in balance after each entry is posted to the accounts. After the transactions are journalized, the information is posted to the accounts using a three-column format. The firm's general ledger is shown in Figure 4-7. A trial balance taken from the general ledger in Figure 4-7 is shown below.

FIGURE 4-6
GENERAL JOURNAL--ACE SECURITY SERVICE

Date	Explanation	Post. Ref.	Debit	Credit
	General Journal			**Page 1**
19X2				
June 1	Cash		25,000	
	Common Stock			25,000
	5,000 shares of common stock were issued			
	to investors.			
1	Prepaid Rent		12,000	
	Cash			12,000
	Paid six months' rent in advance.			
1	Office Supplies on Hand		450	
	Accounts Payable			450
	Purchased office supplies on account.			
3	Cash		1,000	
	Accounts Receivable		5,000	
	Service Revenue			6,000
	Performed services for cash and on account.			
20	Salary Expense		2,500	
	Cash			2,500
	Paid employees for work performed.			
26	Cash		5,000	
	Accounts Receivable			5,000
	Received cash from customers as payment			
	on account.			
30	Dividends Declared		600	
	Cash			600
	Paid cash dividend to stockholders.			
30	Cash		500	
	Unearned Revenue			500
	Received cash for services to be performed.			
30	Accounts Payable		380	
	Cash			380
	Paid cash on account.			
30	Utilities Expense		200	
	Utilities Payable			200
	Received but did not pay the utility bill			
	for June.			

FIGURE 4-7
GENERAL LEDGER--ACE SECURITY SERVICE

Account: Cash   **Account No. 100**

Date	Explanation	Post. Ref.	Debit	Credit	Balance
19X2					
June 1		GJ1	25,000		25,000
1		GJ1		12,000	13,000
3		GJ1	1,000		14,000
20		GJ1		2,500	11,500
26		GJ1	5,000		16,500
30		GJ1		600	15,900
30		GJ1	500		16,400
30		GJ1		380	16,020

Account: Accounts Receivable   **Account No. 110**

Date	Explanation	Post. Ref.	Debit	Credit	Balance
19X2					
June 3		GJ1	5,000		5,000
26		GJ1		5,000	-0-

Account: Prepaid Rent   **Account No. 130**

Date	Explanation	Post. Ref.	Debit	Credit	Balance
19X2					
June 1		GJ1	12,000		12,000

Account: Office Supplies on Hand   **Account No. 140**

Date	Explanation	Post. Ref.	Debit	Credit	Balance
19X2					
June 1		GJ1	450		450

Account: Accounts Payable   **Account No. 200**

Date	Explanation	Post. Ref.	Debit	Credit	Balance
19X2					
June 1		GJ1		450	450
30		GJ1	380		70

Account: Utilities Payable — **Account No. 210**

Date	Explanation	Post. Ref.	Debit	Credit	Balance
19X2					
June 30		GJ1		200	200

Account: Unearned Revenue — **Account No. 230**

Date	Explanation	Post. Ref.	Debit	Credit	Balance
19X2					
June 30		GJ1		500	500

Account: Common Stock — **Account No. 300**

Date	Explanation	Post. Ref.	Debit	Credit	Balance
19X2					
June 1		GJ1		25,000	25,000

Account: Retained Earnings — **Account No. 310**

Date	Explanation	Post. Ref.	Debit	Credit	Balance

Account: Dividends Declared — **Account No. 320**

Date	Explanation	Post. Ref.	Debit	Credit	Balance
19X2					
June 30		GJ1	600		600

Account: Service Revenue — **Account No. 400**

Date	Explanation	Post. Ref.	Debit	Credit	Balance
19X2					
June 30		GJ1		6,000	6,000

Account: Rent Expense — **Account No. 500**

Date	Explanation	Post. Ref.	Debit	Credit	Balance

Account: Salary Expense   **Account No. 510**

Date	Explanation	Post. Ref.	Debit	Credit	Balance
19X2					
June 20		GJ1	2,500		2,500

Account: Utilities Expense   **Account No. 520**

Date	Explanation	Post. Ref.	Debit	Credit	Balance
19X2					
June 20		GJ1	200		200

FIGURE 4-8
TRIAL BALANCE--ACE SECURITY COMPANY

ACE SECURITY COMPANY
Trial Balance
June 30, 19X2

Account Title	Debit	Credit
Cash	$16,020	
Accounts Receivable	-0-	
Prepaid Rent	12,000	
Office Supplies on Hand	450	
Accounts Payable		$ 70
Utilities Payable		200
Unearned Revenue		500
Common Stock		25,000
Dividends Declared	600	
Service Revenue		6,000
Rent Expense	-0-	
Salary Expense	2,500	
Utilities Expense	200	
Totals	$31,770	$31,770

The fact that the sum of the debit column equals the sum of the credit column in the trial balance does not ensure that errors have not been made. For example, a correct amount can be recorded to the wrong account, a transaction may be omitted completely, or a transaction may have been analyzed and entered at the wrong amount. A trial balance is simply a verification that (1) equal debits and credits have been recorded in the accounts and (2) the account balances were computed correctly, based on the recorded data. A trial balance that does not balance is a clear indication that either there are one or more errors in the accounts or there was an error in preparing the trial balance. Locating and correcting errors is covered in the next section of this chapter.

DISCOVERY AND CORRECTION OF ERRORS

Some errors are discovered by chance or during normal operations. For example, if an account receivable is overstated, the customer will usually inform the firm when monthly billings are made. Other errors may be identified through procedures established by the firm to check on the accuracy of its records. For example, a firm prepares a bank reconciliation each month to verify the balance in the Cash account.

A trial balance that does not balance is a clear indication either that one or more errors exist in the accounts or that there was an error in preparing the trial balance. Although there is no one correct procedure for locating all types of errors, the following systematic approach is helpful:

1. Check the accuracy of the trial balance totals by adding the columns again.

2. Certain types of errors may be identified by performing some simple computations. First, compute the difference between the totals and divide it by two. Next, review the trial balance and the journal for each of these amounts. The amount of the difference may be equal to a debit or credit that was omitted; or, if a debit or credit was recorded twice, the erroneous posting will be equal to one-half of the difference. This is also true if a debit account balance is listed accidentally in the trial balance as a credit or vice versa.

   If the difference between the two trial balance totals is evenly divisible by nine, it may be an indication of one or two common errors called transpositions or slides. To illustrate, assume that an expense account should have been debited for $460. If the error is a *transposition,* the order of the digits in a number is altered, as in posting the amount as $640, rather than $460 (e.g., $640 - $460 = $180, which is divisible by 9). In a *slide,* the decimal point is shifted to the left or the right, as by writing $46 instead of $460 (e.g., $460 - $46 = $414, which is divisible by 9).

3. Compare the account balances listed in the trial balance with the ledger accounts to verify that all account balances were included and copied correctly.

4. Recompute the account balances.

5. Verify that the debits equal the credits for each entry in the journal.

6. Trace the entries as recorded in the journal to the ledger accounts, and place a small check mark by each amount in the journal and ledger as each posting is verified. Be alert for the posting of wrong amounts and for debits posted as credits or vice versa. If the error is not found before this process is completed, review the journal and ledger, looking for amounts without a check mark.

Correction of Errors

Once an error is located, it must be corrected. An error in a journal entry discovered before the amount is posted is corrected by crossing out the wrong amount with a single line and inserting the correct amount immediately above it. An error in an amount posted to a correct ledger account is corrected in the same way. Errors should never be erased because the erasures may give the impression that something is being canceled.

Incorrect journal entries that have been posted should be resolved by preparing a new correcting journal entry. For example, assume that the following entry was made in the journal to record the receipt of cash for the performance of a service for a customer and was posted in the ledger.

	General Journal			Page 64
Date	Explanation	Post. Ref.	Debit	Credit
19X2				
Feb. 14	Accounts Receivable		862	
	Service Revenue			862
	To record the performance of service on			
	account.			

A correcting entry is needed to cancel the incorrect debit to Accounts Receivable and to record a correct debit to the Cash account.

Mar. 10	Cash		862	
	Accounts Receivable			862
	To correct an entry recorded on Feb. 14 in			
	which a cash receipt was debited to			
	Accounts Receivable.			

PRACTICE ACTIVITY 4-4

Listed below are several errors that occurred during the accounting period on the books of a business. The errors affect the accounting records in various ways.

1. A $275 credit to Service Revenue was posted as a $257 credit.
2. Receipt of a payment on account from a customer was recorded as a debit to Cash for $135 and a credit to Accounts Payable for $135.
3. A $450 credit to Accounts Receivable was not posted.
4. A $540 debit to Rent Expense was posted as a credit.

Required:

A. For each item listed above:
    1. Indicate whether the errors would cause the trial balance to have unequal totals.
    2. Determine the amount by which the trial balance totals would differ.
    3. Determine whether the error would cause the debit total or the credit total to be larger.
B. Describe how each error should be corrected. Prepare the correcting journal entry where necessary.

SOLUTIONS TO PRACTICE ACTIVITIES

PRACTICE ACTIVITY 4-1

1. data processing, accounting.

2. Step 1: Transactions occur.
   Step 2: Transactions are recorded in the journal, called journalizing.
   Step 3: Journal entries are posted to the ledger.

3. __6__ Financial statements prepared.   __8__ Prepare post-closing trial balance.
    __7__ Journalize and post closing entries.   __3__ Post journal entries.
    __2__ Journalize transactions.   __5__ Journalize and post adjusting entries.
    __1__ Transactions occur.   __4__ Prepare a worksheet.

4. True

PRACTICE ACTIVITY 4-2

I. 1. original   4. True
    2. general journal   5. credited
    3. journalizing   6. Debit, Credit

II.

General Journal				Page 1
Date	Explanation	Post. Ref.	Debit	Credit
Nov. 5	Accounts Receivable		11,400	
	Service Revenue			11,400
	Provided service on account.			
10	Office Equipment		8,000	
	Cash			2,000
	Notes Payable			6,000
	Purchased equipment for cash and issued			
	note for the balance.			

PRACTICE ACTIVITY 4-3

I. 1.   added to, subtracted from

2.   general ledger

3. $5,360 - $800 = $4,560

4.   Account number of account to which the dollar amount was posted.

5.   journalizing, posting

II.

Account: Cash   **Account No. 100**

Date	Explanation	Post. Ref.	Debit	Credit	Balance
19X2					
Oct. 1	Beginning balance				20,000
6		GJ4	2,000		22,000

Account: Accounts Receivable   **Account No. 110**

Date	Explanation	Post. Ref.	Debit	Credit	Balance
19X2					
Oct. 1	Beginning balance				8,200
6		GJ4		2,000	6,200

PRACTICE ACTIVITY 4-4

1. A. 1.   Totals unequal   2.   Difference $18   3.   Debit total larger
    B.   No journal entry is necessary since the error occurred in the posting process. Cross out the incorrect
          posting, and enter the correct amount above it. The balance in the account would be corrected to reflect the
          correct balance.

2. A. 1.   Totals equal   2.   No difference   3.   Debits = credits
    B.   The error would be corrected by making the following journal entry.
          Accounts Payable   135
              Accounts Receivable   135

3. A. 1.   Totals unequal   2.   Difference $450   3.   Debit total larger
    B.   Since the omission occurred in the posting process, no correcting journal entry is required. The $450 credit
          would be posted to the Accounts Receivable account and the account balance decreased to reflect the
          correct amount.

4. A. 1.   Totals unequal   2.   Difference $1,080   3.   Credit total larger
    B.   No journal entry is necessary since the error occurred in the posting process. The Rent Expense ledger
          account would be corrected by crossing out the incorrect credit and the correct debit entered in the account.
          The balance in the account would be corrected.

CHAPTER 5

Accrual Basis and Cash Basis Methods of Accounting

CONTENTS

CHAPTER OVERVIEW AND OBJECTIVES

This chapter discusses the cash basis and accrual basis methods of accounting. When you have completed this chapter, you will be able to:

1. Describe the cash basis method of accounting.
2. Describe the accrual basis method of accounting.

This chapter begins with a discussion of the concept of measuring net income. To comprehend the income statement and adjusting entries that are covered in the next chapter, the concept of *accrual basis net income,* as it is measured by accountants, must be understood. Although all revenues and expenses eventually involve cash receipts and cash payments, the timing of cash receipts and sales and cash payments and expenses is often different. For example, a firm may pay for equipment before it is used in the business to produce revenue. The need for making adjusting entries is related to the use of the accrual basis method of accounting. The account balances developed in the last chapter for the Quality Real Estate Office, Inc., are used as a basis for illustrating the analysis and preparation of both adjusting entries and the adjusted trial balance.

MEASURING NET INCOME

A major objective of a business is to earn a profit (called net income). As discussed in Chapter 1, in order to provide timely information to statement users, the operating life of a business is divided into relatively short intervals of equal length called accounting periods. One important accounting function is measuring the net income earned or the net loss incurred during an accounting period. The amount of net income or loss is the difference between revenues and expenses. Revenues and expenses may be measured on either a cash basis or an accrual basis.

CASH BASIS METHOD OF MEASURING NET INCOME

Under the cash basis method of accounting, revenues are recorded in the period in which cash is received and expenses are recorded in the period in which cash is paid. On a strict cash basis, net income is the excess of cash inflow from revenues over cash outflow for expenses. This method does not recognize revenue from the sale of goods or the performance of a service on credit until the receivable is collected. The costs of goods and services used to produce revenue during the current period are recognized as expenses in the period in which they are paid. They may have been paid for in the current period, may have been paid for in a previous period, or may be paid for in a future period. Thus, the cash basis method of measuring net income often does not properly match the efforts of the firm to produce revenue with the revenues earned.

Although the cash basis approach is used by small businesses and professional people who conduct most of their activities in cash, *it is not generally accepted for use by businesses that conduct a significant portion of their business on credit* or hold a significant amount of inventory (goods bought for resale). The cash basis system is simple to operate and, when transactions are primarily in cash, produces essentially the same results as those produced by accrual accounting.

When the cash method is used, it is often modified to use the accrual method to account for costs of inventory and plant and equipment. Thus, under the modified cash method, inventory costs are expensed when the inventory is sold and plant and equipment costs are expensed through depreciation as the asset is used.

ACCRUAL BASIS METHOD OF MEASURING NET INCOME

Under the accrual basis method of accounting, revenues are recognized in the period in which they are earned--that is, when goods are sold or services are performed--rather than when cash is received. Expenses are recognized when they are incurred--that is, during the period in which goods are used or services are received--rather than when they are paid for. The accrual basis net income for an accounting period is determined by subtracting expenses incurred during the period from revenues earned during the period, in accordance with the revenue principle. The process of associating expenses with revenues generated during the period is called *matching*.

Thus, the process of determining periodic net income involves identifying and measuring the revenues earned during a specific accounting period. Next, expenses associated with producing those revenues are identified and measured. As a result, both revenues earned and the cost of assets used up in the process of producing those revenues (i.e., expenses) are reported in the same income statement. In order to fully understand accrual accounting, the important concepts of revenue and expense must be thoroughly understood.

Accrual Basis Revenues

Revenues are the inflow of assets resulting from the sale of goods or the performance of services. As noted in Chapter 2, revenues for a period are determined by applying the revenue principle. Essentially, the revenue principle asserts that revenue should be recognized under accrual accounting when it is earned, rather than when the actual cash is received. Consequently, it is important to understand what is meant by *earning revenue*.

Some revenue, such as interest revenue and rent revenue, is earned with the passage of time and, therefore, is not difficult to associate with specific time periods. However, revenue such as sales revenue is earned in a continuous process as the operating activities, which give rise to revenue, take place. For example, the earning process (or earning cycle) for a manufacturing firm involves the acquisition of goods and services, the production of a product, and the sale of the finished product. Each of these steps contributes to the earning process, but it is difficult to objectively determine how much revenue is earned at each step.

Accountants have adopted the revenue principle as a practical guide. Thus, revenue is recognized when (1) the earning process is complete or essentially complete and (2) an exchange has taken place. According to this principle, most revenue is recognized when goods are sold (which normally means when they are delivered) or when services are rendered and, thus, can be billed to the customer. At this point, the earning process is considered essentially complete. The only remaining part of the earning cycle is the collection of the sales price, which is considered relatively assured in today's credit-oriented society. The sales price provides the necessary objective evidence of the amount of revenue to be recognized.

The sales price is normally received in cash or as a customer's promise to pay cash at a set time in the future (an account receivable). Occasionally, however, a firm may receive either property or services in payment. In such cases, the amount of revenue recorded is the fair value of the asset or services received. Thus, for a given accounting period, revenue earned is the sum of cash, accounts receivable, and the fair value of other assets received from customers for the sale of goods or the performance of services during that period.

Although most revenue is recognized at the time of sale, two major exceptions are the percentage-of-completion method and the installment sales method. These methods will not be emphasized in this course, but they are presented here to provide an awareness of the exceptions.

The Percentage-of-Completion Method. Businesses often undertake projects that may take two or more years to complete. For example, assume that a company signed a contract to construct a major section of interstate highway, which is expected to take four years to finish. If the basic revenue principle was followed, net income on the project would not be recognized until the end of construction. Such accounting is called the *completed contracts method*. Under this method, annual income statements would clearly be of little use to investors and other users who must make timely decisions. As a result, a departure from the revenue principle is required for long-term projects when estimates of cost to complete and the extent of progress toward completion are reasonably dependable.[1] Estimates are made of the percentage of the project completed each year, and gross profit is recognized in proportion to the work completed. This approach is called the *percentage-of-completion method* of accounting for long-term contracts. This method works as follows.

1. An estimate is made of the total cost expected to be incurred on the project. The difference between the contract price and the total estimated cost is the company's estimated gross profit.

2. At the end of each year, the percentage of the project completed during the year is estimated. This may be done by comparing the actual project costs incurred during the year to the most recent estimate of the total cost of the project, or to an estimate made by engineers or other qualified personnel.

3. The estimated gross profit on the project, as computed in Step 1, is multiplied by the percentage determined in Step 2 to find the amount of gross profit for the year.

4. In the final year of the project, no estimate is needed, because total costs are known. The difference between the actual gross profit and the cumulative amount of gross profit recognized in prior years constitutes the gross profit for the final year.

Assume that Cress Company signed a contract to construct a section of interstate highway at a price of $20,000,000. The project is expected to take three years to complete at an estimated cost of $14,000,000. Therefore, estimated gross profit on the project is $6,000,000. The actual costs incurred and the amount of gross profit recognized each year are as follows.

---

[1] "Long-term Construction-Type Contracts." *Accounting Research Bulletin,* No. 45 (New York: AICPA, 1955), par. 15.

Year	Actual Costs Incurred	÷	Estimated Total Costs	=	Percent Completed	x	Estimated Gross Profit	=	Gross Profit for the Year
1	$4,900,000	÷	$14,000,000	=	35%	x	$6,000,000	=	$2,100,000
2	5,600,000	÷	14,000,000	=	40%	x	6,000,000	=	2,400,000
3	3,700,000		Balance to complete the contract*						1,300,000
Total	$14,200,000								$5,800,000

*Balance to complete the contract:

Contract price	$20,000,000
Actual costs	14,200,000
Actual gross profit	5,800,000
Gross profit recognized in first two years ($2,100,000 + $2,400,000)	4,500,000
Remaining gross profit	$ 1,300,000

In Year 1, the actual cost incurred represented 35% of the estimated total cost of the project. The percentage-of-completion method assumes that incurring costs represent a valid reflection of progress toward completion of the project. Thus, 35% of the estimated gross profit is recognized in Year 1. Similarly, 40% of the total estimated cost was incurred in Year 2, and thus, 40% of the estimated gross profit is recognized. In Year 3, gross profit is recognized in an amount equal to the actual total gross profit on the contract, minus the cumulative amount of gross profit recognized in Years 1 and 2.

The percentage-of-completion method is based on estimates and, therefore, introduces an element of subjectivity into the determination of net income. In spite of this, the financial statements are considered more useful than they would be if none of the profit was recognized until the end of the project.

Although the percentage-of-completion method is appropriate in accounting for long-term contracts expected to produce a profit, it is not appropriate if a loss is expected. When it becomes apparent that a loss will occur, the estimated loss must be recognized immediately under the *conservatism convention.*

The Installment Method. It is common practice in some businesses to make sales on an installment basis. The purchaser normally makes a down payment and agrees to pay the remainder of the purchase price in equal installments at specified times. The seller often retains title to the property until final payment is received, or instead, the seller makes other arrangements to permit the repossession of the property in the event that the purchaser defaults on payment. Even though the sales price is received over an extended period, installment sales ordinarily should be accounted for in the same manner as regular sales on account, and revenue should be recognized at the time of sale.[2] As will be discussed in a later chapter, an appropriate provision should be made for estimated

---

[2] Accounting Principles Board, "Omnibus Opinion--1966," APB Opinion No. 10 (New York: AICPA, 1966), par. 12.

uncollectible accounts. In the relatively rare situations in which collection of the sales price is not reasonably assured, the installment method of accounting may be used.[3]

Under the *installment method*, gross profit (sales price less cost of item sold) is deferred and recognized when payment is received. Each cash receipt consists of a partial recovery of the cost of the property sold and part of gross profit. For example, if the gross profit rate on an installment sale is 40%, each cash receipt is considered to consist of 40% gross profit and 60% recovery of cost of the property sold.

To illustrate, assume that on July 1, 19X2, Franklin Company sold land for $60,000 that had cost $36,000. The gross profit rate is 40% [($60,000 – $36,000)/$60,000]. The purchaser made a down payment of $12,000 and agreed to pay the remaining $48,000 at the rate of $2,000 per month for 24 months, beginning on August 1.[4] The collection of the sales price is not reasonably assured. The amount of gross profit from installment sales recognized in each period, assuming all payments are received when due, is as follows.

Year	Amount Collected	x	Gross Profit Rate	=	Gross Profit
19X2	$22,000*	x	40%	=	$ 8,800
19X3	24,000	x	40%	=	9,600
19X4	14,000	x	40%	=	5,600
Total	$60,000				$24,000
*The $22,000 collected in 1992 consists of the down payment of $12,000 plus five monthly payments of $2,000 each.					

PRACTICE ACTIVITY 5-1

I.   Construction equipment with a cost of $215,000 was sold for $250,000. A $40,000 down payment was received in 19X1, and the purchaser agreed to pay the balance in eight equal quarterly installments during 19X2 and 19X3. Collection of the full sales price is not reasonably assured.

Required:

---

[3] The Internal Revenue Code allows the use of the installment method; it is often used because it permits the deferral of income tax payments until the cash is received.

[4] Installment sales contracts generally provide for interest on the unpaid balance. Although ignored in our illustration, the amount of each payment representing interest is recognized as interest revenue when received.

Determine the amount of gross profit that should be recognized in 19X1, 19X2, and 19X3.

II.   Earth-movers Construction Company signed a contract to construct an office complex at a contract price of $8,000,000. The project is expected to take three years to complete at an estimated total cost of $6,000,000. Actual cost incurred on the project during 19X2 was $2,100,000. Estimates of cost to complete and the extent of progress toward completion are reasonably dependable. Estimated total costs remained $6,000,000 during 1992.

Required:

Compute the amount of gross profit that should be recognized in 19X2.

Accrual Basis Expenses

Costs are incurred as a necessary part of the revenue-generating process. The portion of the cost that is expected to be used in the production of revenue in the future is reported as an asset and is called an unexpired cost. The purchase price (cost) of a delivery truck is an example of an *unexpired cost*. The cost of the truck is debited to an asset account. The asset account is then reduced when the cost of the asset can be identified or matched with the revenue earned during each period. The amount of the reduction is reported in the income statement as an expense (sometimes called an *expired cost*). Expired costs are deducted from revenue in the determination of net income.

The cost can be diagrammed as follows, assuming that a firm paid $3,000 for equipment to be used for 10 years:

Asset (Unexpired Cost)	Activity	Expense (Expired Cost)
Cost incurred to acquire economic resources ($3,000)	Equipment is used during the period to produce revenue	Associate cost of asset used with revenue earned (matching) ($300)

The firm computed the cost of the asset to be matched against revenues of the current period to be $300. The remaining unexpired cost ($2,700) is a measure of the costs of future economic services. Put another way, the $2,700 is an asset to be utilized in future periods to earn revenue. The $2,700 is expensed in future periods as the asset is used.

Thus, assets are the resources owned by the firm, and expenses are the dollar amount of these resources consumed during the period to produce revenue.

Matching Expenses Incurred with Revenues Earned

As noted in the preceding paragraph, the cost of assets must be allocated to both current and future periods in order to provide proper matching of expenses incurred with revenues earned. Some costs, such as the cost of a refrigerator sold by an appliance store, can be directly associated with the revenues of a specific accounting period. Other costs cannot be as directly associated with revenues (e.g., officers' salaries). Still other costs can be associated with revenues of more than one accounting period (e.g., the cost of an office building).

Just as the revenue principle was developed to serve as a guide in the timing of revenues, the matching principle was developed to guide the timing of expense recognition. A hierarchy of three basic rules–associating cause and effect, systematic and rational allocation, and immediate recognition–specifies the bases for recognizing expenses.

Associating Cause and Effect. Some expenses, such as the cost of a computer sold by a computer store and the sales commission earned by the salesperson making the sale, are recognized as having a relatively direct cause and effect association with revenues earned. Therefore, these expenses are recorded in the same period in which the revenues associated with them are recognized. For example, the sale of the computer, the cost of the computer, and the sales commission are all recorded in the same period.

Systematic and Rational Allocation. Many expenses cannot be associated directly with revenue-producing transactions but can be associated with specific accounting periods. For example, the cost of purchasing a building should be allocated to each period the building is used. Although there is no direct association between the specific revenues produced and the use of the building, a portion of its cost should be expensed because the building contributed to revenue. Such a cost is allocated to specific accounting periods in a systematic and rational way. Some examples are depreciation of plant assets and allocation of rent and insurance paid for in advance.

Accounting principles require that the method used to allocate costs to specific accounting periods must be systematic and rational. "Systematic" means that the allocation is based on a prescribed method or formula. "Rational" means that there is some logical relationship between the cost allocated and the benefits received in the current period. For example, a building that is expected to produce equal benefits each year should have an equal amount of its cost expensed each year.

Immediate Recognition. Some expenses are associated with the current accounting period for one of the following reasons:

1. They cannot be directly associated with revenue transactions.

2. They have no discernible benefits for future accounting periods.

3. Their allocation among several accounting periods serves no useful purpose.

According to this rule, costs—such as officers' salaries, advertising expenses, and research and development expenditures—are charged as expenses in the period in which payment is made or liability is incurred. In addition, items carried as assets that are determined to have no discernible benefit for future periods are charged as expenses or losses. One example of such an item is equipment that has become obsolete before the end of its original useful life.

PRACTICE ACTIVITY 5-2

Part 1.

1. Costs that have been incurred for the purpose of generating revenue during the current period are sometimes called _____ costs.

2. That portion of the cost of an asset that has not yet been allocated to an expense is sometimes called an _____ cost.

3. _____ is the process of associating expenses with revenues earned during the accounting period.

4. _____ costs can be found on the balance sheet, whereas _____ costs are reported on the income statement.

5. Under the _____ basis of accounting, revenue is recognized when earned rather than when _____ is received.

6. The _____ basis of accounting is typically used by small businesses and professional organizations.

Part 2.

In the space provided, indicate whether associating cause and effect, systematic and rational, or immediate recognition would serve to associate the expense listed with revenue.

1.	Salaries of supervisors	_____
2.	The cost of a television sold by a retail store	_____
3.	The portion of an insurance contract expiring this period	_____
4.	Sales commissions	_____
5.	Advertising cost paid in the current period	_____
6.	The portion of the cost of a building expensed in the periods the building is used	_____

Part 3.

Selected accounts of X Company contain the following balances at the beginning and the end of its fiscal year:

	Jan. 1	Dec. 31
Prepaid Insurance	$1,200	$1,520
Salaries Payable	1,250	1,425

The following items appear on the income statement for the year ended December 31.

Insurance Expense	$ 1,380
Salaries Expense	37,450

Required:

Compute the amount of cash used during the year to purchase insurance and pay salaries.

Part 4.

X Company began the year with $450 in supplies on hand and purchased an additional $795 during the year. The company reported Supplies Expense in the amount of $870 in the income statement. Compute the supplies on hand at the end of the period.

CASH BASIS VERSUS THE ACCRUAL BASIS

The following situation contrasts cash basis and accrual basis accounting:

1. Systems Company contracted for $60,000 to install an accounting information system for Pinewood Company.

2. Systems started the project in October 19X0 and completed it by December 31, 19X0, its fiscal year-end.

3. Payment for the services was received in January 19X1.

4. Expenses of $36,000 were incurred in 19X0; $24,000 was paid in 19X0 and $12,000 in 19X1.

Net income is measured below for the two periods under both the cash basis and the accrual basis:

Cash Basis	19X0	19X1	Total
Cash receipts	$ -0-	$60,000	$60,000
Cash payments for expenses	24,000	12,000	36,000
Net income (loss)	$(24,000)	$48,000	$24,000
Accrual Basis			
Service revenue	$60,000	$ -0-	$60,000
Expenses	36,000	-0-	36,000
Net income	$24,000	$ -0-	$24,000

This illustration clearly shows the failure of the cash basis method to associate the firm's operating activities with a given accounting period. Although the efforts of the firm to earn the revenue took place in 19X0, revenue under the cash basis method is not reported until cash is received. The cash basis also fails to properly match expenses with revenues. Expenses of $24,000 are reported under the cash basis method in 19X0 even though none of the revenue is reported then. In contrast, the accrual basis recognizes revenue in the period when the economic activity occurs. Expenses are then associated with the earned revenue. This approach is much more useful for evaluating the performance of a firm.

As we shall see throughout the remainder of the book, the application of the accrual basis accounting involves the use of estimates, professional judgment, and assumptions. For example, allocating the cost of long-term assets (such as a building) must be based on estimates because accountants are simply unable to predict with certainty the length of time a building will be used. However, the need for timely information (*the time period assumption*) takes precedence over the lack of precision. Although the estimates should be as accurate as possible, they are only tentative, and the actual results can be determined only when the firm ends its operations. Thus, although the information reported in the financial statements appears to be precise, it can be considered only reasonably accurate. The information is made more meaningful by the explanations presented in the notes immediately following the statements. An effective user of financial statements should be aware of the limits of the statements and understand the basis on which they are prepared.

PRACTICE ACTIVITY 5-3

The following income statement was prepared for Silver Company at the end of its first year of operations:

Silver Company
Income Statement
For the Year Ended December 31, 19X3

Service revenue		$192,000
Expenses:		
Salaries expense	$96,800	
Rent expense	16,500	
Utilities expense	6,300	
Advertising expense	2,500	
Supplies expense	1,500	
Total expenses		123,600
Net income		$ 68,400

The following information about the firm was gathered at year-end.

1. Customers owed Silver Company $4,500 for services performed during December.
2. Salaries earned by employees but not yet paid by Silver totaled $5,200.
3. A telephone bill for $640 and a gas bill for $220 were received on December 31, but they were not paid at year-end.
4. Advertising, at a cost of $500, was run by the local newspaper in December. The bill has not been paid.
5. Rent on the office space is $1,500 per month and had been paid for 19X3 and January 19X4.
6. Customers had paid Silver $10,800 for service contracts for the period January 1, 19X4, through March 31, 19X4. The receipt was included with revenue for 19X3.

Required:

Convert the cash basis income statement to an accrual basis by completing the form given below.

	Cash Basis	Increase Balance	Decrease Balance	Accrual Basis	
Service revenue	$192,000				
Expenses:					
Salaries expense	$96,800				
Rent expense	16,500				
Utilities expense	6,300				
Advertising expense	2,500				
Supplies expense	1,500				
Total expenses	123,600				
Net income	$ 68,400				

SOLUTIONS TO PRACTICE ACTIVITIES
PRACTICE ACTIVITY 5-1

I. Because collection of the sales price is not reasonably assured, the use of the installment method is appropriate in this case.

Sales price	$250,000	100.0%
Cost	215,000	86.0%
Gross profit	$ 35,000	14.0%

Year	Cash Received	Gross Profit %	Gross Profit Recognized
19X1	$ 40,000	14.0	$ 5,600
19X2	105,000	14.0	14,700
19X3	105,000	14.0	14,700
Totals	$250,000		$35,000

II.   The percentage-of-completion method should be used in this part.

Contract price $8,000,000
Estimated cost   6,000,000
Estimated gross profit $2,000,000

Gross profit for 19X2:   Cost incurred / Total estimated cost = % of completion

$2,100,000 / $6,000,000 = 35%

$2,000,000 X 35% =$700,000 gross profit in 19X2

PRACTICE ACTIVITY 5-2

Part 1.
1.   expired
2.   unexpired
3.   matching
4.   unexpired, expired
5.   accrual, cash
6.   cash

Part 2.

1.	Salaries of supervisors	Immediate recognition
2.	The cost of a television sold by a retail store	Associating cause and effect
3.	The portion of an insurance contract expiring this period	Systematic and rational
4.	Sales commissions	Associating cause and effect
5.	Advertising cost paid in the current period	Immediate recognition
6.	The portion of the cost of a building expensed in the periods the building is used	Systematic and rational

Part 3.

Ending balance - Prepaid insurance	$1,520
Insurance expense	1,380
Insurance to account for	2,900
Less: Beginning balance - Prepaid insurance	1,200
Cash paid for insurance	$1,700
Salaries expense	$37,450
Less: Ending balance - Salaries payable	1,425
Cash paid for current year's salaries	36,025
Add: Cash paid for salaries accrued at the beginning of the year	1,250
Cash paid for salaries	$37,275

Part 4.

Beginning balance - Supplies on hand	$ 450
Add: Purchases made during the year	795
Supplies available for use	1,245
Less: Supplies used during the year	870
Ending balance - Supplies on hand	$ 375

PRACTICE ACTIVITY 5-3

	Cash Basis	Increase Balance	Decrease Balance	Accrual Basis	
Service revenue		$192,000	4,500	10,800		$185,700
Expenses:						
Salaries expense	$96,800		5,200		$102,000	
Rent expense	16,500			1,500	15,000	
Utilities expense	6,300		640			
			220		7,160	
Advertising expense	2,500		500		3000	
Supplies expense	1,500				1,500	
Total expenses		123,600				128,660
Net income		$ 68,400				$ 57,040

CHAPTER 6

Preparing Adjusting Entries

CONTENTS

CHAPTER OVERVIEW AND OBJECTIVES

This chapter describes the preparation of adjusting entries and the effect of year-end adjustments on financial statements. The adjusting process, Step 5 in the accounting data processing cycle, is completed at the end of the period. When you have completed the chapter, you should understand:

1. The need for adjusting entries.
2. How to classify adjusting entries into the two broad categories of deferrals and accruals.
3. How to prepare entries to adjust for prepaid expenses.
4. How to prepare entries to adjust for unearned revenues.
5. How to prepare entries to adjust for accrued expenses.
6. How to prepare entries to adjust for accrued revenues.
7. The preparation of an adjusted trial balance.

In Chapter 4, the steps in the accounting cycle *performed during the accounting period* were covered. This involved preparing source documents, analyzing transactions and recording them in the general journal, and posting the transactions in the general ledger. A trial balance can be prepared at any time to verify the equality of debits and credits in the general ledger. In this chapter we begin the coverage of the part of the accounting cycle that is *completed at the end of the accounting period*.

END OF PERIOD PROCESS

During the period, journal entries are made to record the effects of business transactions on a firm's financial statements at the time the transactions occur (external transactions). At the end of the accounting period, financial statements are prepared (Step 6) for use by management and external parties. However, before the account balances can be used in the preparation of financial statements, they must be adjusted for changes that have occurred but are not yet entered in the accounts. The process of updating the accounts to reflect current balances at the end of the accounting period is known as adjusting the accounts (Step 5).

The income statement is prepared for a specific interval of time. Revenue, expense, gain, and loss accounts are subclassifications of the Retained Earnings account and are used to accumulate and summarize information related to the income statement. After the statements are prepared, these accounts are reduced to a zero balance. This is called closing the accounts (Step 7). The net balance in the income statement accounts is the net income or loss for the period, which is transferred to the Retained Earnings account. The result of this process is that income statement accounts begin the next period with a zero balance and are thus prepared for accumulating information in the next period. If this were not done, it may become difficult to identify revenue and expense transactions with a specific period. As part of the closing process, the balance in the Dividends Declared is also transferred to the Retained Earnings account.

An optional step in the process is the preparation of reversing entries. Reversing entries are made to facilitate the preparation of routine transactions in the next period. How these different types of journal entries fit into a sequence of activities is diagrammed below for a firm with a December 31 year-end.

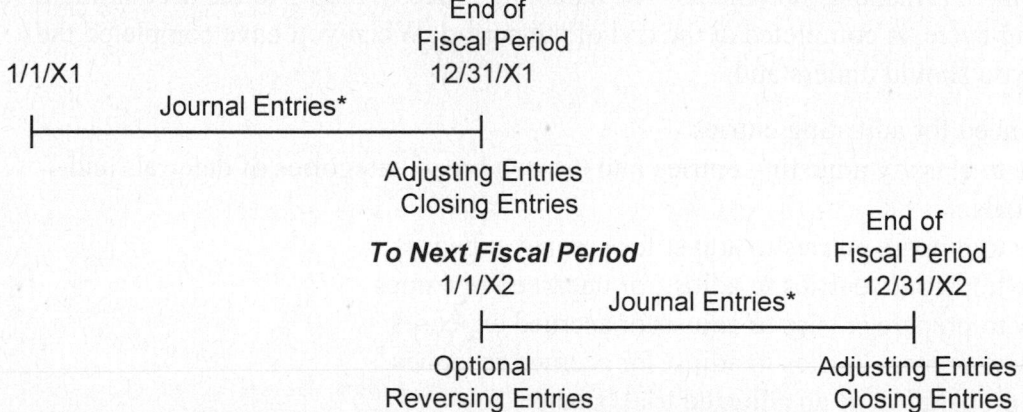

*Journal entries are made throughout each fiscal period to enter effects of transactions.

Adjusting entries are discussed in detail in this chapter. The closing process is illustrated in Chapter 7; reversing entries are covered in Chapter 8. As we shall see in Chapter 7, accountants often use a special form, called a *worksheet*, to accumulate the information needed to complete the accounting cycle at the end of the period.

WHY ADJUSTING ENTRIES ARE NEEDED

During the accounting period, the accountant records external transactions, many of which involve the payment or receipt of cash. In some cases, the period in which the cash flow is recorded coincides with the period in which the revenue is earned or the expense is incurred. In such situations, income measurement is a relatively simple process. However, some cash receipts or payments that are recorded in the current period will affect the firm's net income and financial position for two or more accounting periods. For example, a firm that purchases a 36-month insurance policy pays for the policy in advance of receiving the protection. In the prior chapters, the cost of the insurance coverage was recorded in an asset account. Although the protection expires on a daily basis over several accounting periods, the accountant does not make a series of daily entries to expense the cost of the protection because such a procedure requires too much clerical effort. Although the current account balances are not correct, this is of little concern to the accountant until financial statements are to be prepared. At that time, entries are made to adjust the accounts to their proper balances. For example, an entry is made at the end of the period to expense the cumulative total cost of the protection that has expired during that period. Failure to do so will result in assets being overstated and expenses understated, resulting in net income being overstated.

There are also cases in which revenues and expenses are reported in the current period, even though the cash for them may not be received or paid until the next period. For example, interest on a bank savings account is earned continuously on a daily basis. Cash receipt for the interest earned on the account is received after the interest is earned. All interest earned between the last time interest was recorded and the end of the accounting period should be reported in the current period's financial statements. Again, rather than making a daily journal entry to record the interest earned, one entry will be made at the end of each accounting period to record the accumulation of interest from the last accrual up to the end of the period. As you review the examples that follow, you should note that many adjustments are needed because the firm engaged in such activities that occur continuously during the period rather than as a discrete recordable event.

Whatever the situation, it is important to recognize that under the accrual basis of accounting, the recognition of revenues and expenses often does not occur in the same accounting period as the cash flow. At the end of the period, the account balances may not include the proper amount of revenues earned or expenses incurred during the period or an accurate measure of the asset and liability balances on the last day of the accounting period. Thus, account balances must be adjusted to reflect the transactions that are unrecorded as of the last day of the accounting period. These journal entries are called **adjusting entries.**

The adjusting process involves an analysis of each account and supporting source documents to determine whether entries are needed to adjust account balances to their proper amounts for financial reporting purposes. For example, an insurance policy or the billing invoice received from the insurance company will contain information related to the type of coverage, cost, and period of coverage. It may also be necessary to count some assets such as supplies to verify the amount on hand at the end of the period. Once this analysis is completed, *adjusting journal entries* are recorded in the journal and posted to the accounts. Failure to make the adjusting entries will result in misstatement of both income statement and balance sheet accounts.

In practice, it may take several weeks to gather the information to complete the adjusting process. Although the analysis is performed and the adjusting entries are journalized after the last day of the accounting period, adjusting entries are dated the last day of the accounting period.

CLASSIFYING ADJUSTING ENTRIES

Adjusting entries normally are classified into two major categories with two types of adjustments within each category. The two major categories of adjusting entries are deferrals and accruals. A **deferral** is either (1) an advance payment for an expense in advance of its use or (2) an amount received for revenue prior to earning the revenue. An **accrual** is the recognition of either (1) an expense for benefits received before the cash payment is made or (2) a revenue that has been earned but for which cash has not yet been received. Thus, in the case of a deferral, the cash flow precedes the recognition of an expense or a revenue. The payment or receipt of cash necessitates the recording of a deferral. Conversely, in the case of an accrual, the recognition of an expense or revenue precedes the payment or receipt of cash, and thus, the transactions have not been recorded.

DEFERRALS (PREPAID OR UNEARNED ITEMS)

Prepaid expenses are the costs of resources acquired by a firm before they are used to produce revenue. Prepaid expenses are assets until they are used or consumed in the earning process. They must be allocated to the periods in which they are used to properly match expenses with revenues. Examples include a payment for rent in advance of occupancy of a building and insurance premiums paid for protection to be received in the future. At the end of the period, an adjusting entry is needed to allocate the cost of the resource between an asset and an expense account.

Unearned revenues are cash receipts for the sale of goods or the performance of services before the goods are delivered or the services are performed. Advance receipts of revenues are liabilities until they are earned by the firm. Examples include the receipt of cash by a publishing company for a two-year magazine subscription and a rent payment received from a tenant before the occupancy period occurs. At the end of an accounting period, an adjusting entry is needed to allocate the advance receipt between a liability and a revenue account.

ACCRUALS (UNRECORDED ITEMS)

Accrued expenses are expenses that have been incurred during the current period but have not been recorded or paid for by the firm. To properly match expenses with revenues, expenses should be recognized in the period incurred regardless of when the cash payment is made. Examples include unpaid wages earned by the firm's employees and interest expense that has accumulated on an outstanding note payable. Because the goods or services received have not yet been paid for, an adjusting entry is made at the end of the period to record a liability and an expense.

Accrued revenues are revenues that have been earned for services performed or for goods that have been delivered in advance of collecting the payment from the customers. Under the accrual basis of accounting, revenues should be reported in the period earned, even though the cash has not been received. Examples include sales commissions earned but not yet received and interest revenue accumulated on a note receivable. An adjusting entry is made at the end of the period to record both a receivable from the customer and a revenue item.

The four types of adjusting entries are summarized in Figure 6-1. Note that every adjusting entry affects one balance sheet account and one income statement account. Also note that the **Cash account is never affected** by an adjusting entry.

FIGURE 6-1

SUMMARY OF THE TYPES OF ADJUSTING ENTRIES

Type of Adjustment	Original Entry		Adjusting Entry		Effects on Accounts
Deferrals:					
Prepaid expense-- e.g., rent paid in advance.	Asset Cash	XX XX	Expense Asset For the cost of the asset consumed	XX XX	Increase expense Decrease asset
Unearned revenue-- e.g., rent received from tenant before occupancy.	Cash Liability	XX XX	Liability Revenue For the amount earned	XX XX	Decrease liability Increase revenue
Accruals:					
Accrued expense-- e.g., salaries earned by employees but not paid.	None		Expense Liability For the amount incurred	XX XX	Increase expense Increase liability
Accrued revenue-- e.g., commission earned from selling a product but not received.	None		Asset Revenue For the amount earned	XX XX	Increase asset Increase revenue

PRACTICE ACTIVITY 6-1

I.

1. Journal entries made at the end of the accounting period to ensure that all revenues and expenses are recorded in the proper period are called _____ _____.

2. Expenses that have been incurred but not paid are called _____ _____.

3. An advance receipt for services to be performed is reported as a(n) _____ until earned by the firm.

4. The cost of resources acquired by a firm before they are used to produce revenue is called _____ _____.

II. Complete the chart presented below by filling in the combinations of accounts debited and credited in preparing adjusting entries. The adjustment to prepaid expenses is completed for you as an example.

	Type of account debited	Type of account credited
Deferrals		
Prepaid Expenses	Expense	Asset
Unearned Revenues		
Accruals		
Accrued Revenues		
Accrued Expenses		

ADJUSTING ENTRIES ILLUSTRATED

Adjusting entries are illustrated in this chapter assuming that deferrals are initially recorded in an asset or a liability account. An alternative approach is to record the initial entry for deferrals in income statement accounts. The latter approach is discussed in Chapter 8.

To demonstrate each of the four types of adjusting entries, it will be assumed that the entries for a real estate office, called Quality Real Estate Office, Inc., have been made during 19X2 and that adjusting entries must be prepared at the end of the period. The company began operations on January 1, 19X1. The trial balance prepared on December 31, 19X2, the end of the fiscal period, for Quality is shown in Figure 6-2. Such a trial balance is called an **unadjusted trial balance** because it is prepared from the general ledger before the adjusting entries are posted.

As you study the following examples, keep in mind that these are only representative of the four types of adjustments. In practice, you will encounter many different adjustments within each type. In determining whether an adjusting entry is needed, the accountant must examine the appropriate source documents (for example, an insurance policy or the bill from the insurance company to verify the cost of the policy and its term). The account balances listed in a trial balance are reviewed to compute the amount of the adjustment needed.

ADJUSTMENTS FOR DEFERRALS

In this section, the two types of adjusting entries related to deferrals are discussed. Recall that in the case of deferrals, a previously recorded asset is reduced and an expense account is increased for the amount consumed during the period, or a previously recorded unearned revenue account (a liability) is reduced and a revenue account is increased for the amount of revenue earned during the period.

FIGURE 6-2
UNADJUSTED TRIAL BALANCE

QUALITY REAL ESTATE OFFICE, INC. Unadjusted Trial Balance December 31, 19X2		
Account Title	**Debit**	**Credit**
Cash	$ 31,090	
Accounts Receivable	6,800	
Prepaid Insurance	800	
Office Supplies on Hand	940	
Office Equipment	30,000	
Accumulated Depreciation—Office Equipment		$ 3,000
Accounts Payable		7,200
Unearned Management Fees		900
Capital Stock		25,000
Retained Earnings		8,930
Dividends Declared	10,000	
Commissions Revenue		140,800
Advertising Expense	8,240	
Income Tax Expense	3,800	
Rent Expense	12,000	
Salaries Expense	76,590	
Utilities Expense	5,570	
Total	$185,830	$185,830

PREPAID EXPENSES (ASSET TRANSFERRED TO EXPENSE ADJUSTMENTS)

A business often pays for some expense items (such as rent, insurance, and supplies) in advance of the items' use. Goods and services, such as the purchase of office supplies, which are paid for in advance and are expected to benefit several periods, are normally recorded as assets (unexpired costs) at the time of payment. At the end of the accounting period, the portion of the asset's cost consumed or the cost of a service utilized this period is an expired cost that is transferred to an expense account as a cost of doing business. The remaining unexpired or unused portion of the asset is reported in the balance sheet. Thus, before the financial statements are prepared, the balance in the asset account is analyzed and apportioned between an asset and an expense.

In many cases, however, the prepayment and expiration of the asset occur in the same accounting period. While the costs of such goods and services are considered assets at the time of payment, such payments are charged directly to expense accounts if the items will be consumed in the current period. For example, the payment of one month's rent in advance on the first of the month is normally debited to Rent Expense rather than Prepaid Rent.

Prepaid Insurance

Quality Real Estate Office, Inc., insures its office equipment. At the beginning of the year, the Prepaid Insurance account contained a $200 balance, which is the amount paid in 19X1 for insurance coverage for the period January 1, 19X2, through May 31, 19X2. On June 1, 19X2, a 12-month insurance policy was purchased for $600. This policy provides for coverage to begin on June 1. The transaction was recorded as follows.

June	1	Prepaid Insurance	600	
		Cash		600

Prepaid Insurance

1/1	200	
6/1	600	
12/31 Bal.	800	

(Note that the balance of $800 is the amount reported for the account in Figure 6-2.)

As time passes, a part of this asset is consumed. At the end of the fiscal period, the company has received 12 months of insurance coverage and has prepaid for 5 months protection to be received in the next period. The cost of the coverage received this period is an expense of doing business. The expired cost for the year is computed as follows:

Cost of protection 1/1 - 5/31 (5 months)	$200
Cost of protection 6/1 - 12/31 (7 months) $600 X 7/12	350
Total	$550

The following adjusting entry is made on December 31 to record Insurance Expense and to reduce the Prepaid Insurance account.

(a) Dec.	31	Insurance Expense	550	
		Prepaid Insurance		550
		(The adjusting entries are identified by letters in this illustration for reference purposes only.)		

As discussed earlier, the adjusting entry is dated the last day of the accounting period.

After the adjusting entry is posted, the account balances are:

Prepaid Insurance				**Insurance Expense**	
1/1	200	12/31 (a)	550	12/31 (a)	550
6/1	600				
12/31 Bal.	250				

After making an adjusting entry you should review the results to be sure that the account balances are the appropriate amounts. The Prepaid Insurance account balance of $250 is the unexpired portion of the cost applicable to future periods (5 months X $50 per month) and is reported as an asset. The cost of insurance coverage for 19X2 ($550) is properly matched as an expense with the revenue reported in 19X2. If the adjusting entry were not made, expenses would be understated resulting in an overstatement in net income. In the balance sheet, assets would be overstated as would be owners' equity since income is part of the owners' interest in the business.

The total cost of the policy purchased on June 1 is allocated to two accounting periods as an expense over its life as shown below.

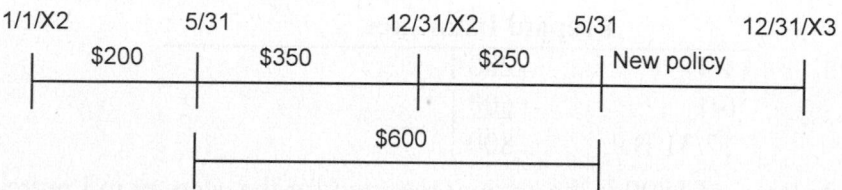

The company will most likely purchase a new policy that begins coverage on June 1, 19X3. The costs of additional policies purchased are debited to the Prepaid Insurance account and allocated to expense by following similar procedures.

Office Supplies on Hand

Quality Real Estate Office, Inc., began the period with $180 in office supplies on hand (an asset). Additional purchases of office supplies are debited to the Office Supplies on Hand account because the supplies are expected to be used over more than one accounting period. The following journal entry was made on June 5 to record the purchase of $760 in office supplies.

June	5	Office Supplies on Hand	760	
		Accounts Payable		760

The cost of office supplies used during the period is a cost of doing business, but recognition of the expense is normally deferred until the end of the accounting period. In other words, no journal entry is made during the period to record the cost of supplies consumed because this information is not needed on a day-to-day basis. If no useful purpose is served by making an expense entry every time supplies are used during the period, why incur the clerical cost of doing so? Before financial statements are prepared, however, an adjusting entry is made to remove the cost of the supplies used from the asset account and increase an expense account.

For control purposes, firms generally keep supplies in a central location. Employees are required to fill out a requisition form that identifies the supplies they have taken or used. The total cost of the supplies is determined for each requisition. The total of these requisitions is the cost of the supplies used during the period. If a requisition system is not used, the cost of the supplies on hand is determined at the end of the period by counting and pricing them, which in turn allows for computation of the cost of supplies used.

Assume that the cost of the supplies Quality Real Estate Office, Inc., had on hand at the end of December 31 was determined to be $240. Therefore, the cost of supplies used during this period was $700, as shown below:

Supplies on hand, January 1	$180
Supplies purchased during the period	760
Supplies available for use*	940
Supplies on hand, December 31	240
Supplies used during the period	$700

*Balance in the Supplies on Hand account at end of the period. (See Figure 6-2.)

The following adjusting entry is made to transfer the cost of supplies used during this period from an asset account to an expense account.

(b)					
Dec.	31	Office Supplies Expense		700	
		Office Supplies on Hand			700

After this entry is posted, the accounts will appear as follows:

Office Supplies on Hand				**Office Supplies Expense**	
1/1	180	12/31 (b)	700	12/31 (b)	700
6/5	760				
12/31	240				

The $240 balance left in the Office Supplies on Hand account is the cost of supplies available for use in future periods (an asset). The $700 balance in the Office Supplies Expense account is the cost of supplies used during the year, which is matched with revenue earned during 19X2 in the income statement.

In future periods, the cost of additional purchases of supplies is debited to the Office Supplies on Hand account. The same analysis and process described above is performed at the end of each subsequent accounting period.

PRACTICE ACTIVITY 6-2

SMU Company purchased a three-year insurance policy on April 1, 19X1. The premium of $3,600 was recorded by debiting Prepaid Insurance. The balance in the Prepaid Insurance account on January 1, 19X1, was $270, which was the prepaid cost of coverage for the period January 1 through March 31, 19X1. The company has a December 31 year-end.

Required:

1. Prepare the December 31, 19X1, adjusting entry.

2. What amount should be reported in the December 31, 19X1 balance sheet for Prepaid Insurance? $_____

3. Assuming no additional insurance was purchased, prepare the adjusting entry for December 31, 19X2.

Depreciation of Equipment

Assets such as office equipment, buildings, automobiles, store fixtures, and machines are acquired by a business for use in performing operating activities. Thus, the firm is buying future service benefits from such assets. Because these assets are used by a business (i.e., the benefits are received) over more than one accounting period, their cost is allocated to the accounting periods that benefit from their use. The portion of the asset's cost assigned to expense in the current period is called **depreciation** or **depreciation expense.**

The adjusting entry to record depreciation is similar to the entries described previously for the allocation of the cost of the insurance policy and office supplies. That is, as an asset is used, an expense account is increased for the portion of the cost allocated to the current period and an asset account is decreased for the same amount. However, unlike the purchase of the insurance policy and the office supplies, which are generally consumed during one or two fiscal periods, items of equipment and buildings are frequently used for extended periods of time, sometimes up to 30 years or longer. The use of an asset for an extended time period results in an inability to determine precisely what portion is consumed in a given accounting period. Depreciation expense must therefore be computed as an estimate based on the following three factors:

1. **Cost of the asset.** The cost of an asset is the amount paid to purchase the asset.

2. **Estimated useful life.** The estimated **useful life** is the time period during which the asset is expected to be used.

3. **Estimated residual value.** The estimated **residual value** is the amount expected to be received at the end of the asset's useful life.

Given these three factors, there are several systematic methods used by accountants to compute depreciation expense. A more complete discussion of computing depreciation is contained in more advanced accounting courses. For this course we will use the *straight-line method* to compute depreciation. This method allocates an equal amount of depreciation to each full accounting period of the asset's useful life. The amount of depreciation for each period is computed as follows:

$$\frac{\text{Cost} - \text{Residual value}}{\text{Useful life}} = \frac{\text{Depreciation expense for}}{\text{the period}}$$

To illustrate, assume that the office equipment purchased by Quality Real Estate Office for $30,000 has a ten-year estimated useful life and a zero residual value at the end of ten years. The expense for the year is computed as follows:

Office Equipment

$$\frac{\$30,000 - \$-0-}{10 \ \textit{years}} = \$3,000 \text{ per year}$$

In making the adjusting entry for depreciation, a separate account, entitled **Accumulated Depreciation**, is credited for the cost associated with the period. This is done instead of making a direct credit to the asset account. The Accumulated Depreciation account is called a **contra account.** A contra account is reported as an offset to or a deduction from a related account. Thus, in the balance sheet, the Accumulated Depreciation account is reported as a deduction from the original cost reported in the related asset account. The use of the contra account preserves the original cost of the asset, while the balance in the Accumulated Depreciation account shows the portion of the cost that has been assigned to expense since the item was purchased. A comparison of the Accumulated Depreciation account balance and the original cost provides useful information about the age of the asset to statement users.

The adjusting entry to record depreciation for the period is:

(c)					
Dec.	31	Depreciation Expense	3,000	
		Accumulated Depreciation--Office Equipment		3,000

The T accounts appear as follows:

Office Equipment			Accumulated Depreciation–Office Equipment	
1/1/X1	30,000		12/31/X1	3,000
			12/31/X2 (c)	3,000
			12/31 Bal.	6,000

Depreciation Expense	
12/31 (c)	3,000

(Recall that Quality Real Estate Office, Inc., began operations on January 1, 19X1. The office equipment was purchased by the company on January 1, 19X1. Thus, the first $3,000 entered in the Accumulated Depreciation account on 12/31/X1 is the depreciation recorded for 19X1. The balance in this account is carried forward to the next period. As discussed in more detail in Chapter 7, the balance in the Depreciation Expense account is reduced to a zero balance at the end of each period as part of the closing process.

The depreciation expense is reported as an expense in the income statement. The accumulated depreciation account is subtracted from the cost of the appropriate asset in the balance sheet. The office equipment is shown in the balance sheet in the property, plant, and equipment section as shown below.

Property, plant, and equipment:

Land		$ XXX
Building	$ XXX	
Less: Accumulated depreciation	XXX	XXX
Office equipment	30,000	
Less: Accumulated depreciation	6,000	24,000
Total property, plant, and equipment		$ XXX

The difference between the original cost of the asset and its accumulated depreciation is called the **book value** of the asset and represents the unexpired cost of the asset.

As long as the asset is in use, an adjusting entry is made for every accounting period until the cost less residual value is fully assigned to expense. Thus, in successive balance sheets, the Accumulated Depreciation–Office Equipment account will increase $3,000 each year. The original cost of the asset remains in the Office Equipment account and does not change.

PRACTICE ACTIVITY 6-3

I.

1. A _____ account is an account that is subtracted from another account.

2. The portion of the cost of a building assigned to expense in the current period is called _____.

3. The estimated _____ _____ is the amount expected to be received at the end of the asset's useful life.

4. The _____ _____ account is credited when depreciation is recorded.

5. The _____ _____ of an asset is equal to its original cost less its accumulated depreciation.

II. Troy Company purchased a delivery truck on January 1, 19X1, for $26,000. The estimated useful life of the truck is five years, and its estimated residual value is $2,000.

Required:

1. Prepare the adjusting entry at December 31, 19X1, to record the annual depreciation on the van.

2. Compute the book value of the van on January 1, 19X3.

UNEARNED REVENUE (LIABILITY TRANSFERRED TO REVENUE ADJUSTMENTS)

A firm may receive payment in advance for services that are to be performed or goods that are to be delivered in the future. Until the service is performed or the goods are delivered, a liability, called unearned revenue, equal to the amount of the advance payment is reported in the balance sheet. Thus, the firm's obligation to perform future services is reported. That is, recognition of the revenue is postponed until the earning cycle is completed by performance of the services or delivery of the goods. If services are not performed, it is assumed that the balance in the account is the amount that would be refunded to settle the account, a liability.

Unearned Management Fees

As an example of unearned revenue, Quality Real Estate Office, Inc., received a $900 advance payment on December 1, 19X2, to manage three single-unit rentals for the period December 1, 19X2, through February 28, 19X3. The following entry was made to record the receipt of cash:

Dec.	1	Cash	900	
		Unearned Management Fees		900

Since the management fee will be earned over a three-month period, the credit is made to an ***unearned revenue*** account (a liability) at the time the cash is received. As the services are performed, the obligation is reduced and revenue is earned. Assuming that the management fee is earned evenly over the three-month period, an adjusting entry to transfer the portion of the advance payment earned in December in the amount of $300 ($900 / 3 months) to revenue is made on December 31. The adjusting entry is as follows:

| (d) Dec. | 31 | Unearned Management Fees | 300 | |
| | | Management Fees Revenue | | 300 |

After the entry is posted, the accounts will appear as follows.

Unearned Management Fees				**Management Fees Revenue**	
12/31 (d)	300	12/1	900	12/31 (d)	300
		12/31 Bal.	600		

The balance in the Unearned Management Fees account shows that Quality has an obligation to perform a service in the future. If the remaining services are performed in the next period ($300 each in January and February), an adjusting entry is made to record the $600 balance as revenue. This results in the revenue being recognized in the period services are performed and earned, instead of reporting all $900 as revenue in December when the cash was received.

The Quality Real Estate Office illustration contains one example of adjusting an unearned revenue account. Some other common unearned revenue items include rent received in advance, magazine subscriptions and advertising fees received in advance by a publisher, and deposits received from customers before merchandise is delivered.

ADJUSTMENTS FOR ACCRUALS

The two types of adjustments for accrued items are discussed in this section. Adjusting entries for accruals are needed to record expenses that were incurred during the period but were unrecorded, and revenues that were earned during the period but were unrecorded.

ACCRUED (UNRECORDED) EXPENSES (LIABILITY AND EXPENSE ADJUSTMENTS)

Most operating expenses are recorded during the period in which they are paid. However, at the end of the accounting period, there are usually some expenses that have been incurred but not recorded because payment has not been made. Such expenses include unpaid employee salaries, utilities, and interest on notes payable.

An adjusting entry is needed to assign the expense to the period in which it is incurred, rather than to the period of payment. A credit is made to a liability account to record the firm's obligation to pay for the goods or services that were received. These items are called *accrued expenses* or *accrued liabilities*. A separate liability account, such as Salaries Payable and Utilities Payable, may be established for each type of accrued expense.

Accrued Payroll Expense

Employees normally are not paid until they perform a service for the firm. Although an expense is incurred each hour that they work, the expense is generally not recognized until it is paid. When salaries are paid, the expense is recorded by making a debit to an expense account and a credit to cash. Quality Real Estate Office, Inc., follows the practice of paying employees every other Friday for the preceding two weeks of service. For example, the following entry was made on Friday, December 23 to record the payment to employees for the work performed during the preceding two weeks.

Dec.	23	Salaries Expense	2,500	
		Cash		2,500
		(Withholdings from the employees' salaries for taxes are ignored for now.)		

A diagram of the salaries earned between this payment and January 6 is presented in Figure 6-3. This pay period does have special problems, however, because the end of the period (December 31) occurs before the next salary payment date (January 6). An adjusting entry is required to provide (1) a proper matching of expenses incurred with revenues earned during the year and (2) a record of the firm's liabilities at the end of December. Even though the employees are not paid until January 6, a portion of the $2,300 payment is for employees' services that were received in December. Employee time cards showed that $1,250 in salaries was earned between December 23 and December 31. The entry to accrue the unpaid wages up to December 31 is:

(e)				
Dec.	31	Salaries Expense	1,250	
		Salaries Payable		1,250

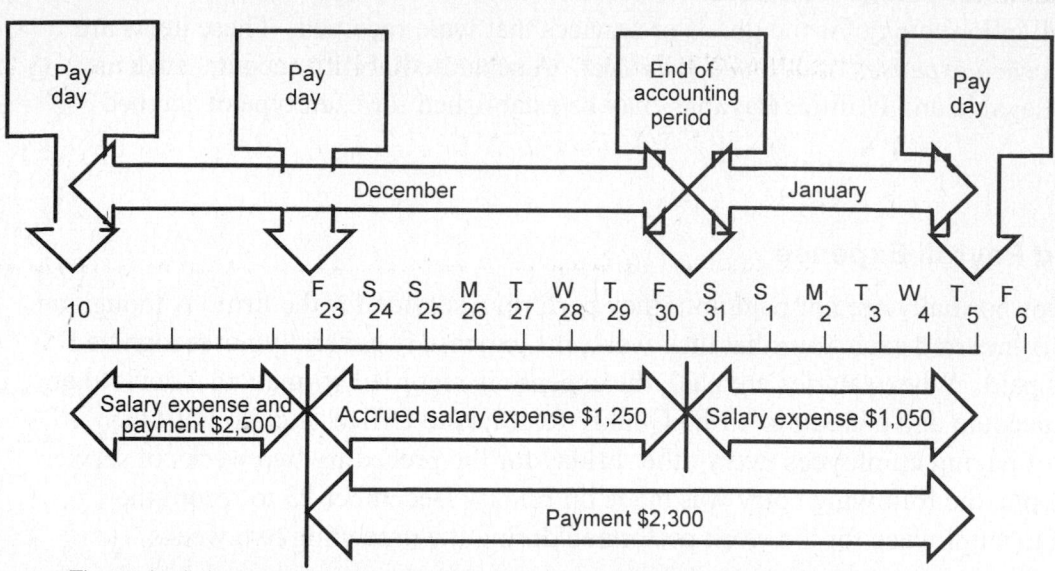

The total salaries vary each pay period because some employees work part-time.

FIGURE 6-3
DIAGRAM OF SALARIES PAID AND ACCRUED

The accounts after the adjusting entry is posted are as follows:

Salaries Payable			Salaries Expense	
	12/31 (e)	1,250	Bal. after	
			12/23	
			payment	76,590
			12/31 (e)	1,250
			12/31 Bal.	77,840

The adjusting entry records an expense of $1,250 for the services received in December. The total salaries expense for 19X2 of $77,840 is reported in the 19X2 income statement. The credit of $1,250 in the Salaries Payable account shows the amount owed to the employees for services performed up to December 31. It is reported as a liability in the balance sheet. Failure to make the December 31 adjusting entry will result in an understatement of expenses and an overstatement of net income for December. In the balance sheet, liabilities will be understated and owners' equity will be overstated.

The $1,250 liability is eliminated on January 6, when the $2,300 employee payroll is paid. The $1,050 earned by the employees in January is recorded as an expense, as shown in the following entry:

Jan.	6	Salaries Payable	1,250	
		Salaries Expense	1,050	
		Cash		2,300

The effect of these entries is to recognize the expense and liability during the period in which the expense was incurred rather than during the period when payment is made to the employees.

PRACTICE ACTIVITY 6-4

Fritz Company pays its employees weekly on Friday for the days of the current week worked. The daily payroll for salaried employees is $17,000, and the employees work a five-day week from Monday through Friday.

Required: I. Assuming that December 31, the last day of the fiscal year, falls on a Tuesday, prepare the year-end adjusting entry.

II. If the adjusting entry on December 31 was omitted, what would be the effect on

1. Net income?
2. Total assets on the year-end balance sheet?
3. Total liabilities on the year-end balance sheet?
4. Total owners' equity on the year-end balance sheet?

Accrued Utilities Expense

A utility company usually bills its customers after the service has been provided. Assume that on January 5 Quality Real Estate Office, Inc., received a bill in the amount of $340 for electricity used in December. The adjusting entry to record the expense in December is:

(f)				
Dec.	31	Utilities Expense	340	
		Utilities Payable		340

This entry increases expenses and liabilities by equal amounts. Note that although the bill was not received until January 5, the journal entry is dated December 31 so that the expense and liability are properly reflected in the December financial statements. However, in practice, when the amounts are immaterial, companies often follow the cash basis for utility expenses and recognize the expense in the period in which the cash is paid.

Accrued Income Tax Expense

Corporations are separate taxable entities. They must file tax returns and pay state and federal tax on their taxable income in accordance with the Internal Revenue Code and the applicable state tax laws. The federal tax laws and some states require that a corporation estimate its tax liability at the beginning of the year and pay the tax in quarterly installments. A simplified tax computation is used here for illustrative purposes. Income taxes are accounted for as an expense of doing business. They are matched against the income to which the tax relates. In the case of Quality Real Estate Office, Inc., assume that the company had made quarterly installments of $3,800 during the year (balance in the Income Tax Expense account, see Figure 6-2) and that at the end of the period income taxes on the taxable income earned this period were computed to be $4,900. Since $1,100 of this amount is unpaid, the following adjusting entry is made to accrue the expense and related liability:

| (g) Dec. | 31 | Income Tax Expense | 1,100 | |
| | | Income Tax Payable | | 1,100 |

ACCRUED (UNRECORDED) REVENUE (ASSET AND REVENUE ADJUSTMENTS)

In most cases, when a service is completed, the firm makes an entry to recognize the transaction. Even if cash is not immediately received, an account receivable is established in order to maintain a record of amounts owed to the firm and to recognize revenue earned. No entry is required at the end of a period since the receivable and the revenue have been recorded.

There are occasions in many firms, however, when revenue has been earned but not recorded. Examples of this include the portion of revenue earned on a partially completed service contract and interest accrued on a note receivable. Earned revenue that is unrecorded at the end of the period must be included in the accounting records by debiting a receivable and crediting a revenue account.

Consider the following illustration. Quality Real Estate Office, Inc., signed an agreement on December 1 to manage an apartment complex for a monthly fee of $875. Although the service fee is earned by the firm in one month, the agreement provides for payment to be made on the fifth day of the following month. No entry was made on December 1, when the agreement was made, because there was no exchange of goods or services and none of the fee was earned at that time. However, as services are performed, a portion of the fee is earned from day to day. By December 31, the full monthly fee of $875 is earned and is recorded by the following entry:

(h) Dec.	31	Accounts Receivable	875	
		Management Fees Revenue		875

Receivables for partially completed service contracts are generally recorded in the Accounts Receivable account. Separate receivable accounts, such as Interest Receivable, may be established for other types of accrued revenues. The Accounts Receivable account is shown in the balance sheet as an asset; the revenue account is reported in the income statement.

PRACTICE ACTIVITY 6-5

Custom Landscape specializes in design, installation, and maintenance of lawns for commercial properties. The company billed and received $175,000 for services performed during the year. Revenues are recorded in an account titled Landscape Revenue. On December 31, the end of the current fiscal year, customers were billed $16,500 for services performed during December. However, no entry was made to record the billings.

Required:

1. Prepare the adjusting entry required, if any, as of December 31.

2. What are the effects on the firm's financial statements if the adjusting entry is omitted?

ADJUSTED TRIAL BALANCE

As stated above, the adjusting entries must be journalized and posted to the ledger accounts. An **adjusted trial balance** is a trial balance taken from the ledger after the adjusting entries have been posted. It is taken to verify the equality of debits and credits in the adjusted ledger accounts. The ledger accounts for Quality Real Estate Office, Inc., are shown after the adjusting entries were posted in T account form in Figure 6-4. An adjusted trial balance taken from the ledger of Quality Real Estate Office, Inc., as of December 31 is presented in Figure 6-5. Financial statements could be prepared from the adjusted trial balance.

FIGURE 6-4
GENERAL LEDGER AFTER ADJUSTING
ENTRIES ARE POSTED

Assets

Cash		100		Accounts Receivable		104
12/31	31,090			12/31	6,800	
				12/31 (h)	875	
				12/31 Bal.	7,675	

Prepaid Insurance		110		Office Supplies on Hand		111
12/31	800	12/31 (a)	550	12/31	940	12/31 (b)	700
12/31 Bal.	250			12/31 Bal.	240		

Office Equipment		170		Accumulated Depr.-Off. Equip.		171
1/1	30,000				12/31	3,000
					12/31 (c)	3,000
					12/31 Bal.	6,000

Liabilities

Accounts Payable		200		Salaries Payable		210
	12/31	7,200			12/31 (e)	1,250

Utilities Payable		216		Unearned Management Fees		220
	12/31 (f)	340	12/31 (d)	300	12/31	900
						600

Income Taxes Payable		225
	12/31 (g)	1,100

Stockholders' Equity

Capital Stock		310		Retained Earnings		310
	12/31	25,000			12/31	8,930

Dividends Declared		320
12/31	10,000	

Revenues

Commissions Revenue		400		Management Fees Revenue		402
	12/31	140,800			12/31 (d)	300
					12/31 (h)	875
						1,175

Expenses

Advertising Expense		500		Depreciation Expense		505
12/31	8,240			12/31 (c)	3,000	

Figure 6-4 continued.

Income Tax Expense		520
12/31	3,800	
12/31 (g)	1,100	
	4,900	

Insurance Expense		525
12/31 (a)	550	

Office Supplies Expense		535
12/31(b)	700	

Rent Expense		540
12/31	12,000	

Salaries Expense		545
12/31	76,590	
12/31 (e)	1,250	
12/31 Bal.	77,840	

Utilities Expense		550
12/31	5,570	
12/31 (f)	340	
12/31 Bal.	5,910	

ADJUSTING ENTRIES NEEDED FOR INTEREST

The number of accounts maintained by Quality Real Estate Office, Inc., was limited in order to focus on the fundamentals of the adjusting process. As such, we have not considered interest transactions and the adjusting entries required for them. We will now consider the basic accounting involved in interest accruals here because it is a very common type of accrual.

Interest is a charge for the use of money over time. It is earned as time passes, regardless of when the actual cash is paid or received. A business can either receive interest (a revenue) or pay interest (an expense). It will receive interest when it makes an investment in an interest paying security (e.g., a bank savings account or a certificate of deposit) or loans money (e.g., a note receivable). Conversely, the firm will pay interest when it borrows money (e.g., a note payable). Thus, interest accruals must be evaluated carefully, because, unlike other adjustments, they can be either a revenue or an expense adjustment.

To illustrate the accrual of interest revenue and interest expense, assume that on May 1 Basic Company received a $10,000 note receivable from a client in exchange for cash. On the same date, the company also borrowed $10,000 from a bank giving a note payable bearing 12% interest. Interest on both notes is due twice a year on October 31 and April 31. Entries for the two transactions are given in Figure 6-6. The entries on October 31 record the receipt or payment of cash for interest accrued during the first six months the notes were outstanding. The formula for computing simple interest is:

Principal x Interest Rate x Fraction of Year = Interest

$10,000 x .12 X 6/12 = $600

It is normally assumed that an interest rate is stated as an annual rate unless otherwise specified.

A problem occurs before cash is received or paid for the second six-month period. In this case, the accounting period ends between the interest entry made on October 31 and the next receipt (or payment) on April 30. An adjusting entry, number (3) in the first column of Figure 6-6, is necessary to record the amount of interest earned and the right to receive cash, an asset (Interest Receivable). The interest receivable will be settled on April 31 when the full six months' interest is received. Note that the right to receive cash for the interest is different from the right to receive cash for the $10,000 loaned, as reflected by the Note Receivable account. The adjusting entry in the second column, related to the Notes Payable, recognizes that the unpaid interest on December 31 must be recorded to bring the expense and liability accounts up to date. The interest payable will be settled on April 31 when the six months' interest ($600) is paid.

FIGURE 6-5
ADJUSTED TRIAL BALANCE

QUALITY REAL ESTATE OFFICE Adjusted Trial Balance December 31, 19X2		
Account Title	Debit	Credit
Cash	$ 31,090	
Accounts Receivable	7,675	
Prepaid Insurance	250	
Office Supplies on Hand	240	
Office Equipment	30,000	
Accumulated Depreciation—Off. Equip.		6,000
Accounts Payable		7,200
Salaries Payable		1,250
Utilities Payable		340
Unearned Management Fees		600
Income Taxes Payable		1,100
Capital Stock		25,000
Retained Earnings		8,930
Dividends Declared	10,000	
Commissions Revenue		140,800
Management Fees Revenue		1,175
Advertising Expense	8,240	
Depreciation Expense	3,000	
Income Tax Expense	4,900	
Insurance Expense	550	
Office Supplies Expense	700	
Rent Expense	12,000	
Salaries Expense	77,840	
Utilities Expense	5,910	
Totals	$192,395	$192,395

Notes Receivable and Interest Revenue			Notes Payable and Interest Expense		

1. To record the lending and borrowing transaction.

| May 1 | Notes Receivable | 10,000 | | Cash | 10,000 | |
| | Cash | | 10,000 | Notes Payable | | 10,000 |

2. To record the receipt or payment of interest due in six months ($10,000 X .12 X 6/12 = $600).

| Oct. 31 | Cash | 600 | | Interest Expense | 600 | |
| | Interest Revenue | | 600 | Cash | | 600 |

3. To adjust the accounts for two months' interest accrued on the notes from November 1 through December 31 ($10,000 X .12 X 2/12 = $200).

| Dec. 31 | Interest Receivable | 200 | | Interest Expense | 200 | |
| | Interest Revenue | | 200 | Interest Payable | | 200 |

4. To record the receipt or payment of interest due in six months.

Apr. 30	Cash	600		Interest Payable	200	
	Interest Receivable		200	Interest Expense	400	
	Interest Revenue		400	Cash		600

FIGURE 6-6
ACCOUNTING FOR INTEREST

PRACTICE ACTIVITY 6-6

Computer Training Inc. conducts training classes on a wide range of popular software packages. Computer Training Inc. permits business customers to pay for the classes six months after the classes are offered. In such cases, Computer requires the business to sign an interest-bearing note. On August 1, 19X3, Computer Training Inc. billed Brooks Corporation $12,000 for classes completed during July. Brooks Corporation signed a 12% note due on February 1, 19X4. Interest on the note is payable in two installments on November 1 and February 1 when the note matures. Both companies have a December 31 fiscal year-end.

Required:

1. Compute the amount of interest due on the note on November 1, 19X3. $_____

2. Compute the amount of interest accrued on the note as of December 31, 19X3. $_____

3. Prepare the journal entries for both firms on:

a. August 1, 19X3. Assume that Brooks Corporation debits the cost of the classes to Employee Training expense.

b. November 1, 19X3. The first interest payment was paid by Brooks.

c. December 31, 19X3. Adjusting entry.

d. February 1, 19x4, assuming that the principal and interest were paid by Brooks.

General Journal for Computer Training Inc.

General Journal for Brooks Corporation

USING A WORKSHEET TO ORGANIZE THE PREPARATION OF ADJUSTING ENTRIES

In the preceding illustration, adjusting entries were analyzed and entered directly in the general journal. A more systematic approach may be useful in more complex situations. One approach is to use a worksheet, such as the one illustrated in Figure 6-7. The advantage of this approach is that it brings together in one place the ledger balances and the changes in the accounts to be recorded in adjusting entries. Such a worksheet is prepared in pencil so that errors can be identified, erased, and corrected before the adjusting entries are recorded in the general journal. It is a tool used by the accountant and does not replace the financial statements or the journal or ledger.

Figure 6-7 contains a column for account titles and three sets of debit and credit columns for (1) the unadjusted trial balance, (2) the adjusting entries, and (3) the adjusted trial balance. The steps in completing the worksheet are as follows:

1. Prepare an unadjusted trial balance from the general ledger.
2. Analyze source documents and account balances, and enter the adjusting entries in the Adjustments columns.
3. Compute the account balances as adjusted, and prepare an adjusted trial balance. **Note that the balances in the Adjusted Trial Balance columns are equal to the ledger account balances in Figures 6-4 and 6-5.**

Once the worksheet is completed, the adjusting entries must be entered in the general journal and then posted to the general ledger.

FIGURE 6-7

ADJUSTING ENTRY WORKSHEET

<table>
<tr><td colspan="7">QUALITY REAL ESTATE OFFICE
Preparation of Adjusting Entries and Adjusted Trial Balance
December 31, 19X2</td></tr>
<tr><td></td><td colspan="2">Unadjusted
Trial Balance</td><td colspan="2">Adjustments</td><td colspan="2">Adjusted
Trial Balance</td></tr>
<tr><td>Account Title</td><td>Debit</td><td>Credit</td><td>Debit</td><td>Credit</td><td>Debit</td><td>Credit</td></tr>
<tr><td>Cash</td><td>31,090</td><td></td><td></td><td></td><td>31,090</td><td></td></tr>
<tr><td>Accounts Receivable</td><td>6,800</td><td></td><td>h) 875</td><td></td><td>7,675</td><td></td></tr>
<tr><td>Prepaid Insurance</td><td>800</td><td></td><td></td><td>a) 550</td><td>250</td><td></td></tr>
<tr><td>Office Supplies on Hand</td><td>940</td><td></td><td></td><td>b) 700</td><td>240</td><td></td></tr>
<tr><td>Office Equipment</td><td>30,000</td><td></td><td></td><td></td><td>30,000</td><td></td></tr>
<tr><td>Accum. Deprec.—Off. Equip.</td><td></td><td>3,000</td><td></td><td>c) 3,000</td><td></td><td>6,000</td></tr>
<tr><td>Accounts Payable</td><td></td><td>7,200</td><td></td><td></td><td></td><td>7,200</td></tr>
<tr><td>Salaries Payable</td><td></td><td>-0-</td><td></td><td>e) 1,250</td><td></td><td>1,250</td></tr>
<tr><td>Utilities Payable</td><td></td><td>-0-</td><td></td><td>f) 340</td><td></td><td>340</td></tr>
<tr><td>Unearned Management Fees</td><td></td><td>900</td><td>d) 300</td><td></td><td></td><td>600</td></tr>
<tr><td>Income Taxes Payable</td><td></td><td>-0-</td><td></td><td>g) 1,100</td><td></td><td>1,100</td></tr>
<tr><td>Capital Stock</td><td></td><td>25,000</td><td></td><td></td><td></td><td>25,000</td></tr>
<tr><td>Retained Earnings</td><td></td><td>8,930</td><td></td><td></td><td></td><td>8,930</td></tr>
<tr><td>Dividends Declared</td><td>10,000</td><td></td><td></td><td></td><td>10,000</td><td></td></tr>
<tr><td>Commissions Revenue</td><td></td><td>140,800</td><td></td><td></td><td></td><td>140,800</td></tr>
<tr><td>Management Fees Revenue</td><td></td><td>-0-</td><td></td><td>d) 300</td><td></td><td></td></tr>
<tr><td></td><td></td><td></td><td></td><td>h) 875</td><td></td><td>1,175</td></tr>
<tr><td>Advertising Expense</td><td>8,240</td><td></td><td></td><td></td><td>8,240</td><td></td></tr>
<tr><td>Depreciation Expense</td><td>-0-</td><td></td><td>c) 3,000</td><td></td><td>3,000</td><td></td></tr>
<tr><td>Income Tax Expense</td><td>3,800</td><td></td><td>g) 1,100</td><td></td><td>4,900</td><td></td></tr>
<tr><td>Insurance Expense</td><td>-0-</td><td></td><td>a) 550</td><td></td><td>550</td><td></td></tr>
<tr><td>Office Supplies Expense</td><td>-0-</td><td></td><td>b) 700</td><td></td><td>700</td><td></td></tr>
<tr><td>Rent Expense</td><td>12,000</td><td></td><td></td><td></td><td>12,000</td><td></td></tr>
<tr><td>Salaries Expense</td><td>76,590</td><td></td><td>e) 1,250</td><td></td><td>77,840</td><td></td></tr>
<tr><td>Utilities Expense</td><td>5,570</td><td></td><td>f) 340</td><td></td><td>5,910</td><td></td></tr>
<tr><td>Totals</td><td>185,830</td><td>185,830</td><td>8,115</td><td>8,115</td><td>192,395</td><td>192,395</td></tr>
</table>

SOLUTIONS TO PRACTICE ACTIVITIES

PRACTICE ACTIVITY 6-1

I. 1. adjusting entries
    2. accrued expenses
    3. liability
    4. prepaid expenses or prepaid assets

II.

	Type of account debited	Type of account credited
Deferrals		
Prepaid Expenses	Expense	Asset
Unearned Revenues	Liability	Revenue
Accruals		
Accrued Revenues	Asset	Revenue
Accrued Expenses	Expense	Liability

PRACTICE ACTIVITY 6-2

1.

Dec. 31	Insurance Expense		1,170	
	Prepaid Insurance			1,170
	$270 + [($3,600 / 36 months) X 9] = $1,170			

2. Prepaid insurance balance on December 31 is $2,700 ($3,600 − $900).

3.

Dec. 31	Insurance Expense		1,200	
	Prepaid Insurance			1,200
	($3,600 / 36 months) X 12 months = $1,200)			

PRACTICE ACTIVITY 6-3

I. 1. contra
    2. depreciation
    3. residual value
    4. accumulated depreciation
    5. book value

II.

Dec. 31	Depreciation Expense–Trucks		4,800	
	Accumulated Depreciation–Trucks			4,800

($26,000 − $2,000) / 5 years = $4,800 per year

2. Book value on January 1, 19X3 = $26,000 − ($4,800 X 2 years depreciation) = $16,400.

PRACTICE ACTIVITY 6-4

I.

Dec. 31	Salaries Expense		34,000	
	Salaries Payable			34,000

II. 1. Net income is overstated by $34,000.
   2. Total assets are correctly stated.
   3. Liabilities are understated by $34,000.
   4. Owners' equity is overstated by $34,000.

PRACTICE ACTIVITY 6-5

1.

Dec. 31	Accounts Receivable		16,500	
	Landscape Revenue			16,500

2. If the adjusting entry is not made, assets, stockholders' equity, revenue, and net income will be understated.

PRACTICE ACTIVITY 6-6

1. Interest due on November 1, 19X3 $12,000 X 12% X 3/12 = $360
2. Interest accrued as of December 31, 19X3 $12,000 X 12% X 2/12 = $240
3. Computer Training Inc.

General Journal for Computer Training Inc.

Aug. 1	Notes Receivable		12,000	
	Computer Training Revenue			12,000
Nov. 1	Cash		360	
	Interest Revenue			360
Dec. 31	Interest Receivable		240	
	Interest Revenue			240
Feb. 1	Cash		12,360	
	Notes Receivable			12,000
	Interest Receivable			240
	Interest Revenue			120

General Journal for Brooks Corporation

Aug. 1	Employee Training Expense		12,000	
	Notes Payable			12,000
Nov. 1	Interest Expense		360	
	Cash			360
Dec. 31	Interest Expense		240	
	Interest Payable			240
Feb. 1	Notes Payable		12,000	
	Interest Payable		240	
	Interest Expense		120	
	Cash			12,360

CHAPTER 7

Preparation of a Worksheet and Completion of the Accounting Data Processing Cycle–Service Firm

Contents

CHAPTER OVERVIEW AND OBJECTIVES

This chapter introduces a worksheet that is commonly used by accountants to assist in accumulating the information needed to complete the cycle. When you have completed this chapter, you will be able to:

1. Prepare and use a worksheet.
2. Journalize adjusting entries using information from the worksheet.
3. Prepare financial statements from the worksheet.
4. Explain the closing process, and prepare closing entries using information from the worksheet.
5. Prepare a post-closing trial balance.

In this chapter, we complete the steps in the accounting cycle for service-type firms. As defined in previous chapters, the *accounting cycle* is a series of steps completed at least once each fiscal period. The complete cycle is discussed and diagrammed in the first section of this chapter. In Chapter 6, (1) an unadjusted trial balance was prepared, (2) account balances were analyzed and adjusting entries were made directly in the journal and then posted to the ledger, after which (3) an adjusted trial balance was prepared. It was noted that financial statements could be prepared from the adjusted trial balance. However, accountants often prepare a worksheet to organize this information. The **worksheet** is a columnar business form designed so that the account balances needed to complete the accounting cycle at the end of the period can be presented in one place. As part of completing a worksheet, an unadjusted trial balance is prepared, adjusting entries are entered first in the worksheet before they are recorded in the journal, and an adjusted trial balance is prepared. The data developed in Chapter 6 for the Quality Real Estate Office, Inc., will be used in this chapter to illustrate (1) the preparation of a worksheet and (2) the use of a worksheet to complete the steps in the accounting cycle.

THE COMPLETE ACCOUNTING CYCLE

The accounting cycle is completed at least once each fiscal year. The steps in the accounting cycle are diagrammed in Figure 7-1 and are as follows:

Steps Performed during the Period

Step 1   **Transactions occur**. Transactions occur, and source documents are prepared to collect information related to the transactions.

Step 2   **Journalize transactions.** Source documents are analyzed to determine accounts affected and the dollar amounts involved. The transactions are recorded in the general journal (or special journals as discussed in Chapter 11).

Step 3   **Post journal entries to ledger accounts.** Debits and credits are transferred to the proper accounts in the ledger.

Performed at the End of the Period

Step 4   **Prepare a worksheet.** An unadjusted trial balance is prepared as part of the worksheet, and the worksheet is completed.

Step 5   **Journalize and post adjusting entries.** Using the information in the worksheet, adjusting entries are journalized and posted to the ledger.

Step 6   **Prepare financial statements.** Using the information in the worksheet, the following financial statements are prepared.

1. Income statement.
2. Retained earnings statement.
3. Balance sheet.
4. A statement of cash flows is also prepared. Preparation of this statement is covered in more advanced accounting courses.

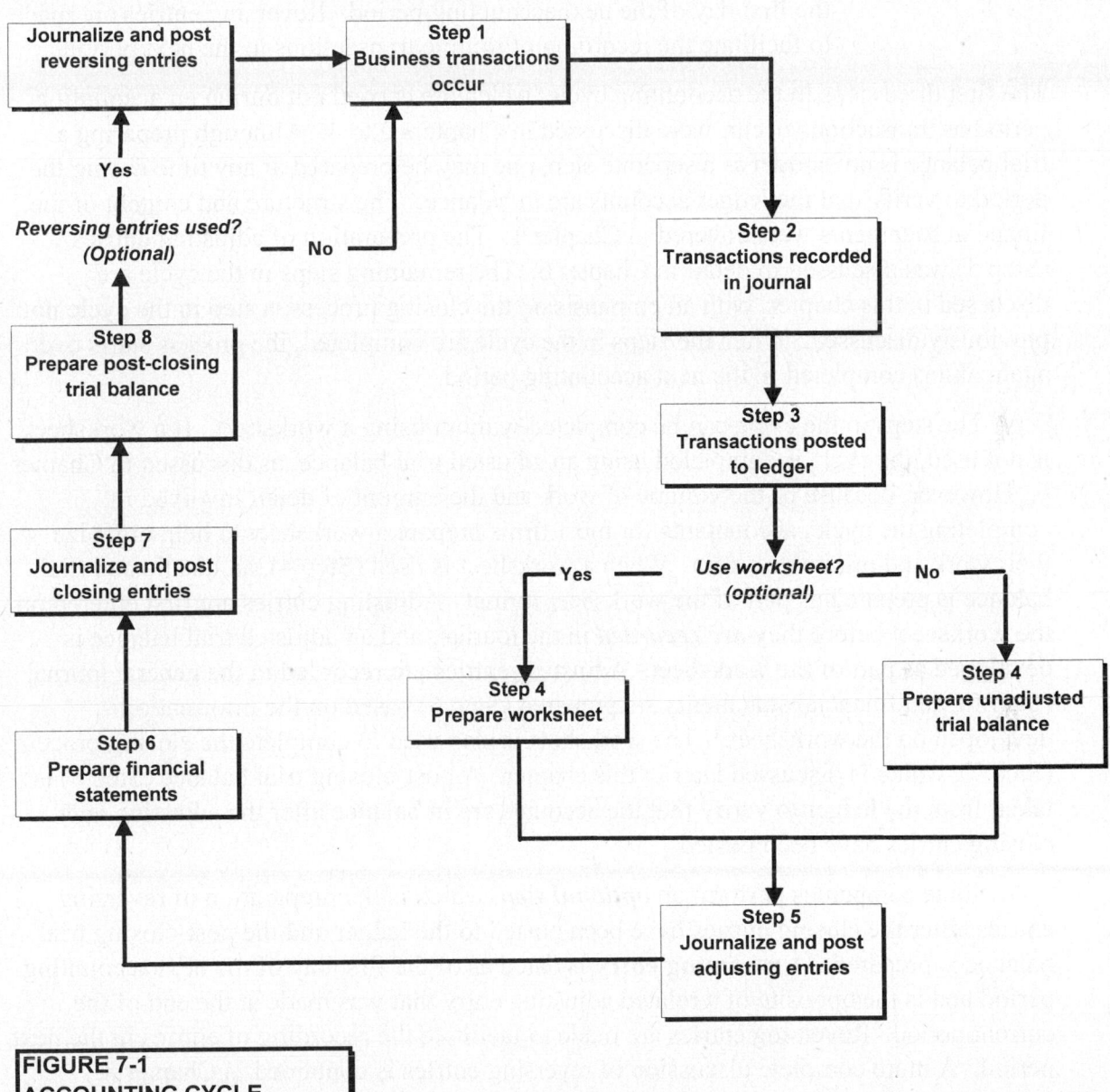

**FIGURE 7-1
ACCOUNTING CYCLE**

Step 7   **Journalize and post closing entries.** Using the information in the worksheet, closing entries are journalized and posted to the ledger.

Step 8   **Prepare post-closing trial balance**. A post-closing trial balance is prepared to verify that accounts are in balance after the adjusting and closing entries have been posted.

Optional Step   **Journalize and post reversing entries.** Reversing entries are dated the first day of the next accounting period. Reversing entries are made to facilitate the recording of routine transactions in the next period.

The first three steps in the accounting cycle, which are carried out during an accounting period as transactions occur, were discussed in Chapters 2 to 4. Although preparing a trial balance is not shown as a separate step, one may be prepared at any time during the period to verify that the ledger accounts are in balance. The structure and content of the financial statements were covered in Chapter 1. The preparation of adjusting entries (Step 5) was discussed in detail in Chapter 6. The remaining steps in the cycle are discussed in this chapter, with an emphasis on the closing process, a step in the cycle not previously discussed. When the steps in the cycle are completed, the process starts over again and is completed in the next accounting period.

The steps in the cycle can be completed without using a worksheet. If a worksheet is not used, the cycle is completed using an adjusted trial balance, as discussed in Chapter 6. However, because of the volume of work and the amount of detail involved in completing the cycle, accountants for most firms prepare a worksheet to help organize their work and minimize errors. When a worksheet is used (Step 4), an unadjusted trial balance is prepared as part of the worksheet format. Adjusting entries are first entered on the worksheet before they *are recorded* in the journal, and an adjusted trial balance is developed as part of the worksheet. Adjusting entries are recorded in the general journal (Step 5), and financial statements are prepared (Step 6) based on the information developed on the worksheet.[1] The worksheet is also used to complete the closing process (Step 7), which is discussed later in this chapter. A post-closing trial balance (Step 8) is taken from the ledger to verify that the accounts are in balance after the adjusting and closing entries have been posted.

Some companies perform an *optional step*, which is the preparation of reversing entries, after the closing entries have been posted to the ledger and the post-closing trial balance is prepared. A **reversing entry** is dated as of the first day of the next accounting period and is the opposite of a related adjusting entry that was made at the end of the current period. Reversing entries are made to facilitate the recording of entries in the next period. A more complete discussion of reversing entries is contained in Chapter 8.

---

[1]Financial statements are prepared based on the data developed in the worksheet. You will find in practice, and in alternative accounting textbooks, that this step is listed either after the adjusting entries are entered in the journal, before adjusting entries are entered in the journal, or after the closing process is complete. What stage the financial statements are prepared is a matter of personal preference.

STEP 4: PREPARATION OF A WORKSHEET

As noted earlier, a worksheet is a device designed to bring together in one place the information needed to record the adjusting entries, to prepare formal financial statements (except for the statement of cash flows), and to prepare closing entries. A worksheet is generally prepared in pencil so that errors can be erased and corrected before the entries are recorded in the journal. Here are some facts about a worksheet: (1) it is not prepared for use by the owners or management of the firm; (2) it replaces neither the financial statements nor the necessity to journalize and post the adjusting and closing entries; (3) it is simply a tool used to gather and organize the information needed to complete the accounting cycle.

PREPARATION OF THE WORKSHEET ILLUSTRATED

The basic format of a worksheet is shown in Figure 7-2. The heading contains the usual three parts: the name of the firm, the title of the form, and the period covered. The first column is used for the account titles. This column is followed by five sets of debit and credit columns provided for (1) the unadjusted trial balance, (2) the adjusting entries, (3) the adjusted trial balance, (4) the income statement, and (5) the balance sheet. Each set consists of a debit column and a credit column, making a total of 10 columns for entering dollar amounts.

The steps followed in preparing a worksheet will be illustrated and described by using the information developed in Chapter 6 for the Quality Real Estate Office, Inc. The following five steps in the preparation of a worksheet are shown in Figure 7-2.

1. Prepare an unadjusted trial balance from the general ledger.

2. Enter the adjusting entries in the Adjustments columns.

3. Compute the account balances as adjusted, and prepare an adjusted trial balance.

4. Extend account balances from the Adjusted Trial Balance columns to the proper Income Statement and Balance Sheet columns.

5. (a) Total the two Income Statement columns and the two Balance Sheet columns. (b) Compute the net income or net loss from the Income Statement columns, and enter this as the balancing amount in the two set of columns. (c) Recompute column totals.

Step 4-1. Enter the ledger account titles and dollar amounts in the Account Title and Unadjusted Trial Balance columns. After all of the transactions that occurred during the period have been posted, a trial balance is prepared to verify the equality of debit and credit account balances, as shown in Figure 7-2. The unadjusted trial balance is taken directly from the general ledger. In this trial balance, all accounts in the general ledger are listed even though some accounts currently have a zero balance. Another approach commonly used is to list accounts with account balances only. Additional accounts needed to complete the adjusting process are added after the listed accounts.

FIGURE 7-2
WORKSHEET FORMAT WITH UNADJUSTED TRIAL BALANCE ENTERED (STEP 1 IN THE PREPARATION OF WORKSHEET)

QUALITY REAL ESTATE OFFICE, INC.
Worksheet
For the Month Ended December 31, 19X2

Heading:
Company name
Title
Period covered

Account Title	Unadjusted Trial Balance Debit	Unadjusted Trial Balance Credit	Adjustments Debit	Adjustments Credit	Adjusted Trial Balance Debit	Adjusted Trial Balance Credit	Income Statement Debit	Income Statement Credit	Balance Sheet Debit	Balance Sheet Credit
Cash	29,930									
Accounts Receivable	6,800									
Prepaid Insurance	1,200									
Office Supp. on Hand	940									
Land	20,000									
Building	70,000									
Accumulated Depr .										
Building		-0-								
Office Equipment	12,000									
Accumulated Depr.										
Office Equipment		-0-								
Accounts Payable		7,000								
Salaries Payable		-0-								
Commissions Payable		-0-								
Interest Payable		-0-								
Utilities Payable		-0-								
Unearned Management										
Fees		300								
Income Taxes Payable		-0-								
Mortgage Note Payable		80,000								
Capital Stock		45,000								
Retained Earnings		-0-								
Dividends Declared	600									
Commissions Revenue		12,000								
Management Fees										
Revenue		-0-								
Salaries Expense	2,500									
Commissions Expense										
Utilities Expense	90									
Advertising Expense	240									
Insurance Expense	-0-									
Office Supp. Expense	-0-									
Depreciation Expense	-0-									
Interest Expense	-0-									
Income Tax Expense	-0-									
Totals	144,300	144,300								

Five sets of money columns with headings.

Step 3: Extend balances from unadjusted trial balance increased or decreased by amounts of adjustments.

Step 2: Enter amounts of adjusting entries.

Step 4: Extend each adjusted account balance to the proper income statement or balance sheet column.

Step 5: Total columns, compute net income or loss, and recompute column totals.

Step 1: Prepare an unadjusted trial balance directly from the general ledger.

Step 4-2. Enter the necessary adjusting entries in the Adjustments columns.
The adjusting entries are entered first on the worksheet in the Adjustments columns.
After the worksheet is completed, the adjusting entries are recorded in the general journal.
To aid in journalizing the entries and locating errors, each adjusting entry is identified by
a separate letter so that the debit part of the entry can be cross-referenced to the credit part
of the entry. The adjustments made in Figure 7-3 are the same as those explained in
detail in Chapter 6. Adjustments were required for the following items.

Entry (a)	Prepaid insurance expired, $550.
Entry (b)	Office supplies used, $700.
Entry (c)	Depreciation on office equipment, $3,000.
Entry (d)	Management fees earned, $300.
Entry (e)	Salaries earned by employees but not yet paid, $1,250.
Entry (f)	Utilities used but not yet paid, $340.
Entry (g)	Unpaid income taxes at the end of the period, $1,100.
Entry (h)	Revenue earned from management of apartment complex but not yet received, $875.

After all of the adjustments are entered, the two Adjustments columns are added to
prove that the total debit adjustments equal the total credit adjustments. Adding the
amounts entered in a vertical column is called footing the column.

QUALITY REAL ESTATE OFFICE, INC.
Worksheet
For the Month Ended December 31, 19X2

Account	Unadjusted Trial Balance Debit	Unadjusted Trial Balance Credit	Adjustments Debit	Adjustments Credit	Adjusted Trial Balance Debit	Adjusted Trial Balance Credit	Income Statement Debit	Income Statement Credit	Balance Sheet Debit	Balance Sheet Credit
Cash	31,090									
Accounts Receivable	6,800		h) 875							
Prepaid Insurance	800			a) 550						
Office Supplies on Hand	940			b) 700						
Office Equipment	30,000									
Accum.Deprec.— Off. Equip.		3,000		c) 3,000						
Accounts Payable		7,200								
Salaries Payable		-0-		e) 1,250						
Utilities Payable		-0-		f) 340						
Unearned Management Fees		900	d) 300							
Income Taxes Payable		-0-		g) 1,100						
Capital Stock		25,000								
Retained Earnings		8,930								
Dividends Declared	10,000									
Commissions Revenue		140,800								
Management Fees Revenue		-0-		d) 300 h) 875						
Advertising Expense	8,240									
Depreciation Expense	-0-		c) 3,000							
Income Tax Expense	3,800		g) 1,100							
Insurance Expense	-0-		a) 550							
Office Supplies Expense	-0-		b) 700							
Rent Expense	12,000									
Salaries Expense	76,590		e) 1,250							
Utilities Expense	5,570		f) 340							
Totals	185,830	185,830	8,115	8,115						
Net income for the period										
Totals										

FIGURE 7-3
**ADJUSTING ENTRIES ENTERED IN THE ADJUSTMENTS COLUMNS
(STEP 2 IN THE PREPARATION OF A WORKSHEET)**

    Step 4-3. Prepare an adjusted trial balance. In this step, each account balance in the Unadjusted Trial Balance columns is combined with the corresponding adjustments, if any, in the Adjustments columns, and the resulting balance is extended on the same line to the proper Adjusted Trial Balance column, as shown in Figure 7-4. The combined amounts entered in these two columns will be the same as the ledger account balances after the adjusting entries are recorded in the journal and posted to the ledger. (To verify this, refer back to the adjusted trial balance of Quality Real Estate Office, Inc., in Figure 6-5.) Combining the amounts entered on each line--that is, adding or subtracting across the worksheet horizontally--is called **crossfooting**.

For those accounts unaffected by the adjustments–such as Cash, Accounts Payable, and Commissions Revenue–the balance is simply extended directly to the appropriate debit or credit column in the Adjusted Trial Balance columns. If an account has a debit balance in the Unadjusted Trial Balance column, a debit adjustment will increase the balance (see the Salaries Expense account), whereas a credit adjustment will decrease the balance (see the Prepaid Insurance account). An account with a credit balance is increased by a credit adjustment and decreased by a debit adjustment. In some cases, an account may not have a balance in the Unadjusted Trial Balance columns, but an adjustment is made to the account. In such cases, the amount of the adjustment is extended directly to the appropriate Adjusted Trial Balance column (see the Salaries Payable account). After all adjusted account balances have been determined, the equality of debits and credits is verified by footing the two Adjusted Trial Balance columns.

QUALITY REAL ESTATE OFFICE, INC.
Worksheet
For the Month Ended December 31, 19X2

Account	Unadjusted Trial Balance		Adjustments		Adjusted Trial Balance		Income Statement		Balance Sheet	
	Debit	Credit	Debit	Credit	Debit	Credit	Debit	Credit	Debit	Credit
Cash	31,090				31,090					
Accounts Receivable	6,800		h) 875		7,675					
Prepaid Insurance	800			a) 550	250					
Office Supplies on Hand	940			b) 700	240					
Office Equipment	30,000				30,000					
Accum.Deprec.— Off. Equip.		3,000		c) 3,000		6,000				
Accounts Payable		7,200				7,200				
Salaries Payable		-0-		e) 1,250		1,250				
Utilities Payable		-0-		f) 340		340				
Unearned Management Fees		900	d) 300			600				
Income Taxes Payable		-0-		g) 1,100		1,100				
Capital Stock		25,000				25,000				
Retained Earnings		8,930				8,930				
Dividends Declared	10,000				10,000					
Commissions Revenue		140,800				140,800				
Management Fees Revenue		-0-		d) 300 h) 875		1,175				
Advertising Expense	8,240				8,240					
Depreciation Expense	-0-		c) 3,000		3,000					
Income Tax Expense	3,800		g) 1,100		4,900					
Insurance Expense	-0-		a) 550		550					
Office Supplies Expense	-0-		b) 700		700					
Rent Expense	12,000				12,000					
Salaries Expense	76,590		e) 1,250		77,840					
Utilities Expense	5,570		f) 340		5,910					
Totals	185,830	185,830	8,115	8,115	192,395	192,395				
Net income for the period										
Totals										

FIGURE 7-4
ACCOUNT BALANCES EXTENDED TO THE ADJUSTED TRIAL BALANCE COLUMNS (STEP 3 IN THE PREPARATION OF A WORKSHEET)

Step 4-4. Extend every account balance listed in the Adjusted Trial Balance columns to its proper financial statement column. Every account balance listed in the Adjusted Trial Balance columns is extended to either the Balance Sheet columns or the Income Statement columns, as shown in Figure 7-5. The accounts are extended as follows:

Type of Account	Column Extended to
Asset	Balance Sheet Debit
Liability	Balance Sheet Credit
Paid-in Capital	Balance Sheet Credit
Retained Earnings	Balance Sheet Credit
Dividends Declared	Balance Sheet Debit
Revenue	Income Statement Credit
Expense	Income Statement Debit

In other words, in this part of the process, accounts are sorted on the basis of their financial statement classification. The account balances extended to the Income Statement columns will be used to prepare the income statement. The Balance Sheet columns will contain data needed to prepare both the statement of retained earnings and the balance sheet. *Note that the Dividends Declared account is extended to the Balance Sheet debit column*, rather than to the Income Statement debit column, because it is not an expense.

PRACTICE ACTIVITY 7-1

Listed below are the ledger accounts appearing in the adjusted trial balance columns of a worksheet.

_3_	Cash	____	Unearned Revenues
____	Dividends Declared	____	Service Revenue
____	Prepaid Insurance	____	Retained Earnings
____	Utilities Expense	____	Accumulated Depreciation–Building

Required:
In the blank provided, indicate the column of the worksheet in which the amount in each account would be extended by entering the following code numbers.

    1 = Income Statement, debit   3 = Balance Sheet, debit
    2 = Income Statement, credit   4 = Balance Sheet, credit
The first account is completed as an example.

QUALITY REAL ESTATE OFFICE, INC.
Worksheet
For the Month Ended December 31, 19X2

Account	Unadjusted Trial Balance Debit	Unadjusted Trial Balance Credit	Adjustments Debit	Adjustments Credit	Adjusted Trial Balance Debit	Adjusted Trial Balance Credit	Income Statement Debit	Income Statement Credit	Balance Sheet Debit	Balance Sheet Credit
Cash	31,090				31,090				31,090	
Accounts Receivable	6,800		h) 875		7,675				7,675	
Prepaid Insurance	800			a) 550	250				250	
Office Supplies on Hand	940			b) 700	240				240	
Office Equipment	30,000				30,000				30,000	
Accum.Deprec.—										
Off. Equip.		3,000		c) 3,000		6,000				6,000
Accounts Payable		7,200				7,200				7,200
Salaries Payable		-0-		e) 1,250		1,250				1,250
Utilities Payable		-0-		f) 340		340				340
Unearned Management Fees		900	d) 300			600				600
Income Taxes Payable		-0-		g) 1,100		1,100				1,100
Capital Stock		25,000				25,000				25,000
Retained Earnings		8,930				8,930				8,930
Dividends Declared	10,000				10,000				10,000	
Commissions Revenue		140,800				140,800		140,800		
Management Fees Revenue		-0-		d) 300 h) 875		1,175		1,175		
Advertising Expense	8,240				8,240		8,240			
Depreciation Expense	-0-		c) 3,000		3,000		3,000			
Income Tax Expense	3,800		g) 1,100		4,900		4,900			
Insurance Expense	-0-		a) 550		550		550			
Office Supplies Expense	-0-		b) 700		700		700			
Rent Expense	12,000				12,000		12,000			
Salaries Expense	76,590		e) 1,250		77,840		77,840			
Utilities Expense	5,570		f) 340		5,910		5,910			
Totals	185,830	185,830	8,115	8,115	192,395	192,395	113,140	141,975	79,255	50,420
Net income for the period							28,835			28,835
Totals							141,975	141,975	79,255	79,255

FIGURE 7-5
ACCOUNT BALANCES EXTENDED TO THE FINANCIAL STATEMENT COLUMNS AND TOTALS
COMPUTED (STEPS 4 AND 5 IN THE PREPARATION OF A WORKSHEET)

Step 4-5. Add the two Income Statement columns and the two Balance Sheet columns. Compute the difference between the totals of the two Income Statement columns, and enter this as a balancing amount in both the Income Statement and Balance Sheet columns. Add the four columns again with the balancing amount included. After all the amounts have been extended to either the Income Statement or the Balance Sheet columns, the four columns are added and their total entered at the bottom of each column. The net income or net loss for the period is determined by computing the difference between the totals of the two Income Statement columns, as shown in Figure 7-5. The computation in this illustration is:

Total of the credit column (revenues)	$141,975
Total of the debit column (expenses)	113,140
Difference (net income)	$ 28,835

In this illustration, the revenues earned ($141,975) exceeded the expenses incurred ($113,140), resulting in a net income of $28,835. This difference is entered in the Income Statement debit column to balance the two columns.

The net income is also entered on the same line in the Balance Sheet credit column to balance the debit and credit subtotals. The balance sheet subtotals are not equal because net income for the period is an increase in owners' equity that *has not been transferred* to the Retained Earnings account at this stage in the accounting cycle. Stated another way, except for the Retained Earnings account, which shows the balance at the beginning of the period, all of the account balances extended to the Balance Sheet columns are end-of-period balances. Extending the net income amount to the Balance Sheet credit column recognizes that operations increased stockholders' equity this period; extending the revenue and expense transactions to the Income Statement columns determines the net income for the period. The other change in retained earnings (a decrease due to the distribution of a cash dividend to the stockholders) is reported in the Balance Sheet debit column. The ending retained earnings balance to be reported in the balance sheet ($27,765) can now be determined directly from the worksheet by adding the net income ($28,835 credit) to, and subtracting the dividends declared ($10,000 debit) from, the beginning retained earnings balance ($8,930).

The four columns are added again with the net income of $28,835 included as a balancing amount in the columns. If the debit and credit columns under Balance Sheet are not equal, there is an error in extending the amounts from the Adjusted Trial Balance columns.

If the Income Statement debit column had exceeded the Income Statement credit column, a net loss for the period would be indicated. In that case, the difference between the two columns would be captioned "Net Loss for the Period" and that difference entered in the Income Statement credit column and the Balance Sheet debit column.

Adding the debit and credit columns to verify the equality of debits and credits as work proceeds across the worksheet does not ensure that the balances are correct. For example, an adjustment may have been omitted entirely or the wrong adjusting amount may have been entered on the worksheet. In Step 4-4, an amount may be extended to the wrong column (e.g., the credit balance in the Unearned Management Fees account, a liability, may have been extended to the Income Statement credit column). This will not destroy the equality of debits and credits, but it will result in (1) an overstatement of revenues in the income statement and (2) an understatement of liabilities and an overstatement of stockholders' equity in the balance sheet.

Once the worksheet is complete, it is used to journalize the adjusting entries, prepare the financial statements, and journalize the closing entries.

PRACTICE ACTIVITY 7-2

Part I.

1. In the worksheet as it is described in this chapter, a net income for the period is entered in which columns? _____

2. Adjusting entries are not recorded in the journal since they are entered in the worksheet. True or False _____

3. _____ is the process of adding or subtracting horizontally across a worksheet.

Part II.

A worksheet for the Baxter Consulting Company with the Unadjusted Trial Balance completed is given on the next page. You are to complete the worksheet using the following information for making adjustments.

a. Rent for the year was $320.
b. Office supplies on hand December 31 per physical count, $120.
c. A utility bill for $60 was received, but not paid.
d. Unpaid salaries at the end of the year were $300.
e. Estimated depreciation on the equipment, $240.

Worksheet for Part 2 of Practice Activity 7-2.

BAXTER CONSULTING COMPANY
Worksheet
December 31, 19X2

Account Titles	Unadjusted Trial Balance		Adjustments		Adjusted Trial Balance		Income Statement		Balance Sheet	
	Debit	Credit	Debit	Credit	Debit	Credit	Debit	Credit	Debit	Credit
Cash	1,200									
Accounts Receivable	600									
Prepaid Rent	520									
Office Supplies	200									
Equipment	6,000									
Acc. Depr. — Equip.		720								
Accounts Payable		400								
Salaries Payable		-0-								
Utilities Payable		-0-								
Capital Stock		3,600								
Retained Earnings		1,100								
Dividends Declared	600									
Consulting Revenue		9,160								
Depreciation Expense	-0-									
Office Supp. Expense	-0-									
Rent Expense	400									
Salaries Expense	5,200									
Utilities Expense	260									
Totals	14,980	14,980								

STEP 5: RECORDING AND POSTING ADJUSTING ENTRIES

The adjusting entries are entered in the general journal as shown in Figure 7-6. The necessary information is available directly from the Adjustments columns of the worksheet. Note that the entries are dated on the last day of the accounting period, and generally, the caption "Adjusting Entries" is written in the general journal to separate these entries from other transactions. After the adjusting entries are posted, the ledger account balances should agree with the balances reported in the Adjusted Trial Balance columns of the worksheet. The adjusting entries are posted to the general ledger in Figure 7-13.

General Journal					Page 3
Date		Accounts and Explanation	Post. Ref.	Debit	Credit
		ADJUSTING ENTRIES			
Dec.	31	Insurance Expense	525	550	
		Prepaid Insurance	110		550
		To record insurance expense for June.			
	31	Office Supplies Expense	535	700	
		Office Supplies on Hand	111		700
		To record office supplies used in June.			
	31	Depreciation Expense	505	3,000	
		Accumulated Depreciation — Office Equipment	171		3,000
		To record depreciation for June on office equipment.			
	31	Unearned Management Fees	220	300	
		Management Fees Revenue	402		300
		To record fees earned for services performed during June.			
	31	Salaries Expense	545	1,250	
		Salaries Payable	210		1,250
		To record unpaid salaries at the end of June.			
	31	Utilities Expense	550	340	
		Utilities Payable	216		340
		To record unpaid utilities at the end of June.			
	31	Income Tax Expense	520	1,100	
		Income Taxes Payable	225		1,100
		To record income taxes accrued on net income earned during June.			
	31	Accounts Receivable	104	875	
		Management Fees Revenue	402		875
		To record revenue earned but not yet billed for management of apartment complex during June.			

FIGURE 7-6
RECORDING ADJUSTING ENTRIES IN THE GENERAL JOURNAL

STEP 6: PREPARATION OF FINANCIAL STATEMENTS

Because the worksheet format provides for sorting account balances between the income statement and the balance sheet, preparation of the formal financial statements–such as the income statement, the retained earnings statement, and the balance sheet–is a relatively easy step. However, as noted earlier, the worksheet is not designed to accumulate information to be used in the preparation of a statement of cash flows.

The income statement in Figure 7-7 is prepared from account balances listed in the two Income Statement columns in the worksheet prepared in Figure 7-5. The retained earnings statement, illustrated in Figure 7-8, and the balance sheet, illustrated in Figure 7-9, are prepared from items contained in the Balance Sheet columns of Figure 7-5.

QUALITY REAL ESTATE OFFICE, INC.
Income Statement
For the Year Ended December 31 ,19X2

Revenues:		
Commissions		$140,800
Management fees		1,175
Total revenues		141,975
Expenses:		
Advertising expense	$ 8,240	
Depreciation expense	3,000	
Insurance expense	550	
Office supplies expense	700	
Rent expense	12,000	
Salaries expense	77,840	
Utilities expense	5,910	
Total expenses		108,240
Income before income taxes		33,735
Income tax expense		4,900
Net income		$ 28,835
Earnings per share*		$5.77

*($28,835 / 5,000 shares)

FIGURE 7-7
INCOME STATEMENT

QUALITY REAL ESTATE OFFICE, INC.
Retained Earnings Statement
For the Year Ended December 31 ,19X2

Retained earnings, January 1, 19X2	$ 8,930
Add: Net income for the year	28,835
Total	37,765
Less: Dividends paid to stockholders	10,000
Retained earnings, December 31, 19X2	$ 27,765

FIGURE 7-8
RETAINED EARNINGS STATEMENT

QUALITY REAL ESTATE OFFICE, INC.
Balance Sheet
December 31, 19X2

Assets

Current assets:
Cash		$31,090
Accounts receivable		7,675
Prepaid insurance		250
Office supplies on hand		240
Total current assets		39,255

Property, plant, and equipment:
Office equipment	$30,000	
Less: Accumulated depreciation	6,000	
Total property, plant, and equipment		24,000
Total assets		$63,255

Liabilities and Stockholders' Equity Liability

Current liabilities:
Accounts payable		$ 7,200
Salaries payable		1,250
Income taxes payable		1,100
Utilities payable		340
Unearned management fees		600
Total current liabilities		10,490

Stockholders' Equity

Capital stock (5,000 shares outstanding)	$25,000	
Retained earnings	27,765	
Total stockholders' equity		52,765
Total liabilities and stockholders' equity		$63,255

FIGURE 7-9
BALANCE SHEET

STEP 7: RECORDING AND POSTING CLOSING ENTRIES

The income statement is prepared for a specific period of time, compared to the balance sheet, which is prepared at a specific date. For example, the income statement for a fiscal period covers a 12-month period. The income statement reports the firm's accomplishments (revenue) from delivery of goods or the performance of services and expenses incurred to produce the reported revenue. Net income or net loss is the difference between the two. Revenues increase assets and owners' equity; expenses decrease assets or increase liabilities (e.g., salaries payable) and decrease owners' equity. Thus, revenue is in effect a credit to owners' equity, and expenses are in effect a debit to owners' equity. Recall that the net effect of income transactions is reported in the Retained Earnings account.

To facilitate the preparation of the income statement and the computation of net income or loss, like operating transactions are accumulated in individual revenue and expense accounts. For example, all revenues earned from performing services are recorded in the Service Revenue account, all payments to employees for salaries are recorded in the Salaries Expense account, and all expired insurance costs are recorded in the Insurance Expense account. Once the income statement has been prepared for the current period, the balances in the revenue and expense accounts are no longer needed. These accounts are reduced to a zero balance at the end of the period so that they will *start the next period with a zero balance*. Obviously, if the accounting equation is to remain in balance, the net balance in the revenue and expense accounts is transferred to another account as discussed and illustrated below. If this were not done, the income statement accounts would contain information from previous accounting periods and it would become difficult to summarize the effects of the transactions that occurred in any one period.

This step in the accounting cycle is referred to as the **closing process**, and journal entries made to close the accounts are called **closing entries**. Because the revenue and expense accounts are reduced to a zero balance at the end of each fiscal period, they are called **temporary accounts** or **nominal accounts**. Balance sheet accounts are not closed. Their ending balances of one period are carried forward and become the beginning balances of the next period. Balance sheet accounts are called **permanent accounts** or **real accounts**.

A new temporary clearing account, called the **Income Summary** account, is normally established to summarize the balances in the revenue and expense accounts. The Income Summary account is a temporary account used for a specific purpose. The closing process *is the only time* in the accounting process when this account is used. Closing entries are generally made in the following sequence:

1. All revenue accounts are closed by debiting each revenue account for the balance in the account and crediting the Income Summary account for the sum of the individual debits. The effect of this entry is to reduce each revenue account to a zero balance and transfer the sum of the balances in the revenue accounts to the credit side of the Income Summary account.

2. All expense accounts are closed by crediting each expense account for the balance in the account and debiting the Income Summary account for the sum of the individual credits. The effect of this entry is to reduce each expense account to a zero balance and transfer the sum of the balances in the expense accounts to the debit side of the Income Summary account.

3. After the first two closing entries have been posted, the balance in the Income Summary account will be equal to the net income or net loss for the period. The balance in the account is transferred to the Retained Earnings account.

4. The Dividends Declared account is closed by crediting the Dividends Declared account and debiting the Retained Earnings account. The effect of this entry is to reduce the Dividends Declared account to a zero balance and transfer its balance to the debit side of the Retained Earnings account.

In applying accounting procedures, there are sometimes alternative approaches used in practice to accomplish an intended accounting objective. Which approach to use is an accounting policy decision rather than a conceptual issue. For example, in practice you may find a firm that makes the second entry listed above as the first entry. The purpose for making the entries is the same, and that is to reduce the revenue and expense accounts to a zero balance. The net effect on the Income Summary is the same.

It is also possible to complete the process by not using the Income Summary account. The process could be completed by making one compound journal entry as follows:

Revenue (debit individual revenue accounts)	XX	
Dividends Declared		XX
Expense (credit individual expense accounts)		XX
Retained Earnings (balancing amount)		XX

For a large corporation, this entry could involve numerous accounts and the entry becomes unwieldy. Performing the closing process in the four steps listed above is considered by most accountants to be more convenient and systematic.

The information needed to prepare the closing entries is conveniently available from the Income Statement columns of the worksheet. The process is diagrammed in Figure 7-10 in T account format, using totals from the Income Statement columns in the worksheet presented in Figure 7-5.

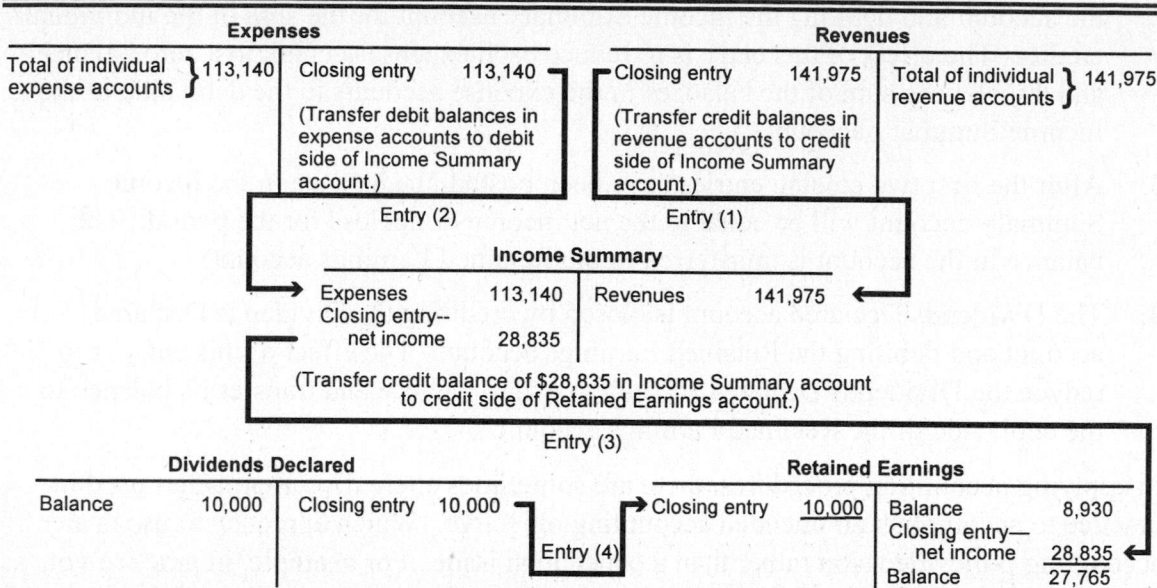

FIGURE 7-10
DIAGRAM OF CLOSING PROCESS

CLOSING ENTRIES ILLUSTRATED

Closing entries for Quality Real Estate Office, Inc., are illustrated in Figures 7-11 and 7-12. The related postings are shown in T account format. In the general journal, the closing entries are separated from the adjusting entries by the caption "Closing Entries." For illustrative purposes only, the closing entries are identified in this chapter by a reference number in the date column of the ledger and in the T accounts.

Closing the Revenue Accounts

A revenue account normally has a credit balance. Therefore, to close the account requires debiting it for an amount equal to its balance. The offsetting credit is made to the Income Summary account. The compound journal entry needed to close the revenue accounts is shown in Figure 7-11. The effect of this entry is to transfer the sum of the credit balances in the revenue accounts to the credit side of the Income Summary account and reduce the revenue accounts to a zero balance for the start of the next period, as shown in Figure 7-11.

Closing the Expense Accounts

Expense accounts normally have debit balances. Each expense account is therefore credited for an amount equal to its balance, and the Income Summary account is debited for the sum of the individual balances. The compound journal entry is shown in Figure 7-11. This entry transfers the sum of the debit balances of $113,140 as a debit to the Income Summary account and reduces each expense account to a zero balance.

Closing the Income Summary Account

After the first two closing entries are posted, the balances formerly reported in the individual revenue and expense accounts are summarized in the Income Summary account. If revenues exceed expenses, a net income is earned and the Income Summary account will contain a credit balance. If expenses exceed revenues, a net loss is incurred and the account will have a debit balance. In either case, the balance is transferred to the Retained Earnings account. In other words, stockholders' equity, specifically the Retained Earnings account, is increased by revenues and decreased by expenses. However, because they are recorded in separate temporary accounts rather than directly to the Retained Earnings account, journal entries are needed at the end of the period to transfer the net effect of the revenues and expenses to the Retained Earnings account.

The Quality Real Estate Office, Inc., earned a net income during 19X2. The credit balance of $28,835 in the Income Summary account is closed to the Retained Earnings account as shown by entry (3) in Figure 7-12. The effect of this entry is to recognize that the net assets (i.e., assets minus liabilities) of the company increased $28,835 this period due to profitable operations. This increase in net assets adds to the owners' interest in the firm. Conversely, if a net loss is reported, the Income Summary account is credited to reduce the account to a zero balance and the Retained Earnings account is debited to reflect a decrease in stockholders' equity from operations.

Closing the Dividends Declared Account

The debit balance in the Dividends Declared account ($10,000) represents a reduction in the stockholders' interest due to the distribution of a cash dividend to them during the period. The balance in the account is transferred directly to the Retained Earnings account (see entry 4 in Figure 7-12). Note that the Dividends Declared account is not closed to the Income Summary account, because the distribution of assets to the owners is not an expense of doing business.

A complete ledger in T account format after the closing entries have been posted is presented in Figure 7-13 for Quality Real Estate Office, Inc. Note in Figure 7-13 that after the closing process is complete, all of the revenue, expense, income summary, and dividends declared accounts have zero balances and are ready for recording transactions in the next period. As a result, the retained earnings balance of $27,765 is equal to the ending balance reported in the balance sheet in Figure 7-9. The balances in the balance sheet accounts are carried forward to the next period and are the only accounts that have a balance.

GENERAL JOURNAL

Page 4

Date		Accounts and Explanation	Post. Ref.	Debit	Credit
(1)		Closing Entries			
Dec.	31	Commissions Revenue	400	140,800	
		Management Fees Revenue	402	1,175	
		Income Summary	350		141,975
		To close the revenue accounts.			
(2)					
Dec.	31	Income Summary	350	113,140	
		Advertising Expense	500		8,240
		Depreciation Expense	505		3,000
		Income Tax Expense	520		4,900
		Insurance Expense	525		550
		Office Supplies Expense	535		700
		Rent Expense	540		12,000
		Salaries Expense	545		77,840
		Utilities Expense	550		5,910
		To close the expense accounts.			

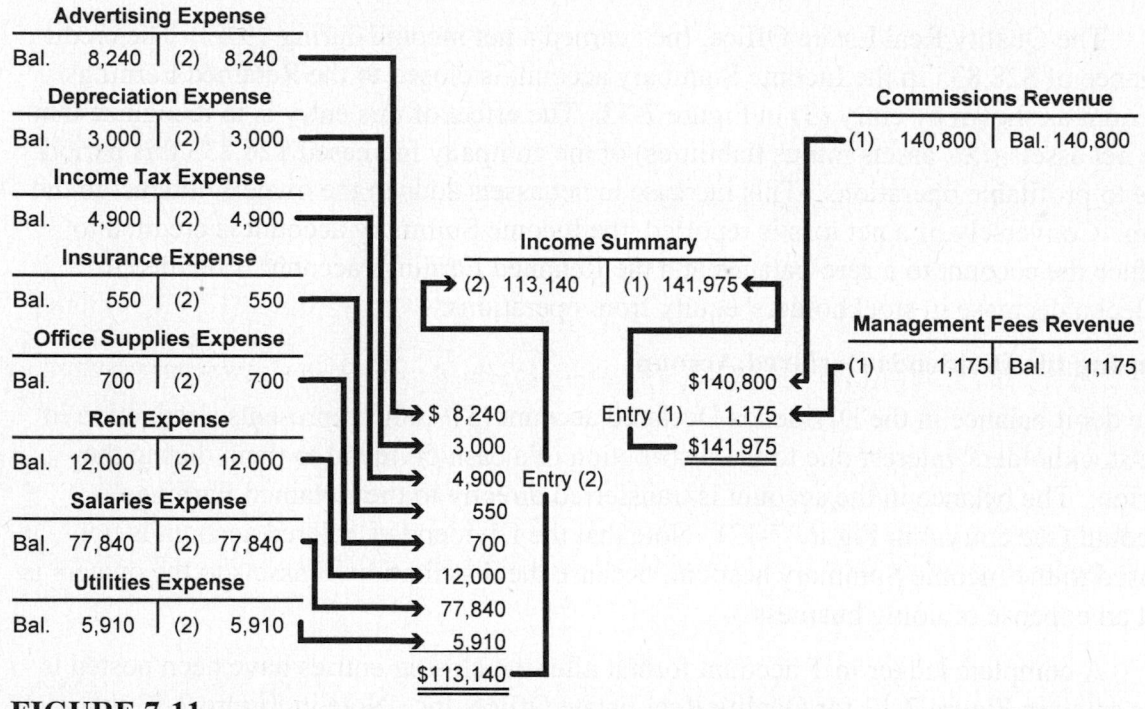

FIGURE 7-11
CLOSING THE REVENUE AND EXPENSE ACCOUNTS

GENERAL JOURNAL

Page 4

Date		Accounts and Explanation	Post. Ref.	Debit	Credit
(3) Dec.	31	Income Summary	350	28,835	
		Retained Earnings	310		28,835
		To close the Income Summary account.			
(4) Dec.	31	Retained Earnings	310	10,000	
		Dividends Declared	320		10,000
		To close the Dividends Declared account.			

Entry (4)

Income Summary	Retained Earnings	Dividends Declared
(2) 113,140 | (1) 141,975	(4) 10,000 | Bal. 8,930	Bal. 10,000 | (4) 10,000
(3) 28,835 |	(3) 28,835	
	Bal. 27,765	

Entry (3)

FIGURE 7-12
CLOSING THE INCOME SUMMARY AND
DIVIDENDS DECLARED ACCOUNTS

PRACTICE ACTIVITY 7-3

1. Balance sheet accounts are called _____ accounts because they are not closed at the end of the period.

2. The following T accounts were taken from the ledger of AAA Tool Company:

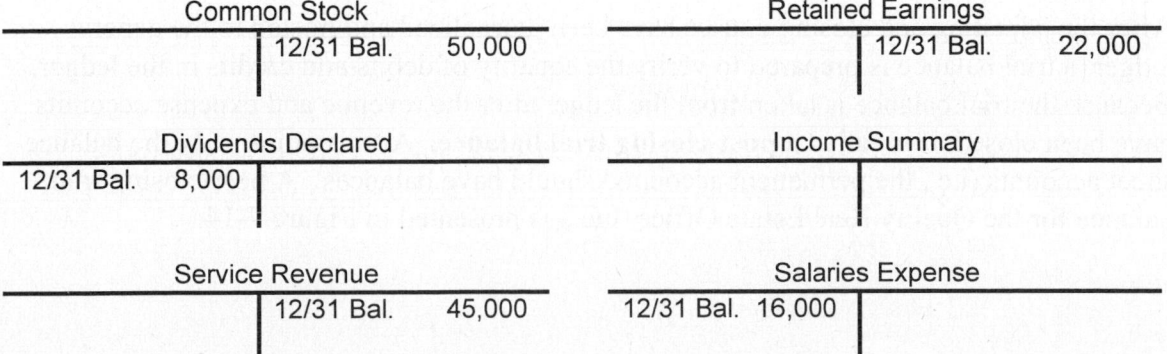

Common Stock	Retained Earnings
12/31 Bal. 50,000	12/31 Bal. 22,000

Dividends Declared	Income Summary
12/31 Bal. 8,000	

Service Revenue	Salaries Expense
12/31 Bal. 45,000	12/31 Bal. 16,000

Rent Expense			Utilities Expense	
12/31 Bal. 14,000			12/31 Bal. 5,000	

Required:

A. Prepare the closing entries in general journal format.

B. Post the closing entries to the T accounts.

C. Compute the balance in the Retained Earnings account. $_____

General Journal					Page 1
Date	Explanation	Post. Ref.	Debit	Credit	

STEP 8: THE POST-CLOSING TRIAL BALANCE

After the adjusting and closing entries have been journalized and posted to the general ledger, a trial balance is prepared to verify the equality of debits and credits in the ledger. Because the trial balance is taken from the ledger after the revenue and expense accounts have been closed, it is called a **post-closing trial balance**. At this point, only the balance sheet accounts (i.e., the permanent accounts) should have balances. A post-closing trial balance for the Quality Real Estate Office, Inc., is presented in Figure 7-14.

PREPARING INTERIM STATEMENTS
WITHOUT CLOSING THE ACCOUNTS

It is common practice for a firm to prepare monthly financial statements for use by management. In addition, most large firms issue quarterly statements to external statement users. Such statements are called *interim statements* because they are prepared between the annual reports issued at the fiscal year-ends. Information needed to prepare interim financial statements is accumulated on the worksheet only. Most firms journalize and post adjusting and closing entries at the end of the fiscal period only. In other words, most accountants make adjustments on the worksheet, but they do not enter them in the accounting records or close the accounts until the end of the fiscal period.

Assets

Cash			100
12/31	31,090		

Accounts Receivable			104
12/31	6,800		
12/31 (h)	875		
12/31 Bal.	7,675		

Prepaid Insurance			110
12/31	800	12/31 (a)	550
12/31 Bal.	250		

Office Supplies on Hand			111
12/31	940	12/31 (b)	700
12/31 Bal.	240		

Office Equipment			170
12/31	30,000		

Accumulated Depr. — Off. Equip.			171
		12/31/X1	3,000
		12/31/X2 (c)	3,000
		12/31 Bal.	6,000

Liabilities

Accounts Payable			200
		12/31	7,200

Salaries Payable			210
		12/31 (e)	1,250

Utilities Payable			216
		12/31 (f)	340

Unearned Management Fees			220
12/31 (d)	300	12/31	900
			600

Income Taxes Payable			225
		12/31 (g)	1,100

Stockholders' Equity

Capital Stock			310
		12/31	25,000

Retained Earnings			310
12/31 (4)	10,000	12/31	8,930
		12/31 (3)	28,835
		12/31 Bal.	27,765

Dividends Declared			320
12/31	10,000	12/31 (4)	10,000

Income Summary			350
12/31 (2)	113,140	12/31 (1)	141,975
12/31 (3)	28,835		
12/31 Bal.	-0-		

Revenues

	Commissions Revenue		400		Management Fees Revenue		402
12/31 (1)	140,800	12/31	140,800	12/31 (1)	1,175	12/31 (d)	300
		12/31 Bal.	-0-			12/31 (h)	875
						12/31 Bal.	-0-

Expenses

	Advertising Expense		500		Depreciation Expense		505
12/31	8,240	12/31 (2)	8,240	12/31 (c)	3,000	12/31 (2)	3,000
12/31 Bal.	-0-			12/31 Bal.	-0-		

	Income Tax Expense		520		Insurance Expense		525
12/31	3,800	12/31 (2)	4,900	12/31 (a)	550	12/31 (2)	550
12/31 (g)	1,100			12/31 Bal.	-0-		
12/31 Bal.	-0-						

	Office Supplies Expense		535		Rent Expense		540
12/31(b)	700	12/31 (2)	700	12/31	12,000	12/31 (2)	12,000
12/31 Bal.	-0-			12/31 Bal.	-0-		

	Salaries Expense		545		Utilities Expense		550
12/31	76,590	12/31 (2)	77,840	12/31	5,570	12/31 (2)	5,910
12/31 (e)	1,250			12/31 (f)	340		
12/31 Bal.	-0-			12/31 Bal.	-0-		

FIGURE 7-13
GENERAL LEDGER AFTER CLOSING PROCESS

QUALITY REAL ESTATE OFFICE, INC.
Post-Closing Trial Balance
December 31, 19X2

Account Title	Account Balance	
	Debit	Credit
Cash	$ 31,090	
Accounts Receivable	7,675	
Prepaid Insurance	250	
Office Supplies on Hand	240	
Office Equipment	30,000	
Accumulated Depreciation — Office Equipment		$ 6,000
Accounts Payable		7,200
Salaries Payable		1,250
Utilities Payable		340
Unearned Management Fees		600
Income Taxes Payable		1,100
Capital Stock		25,000
Retained Earnings		27,765
Total	$69,255	$69,255

FIGURE 7-14
POST-CLOSING TRIAL BALANCE

SOLUTIONS TO PRACTICE ACTIVITIES

PRACTICE ACTIVITY 7-1

3	Cash		4	Unearned Revenues
3	Dividends Declared		2	Service Revenue
3	Prepaid Insurance		4	Retained Earnings
1	Utilities Expense		4	Accumulated Depreciation–Building

PRACTICE ACTIVITY 7-2

Part I.
1.   Income statement debit column and balance sheet credit column.
2.   False
3.   Crossfooting

Part II.   Solution is on the next page.

PRACTICE ACTIVITY 7-2 PART 2

BAXTER CONSULTING COMPANY
Worksheet
December 31, 19X2

Account Titles	Unadjusted Trial Balance Debit	Credit	Adjustments Debit	Credit	Adjusted Trial Balance Debit	Credit	Income Statement Debit	Credit	Balance Sheet Debit	Credit
Cash	1,200				1,200				1,200	
Accounts Receivable	600				600				600	
Prepaid Rent	520			a) 320	200				200	
Office Supplies	200			b) 80	120				120	
Equipment	6,000				6,000				6,000	
Acc. Depr. – Equip.		720		e) 240		960				960
Accounts Payable		400				400				400
Salaries Payable		-0-		d) 300		300				300
Utilities Payable		-0-		c) 60		60				60
Capital Stock		3,600				3,600				3,600
Retained Earnings		1,100				1,100				1,100
Dividends Declared	600				600				600	
Consulting Revenue		9,160				9,160		9,160		
Depreciation Expense	-0-		e) 240		240		240			
Office Supp. Expense	-0-		b) 80		80		80			
Rent Expense	400		a) 320		720		720			
Salaries Expense	5,200		d) 300		5,500		5,500			
Utilities Expense	260		c) 60		320		320			
Totals	14,980	14,980	1,000	1,000	15,580	15,580	6,860	9,160	8,720	6,420
Net income for period							2,300			2,300
Totals							9,160	9,160	8,720	8,720

PRACTICE ACTIVITY 7-3

1.   Permanent or real

2.

Common Stock				Retained Earnings			
		12/31 Bal.	50,000	12/31 (4)	8,000	12/31 Bal.	22,000
						12/31(3)	10,000

Dividends Declared				Income Summary			
12/31 Bal.	8,000	12/31 (4)	8,000	12/31 (2)	35,000	12/31 (1)	45,000
				12/31 (3)	10,000		

Service Revenue				Salaries Expense			
12/31 (1)	45,000	12/31 Bal.	45,000	12/31 Bal.	16,000	12/31 (2)	16,000

Rent Expense				Utilities Expense			
12/31 Bal.	14,000	12/31 (2)	14,000	12/31 Bal.	5,000	12/31 (2)	5,000

General Journal				Page 1
Date	Explanation	Post. Ref.	Debit	Credit
	(Entry (1)--Used here to refer to posting in T accounts)			
Dec. 31	Service Revenue		45,000	
	Income Summary			45,000
	(Entry 2)			
31	Income Summary		35,000	
	Salaries Expense			16,000
	Rent Expense			14,000
	Utilities Expense			5,000
	(Entry 3)			
31	Income Summary		10,000	
	Retained Earnings			10,000
	(Entry 4)			
31	Retained Earnings		8,000	
	Dividends Declared			8,000

Retained earnings balance   = $22,000 + $10,000 – $8,000
$24,000

CHAPTER 8

An Alternative Method of Recording Deferrals and Preparing Reversing Entries

CONTENTS

- Chapter Overview and Objectives
- An Alternative Method of Recording Deferrals
- Payments for Prepaid Expenses Recorded in Expense Accounts
- Revenues Collected in Advance Recorded in Revenue Accounts
- Reversing Entries
- Reversing Adjustments of Deferrals Recorded in Income Statement Accounts
- Reversing Entries Related to Adjustments for Accruals

CHAPTER OVERVIEW AND OBJECTIVES

In this chapter, an alternative method of recording deferrals and the preparation of reversing entries is presented. When you have completed this chapter, you will be able to:

1. Prepare adjusting entries when the initial cash payments or receipts for deferrals are recorded in temporary accounts rather than balance sheet accounts.
2. Prepare reversing entries.

In Chapter 6, the prepayment of an expense or the advance receipt of revenue (deferrals) was recorded initially in balance sheet accounts. For convenience, we will call this the *balance sheet method*. An alternative approach for recording prepayments and adjusting the accounts is covered in this chapter. A second topic covered in this chapter is the preparation of *reversing entries*. The preparation of reversing entries is an optional step in the accounting cycle. A reversing entry is an entry dated the first day of an accounting period and is the opposite of a related adjusting entry that was made at the end of the previous accounting period.

AN ALTERNATIVE METHOD OF RECORDING DEFERRALS

In the preceding chapters, a cash payment made for an expense consumed in the year in which the cash flow occurred was recorded directly in an expense account (e.g., rent for one month paid at the beginning of the month was debited to rent expense). In the case of a revenue transaction, a cash receipt from a client for services performed in the period that the cash was received was recorded directly in a revenue account. As shown in Chapter 2, this procedure avoids the need to make two entries. For example, if the prepayment of an expense is recorded as an asset, a second entry is needed later to record an expense when the asset is consumed. When the payment and the use occur in the same period, debiting an expense account at the time of payment will produce the same net result, a debit to expense and a credit to cash.

When a payment was for a good or a service that was expected to provide benefits over several periods, the cost was initially recorded by debiting a prepaid asset account. Likewise, a receipt of cash for services to be performed in future periods was initially recorded in a liability account because at the time of the receipt the firm is obligated to perform future services. [Recall that the liability was called a *deferred revenue* (sometimes referred to as unearned revenue) because the recognition of revenue is deferred (postponed) until it is earned.] At the end of the period, each asset account was analyzed and an adjustment made when needed to transfer the portion of the asset consumed during the period to an expense account. Similarly, an adjusting entry was made to transfer the revenue earned from the liability account to a revenue account.

To review this procedure, which is the balance sheet method, assume that on December 1 a company paid $300 for three months' rent beginning on that date and also received $300 for revenue to be earned evenly over a three-month period beginning on December 1. The entries to record the initial cash payment or receipt are:

Prepaid Rent	300		Cash		300
Cash		300	Unearned Revenue		300

At the end of the fiscal period, December 31 in this case, the following adjusting entries are needed to adjust the deferred account balances:

Rent Expense	100		Unearned Revenue	100	
Prepaid Rent		100	Revenue		100

The accounts appear as follows after the adjusting entry is posted.

	Prepaid Rent					**Unearned Revenue**			
12/1	300	12/31	100		12/31	100	12/31	300	
Bal.	200						Bal.	200	

	Rent Expense					**Revenue**		
12/31	100						12/31	100

The $200 balance left in the asset account has future economic value (an asset), and the $200 balance left in the unearned revenue account shows the firm's obligation to perform future services. The $100 balance in the revenue account shows the amount earned during December of this period and is reported in the income statement; the $100 reported in the Rent Expense is the cost of December rent and is reported in the income statement.

Another approach is sometimes used to record the initial transaction related to the prepayment of an expense or the receipt of unearned revenue. Some businesses find it more convenient to record *all payments for goods or services in expense accounts*, regardless of whether a particular cost will benefit the current period only or several accounting periods. Consistent with this approach, *all receipts of cash for services are recorded directly in revenue accounts*. We will call this approach the *income statement method*.

The advantage of the income statement method is that it standardizes the recording process. The person analyzing the transactions does not have to be concerned with whether the transaction affects one or more periods but will record all cash receipts and disbursements in the same manner. As with the balance sheet method illustrated in Chapter 6, the income statement method results in incorrect account balances in a number of accounts during the accounting period. At the end of the period, adjustments are made to derive the correct account balances before the financial statements are prepared. However, the analysis is somewhat different in that the *unused portion of the expense* must be transferred at the end of the period from an expense account to an asset account and the *unearned revenue* is transferred from a revenue account to a liability account in the balance sheet.

Before we illustrate the income statement method, a few points need to be emphasized. First, either method used for recording and adjusting deferrals properly applied will result in the same final account balances. That is, the objective of the adjusting process is to report the correct account balances. Although the initial entry to record the cash payment or receipt varies, depending on the method applied, the year-end adjusting entries are modified resulting in the account balances and the financial statements being the same for both methods. As noted on other occasions, there are sometimes different data processing alternatives to select from to accomplish an accounting objective. Which method to use is an accounting policy decision that does not alter the accounting objective or the end results.

Second, the two alternative methods vary as to the accounting for prepaid expenses or unearned revenues only (deferrals). Accruals are adjustments for accrued expenses or revenues that have not been entered on the books. There is only one way to record each type of accrual. For example, the entries to accrue $100 of accrued interest expense or interest revenue are:

To Accrue an Expense		To Accrue a Revenue	
Interest Expense	100	Interest Receivable	100
Interest Payable	100	Interest Revenue	100

In other words, it is the two ways that the initial cash payment or receipt for deferrals can be recorded that requires the adjusting entries for deferrals to vary depending on whether the balance sheet or income statement method is used. The adjusting entries for accruals are the same for either methods.

PAYMENTS FOR PREPAID EXPENSES
RECORDED IN EXPENSE ACCOUNTS

To illustrate recording prepaid expenses in expense accounts (income statement method), assume that the policy of Quality Real Estate Office, Inc., is to record payments for insurance policies in an Insurance Expense account. Quality began 19X2 with a balance of $200 in the expense account, which is the amount paid in 19X1 for insurance coverage for the period January 1, 19X2, through May 31, 19X2. (The balance in the account is from a reversing entry made on January 1. Reversing entries are discussed later in this chapter.) On June 1, 19X2, a 12-month policy was purchased for $600 for insurance protection to begin on June 1. The entry on June 1 to record the payment is:

| June | 1 | Insurance Expense | 600 | |
| | | Cash | | 600 |

The balances in the insurance related accounts at the end of the period are:

Prepaid Insurance			Insurance Expense	
12/31 Bal.	-0-		1/1	200
			6/1	600
			12/31	800

The $200 paid for coverage received during the period January 1 - May 31 is an expired cost of this period and is properly reported as an expense in 19X2. The policy purchased on June 1 for $600 provides coverage for 12 months, which overlaps two separate accounting periods. This $600 cost must be apportioned between 19X2 and 19X3, the periods receiving insurance protection. The monthly cost of this policy is $50 ($600/12 months). Seven months of the coverage expired during 19X2 leaving 5 months prepaid for next year. Since the full cost is in the expense account, an adjusting entry is needed to remove the unexpired portion of the insurance coverage from the expense account and transfer it to an asset account. The unexpired portion at December 31 is:

$$\text{Prepaid insurance} = 5 \text{ months x } \$50$$
$$= \$250$$

The adjusting entry is:

| Dec. | 31 | Prepaid Insurance | 250 | |
| | | Insurance Expense | | 250 |

After this adjusting entry is posted, the two accounts appear as follows:

Prepaid Insurance		Insurance Expense	
12/31 A.E. 250		1/1 200	12/31 A.E. 250
		6/1 600	
		12/31 550	

(The notation A.E. is used in this chapter to identify an adjusting entry.)

You should always review the account balances to be sure that the adjusting entries result in correct balances. In this case, the prepaid asset balance of $250 is the portion of the cost allocated to coverage to be received next period. The $550 balance left in the Insurance Expense account is the cost paid for insurance coverage in the current period. This can be verified as follows:

Cost for the period 1/1 - 5/31	$200
Cost for the period 6/1 - 12/31 (7 months X $50)	350
Total expense for the period	$550

Failure to make the adjusting entry would result in expenses being overstated and net income understated by $250. In the balance sheet, assets would be understated $250 as would owners' equity since net income is part of the owners' interest in the firm.

Both the balance sheet and income statement methods are shown in Figure 8-1 so that you contrast the two methods and verify that they produce the same results. Note that after the adjusting entries are journalized and posted, the account balances are the same for either approach: Ending balance in the Prepaid Insurance account, $250; Insurance Expense for 19X2, $550.

Balance Sheet Method		**Income Statement Method**

1. Initial journal entry to record the payment for the 12-month policy purchased on June 1.

June 1	Prepaid Insurance	600	
	Cash		600

	Insurance Expense	600	
	Cash		600

Prepaid Insurance

1/1	200
6/1	600

Insurance Expense

Prepaid Insurance

Insurance Expense

1/1	200
6/1	600

2. Adjusting entry made at the end of the period.

The adjusting entry for the balance sheet method transfers the **expired cost** from a prepaid asset account to an expense account.

The adjusting entry for the income statement method transfers the **unexpired portion** from the expense account to a prepaid asset account.

Dec. 31	Insurance Expense	550	
	Prepaid Insurance		550

	Prepaid Insurance	250	
	Insurance Expense		250

Account balances after posting adjusting entries.

Prepaid Insurance

1/1	200	12/31 A.E.	550
6/1	600		——
Bal.	250		

Prepaid Insurance

12/31 A.E.	250

Insurance Expense

12/31 A.E.	550

Insurance Expense

1/1	200	12/31 A.E.	250
6/1	600		——
Bal.	550		

FIGURE 8-1
COMPARISON OF BALANCE SHEET AND INCOME STATEMENT METHODS–PREPAID EXPENSE

REVENUES COLLECTED IN ADVANCE
RECORDED IN REVENUE ACCOUNTS

To illustrate the adjustment of unearned revenue when the receipt is recorded initially in a revenue account (income statement method), assume that Quality Real Estate Office, Inc., received $900 advance payment on December 1, 19X2, to manage three rental units for the period December 1, 19X2, through February 28, 19X3. The following entry was made on December 1 to record the receipt of cash.

Dec.	1	Cash	900	
		Management Fees Revenue		900

As of December 31, the revenue account is overstated because two months of revenue (January and February of 19X3) have not been earned. An adjusting entry is needed to transfer the unearned portion of the revenue from the Management Fees Revenue account to a liability account. The amount of the adjusting entry is computed as follows:

$900 \div 3$ months = $300 of revenue earned per month
$300 x 2 months unearned = $600 unearned at the end of December

The adjusting entry is:

Dec.	31	Management Fees Revenue	600	
		Unearned Management Fees		600

After the adjusting entry is posted, the accounts will show:

Unearned Management Fees		Management Fees Revenue		
	12/31 A.E. 600	12/31 A.E. 600	12/1	900
			Bal.	300

The Unearned Management Fees account, a liability, now reflects the obligation of the firm to perform two months of service or refund cash to the client; the revenue account shows the cash received for services rendered in December.

A comparison of the balance sheet and income statement methods for this example is shown in Figure 8-2. Once again note that the results are the same for both methods.

Balance Sheet Method	Income Statement Method

1. Initial journal entry to record the receipt of cash for services to be performed for a three-month period.

Dec. 1	Cash	900	
	Unearned Management		
	Fees		900

Dec. 1	Cash	900	
	Management Fees		
	Revenue		900

Unearned Management Fees

		12/1	900

Management Fees Revenue

Unearned Management Fees

Management Fees Revenue

		12/1	900

2. Adjusting entry made at the end of the period.

The adjusting entry for the balance sheet method transfers the **earned revenue** from a liability account to a revenue account.

The adjusting entry for the income statement method transfers the **unearned portion** from the revenue account to a liability account.

Dec. 31	Unearned Management		
	Fees	300	
	Management Fees		
	Revenue		300

	Management Fees		
	Revenue	600	
	Unearned Management		
	Fees		600

Account balances after posting adjusting entries.

Unearned Management Fees

12/31 A.E.	300	12/1	900
		Bal.	600

Unearned Management Fees

		12/31 A.E.	600

Management Fees Revenue

		12/31 A.E.	300

Management Fees Revenue

12/31 A.E.	600	12/1	900
		Bal.	300

FIGURE 8-2
COMPARISON OF BALANCE SHEET AND INCOME STATEMENT METHODS—DEFERRED REVENUE

PRACTICE ACTIVITY 8-1

Part I.

Modern Day Living is a monthly magazine published by Brady Publishing. Brady is a calendar year company. During 19X2 the company received $465,000 from subscribers. The company records all cash receipts for subscriptions in Subscriptions Revenue. A review of the customers' subscription forms performed on December 31, 19X2, reveals that $182,000 of the cash received was for magazines to be published in 19X3 and 19X4.

Required:

1. Open T accounts for Unearned Subscriptions Revenue and Subscriptions Revenue, and enter the prepayment in the proper account.

Unearned Subscriptions Revenue	Subscriptions Revenue

2. What amount should be reported in the 19X2 income statement for subscription revenue? $_____

3. What amount should be reported in the December 31, 19X2, balance sheet for unearned revenue? $_____

4. Prepare the adjusting entry needed on December 31, 19X2, and post the entry to the two T accounts opened in Part 1.

Part II.

Now assume that the Unearned Subscriptions Revenue account is credited when cash for subscriptions is received (balance sheet method).

1. Open T accounts for Unearned Subscriptions Revenue and Subscriptions Revenue, and enter the prepayment in the proper account.

Unearned Subscriptions Revenue	Subscriptions Revenue

2. What amount should be reported in the 19X2 income statement for subscription revenue? $_____

3. What amount should be reported in the December 31, 19X2, balance sheet for unearned revenue? $_____

4. Prepare the adjusting entry needed on December 31, 19X2, and post the entry to the two T accounts opened in Part 1.

Part III.

Compare the amounts reported for Subscriptions Revenue and for Unearned Subscriptions Revenue in Parts I and II. Are they the same or are they different? If they are the same, explain why.

_____

_____

_____

_____

_____

_____

REVERSING ENTRIES

In the Quality Real Estate Office, Inc., illustration in Chapter 7, the preparation of a post-closing trial balance was the last step in the accounting cycle. After the adjusting and closing entries have been posted, the accounts are ready for recording daily transactions in the next period. Prior to entering the daily transactions in the next period, some firms add another step, reversing entries to the cycle. Reversing entries are dated as of the first day of the accounting period. A reversing entry is a journal entry that is the opposite of a related adjusting entry that was made at the end of the just completed period.

A discussion of reversing entries is presented here because they are used in practice by some companies. It should be emphasized that the reversing process *is an optional bookkeeping technique made to simplify the recording of routine transactions in the current accounting period*. (Reversing entries are another example of an accounting data processing decision that does not alter the end product of the process.) What is sometimes confusing is that not all adjusting entries are reversed. All accruals, but only deferrals initially recorded in income statement (temporary) accounts, are reversed. Reversing entries are not made for deferrals initially recorded in balance sheet (permanent) accounts. *As a general rule, a reversing entry should be made for any adjusting entry that increased an asset (a debit) or liability account (a credit).*

REVERSING ADJUSTMENTS OF DEFERRALS RECORDED IN INCOME STATEMENT ACCOUNTS

In the first section of this chapter, expenses paid in advance and revenues collected in advance were originally recorded in income statement (temporary) accounts. When the income statement method is used, adjusting entries are normally reversed on the first day of the next accounting period.

The Quality Real Estate Office, Inc., example covered earlier in this chapter will be continued. In the case of the prepaid insurance, the following adjusting entry was made by Quality Real Estate Office, Inc.

| Dec. | 31 | Prepaid Insurance | 250 | |
| | | Insurance Expense | | 250 |

The next step in the accounting cycle is the closing process. The two insurance accounts will appear as follows after the adjusting and closing entries are posted:

Prepaid Insurance			Insurance Expense		
12/31 A.E.	$250		12/31	800	12/31 A.E.	250
					12/31 C.E.	550
				800		800
			Bal.	-0-		

(The notation C.E. is used in this chapter to identify a closing entry.)

Notice that the $550 balance in the Insurance Expense account has been closed leaving a zero balance in the account, but the Prepaid Insurance account shows a balance of $250. Recall that balance sheet accounts are not closed.

The company has elected to use the income statement method. Accordingly, the purchase of other insurance policies is debited to an expense account. This will result in the cost of the old policy being in the Prepaid Insurance account and the cost of new policies entered in the Insurance Expense account. This makes the subsequent analysis of insurance expense more difficult and could result in an error. It is therefore desirable to get all insurance related balances into the expense account. (The advantage of making reversing entries is explained in more detail on pages 8 to14.) We accomplish this by making a reversing entry. The following reversing entry is made on January 1, 19X3, to return the prepaid portion of the premium of $250 to the Insurance Expense account.

| Jan. | 1 | Insurance Expense | 250 | |
| | | Prepaid Insurance | | 250 |

Compare this reversing entry to the adjusting entry on December 31. Note that the debit and credit amounts are the same in both entries, but the account debited (Prepaid Insurance) in the adjusting entry is credited in the reversing entry, whereas the account credited (Insurance Expense) in the adjusting entry is debited in the reversing entry. In other words, the reversing entry is the opposite of the adjusting entry.

After the reversing entry is posted, the Prepaid Insurance account balance is zero and the Insurance Expense account balance is $250 as shown below.

Prepaid Insurance				Insurance Expense			
12/31 A.E.	250	1/1 R.E.	250	12/31	800	12/31 A.E.	250
					___	12/31 C.E.	550
					800		800
				1/1 R.E.	250		

(The notation R.E. is used in this chapter to identify a reversing entry.)

Making a reversing entry on January 1 produces an incorrect balance in the expense account because the asset has not been consumed at this point in time. However, again this is of little concern until financial statements are prepared. Additional payments for insurance premiums are then added to the beginning balance in the Insurance Expense account. At the end of the reporting period, the account is analyzed and the prepaid portion is removed, as was done with an entry in an earlier section of this chapter (see page 4).

Reversing entries are also made for deferred revenues initially recorded in a revenue account. The adjusting entry for Quality Real Estate Office, Inc., is reproduced below for illustration:

Dec.	31	Management Fees Revenue	600	
		Unearned Management Fees		600

The revenue account is closed at the end of the period leaving the following balances in the accounts.

Unearned Management Fees			Management Fees Revenue			
	12/31 A.E.	600	12/31 A.E.	600	12/1	900
			12/31 C.E.	300		___
				900		900
					Bal.	-0-

Given that the company records cash receipts for management fees in the revenue account, it is desirable to get all related amounts into one account. To do so, the adjusting entry for the unearned revenue is reversed by the following entry:

Jan.	1	Unearned Management Fees	600	
		Management Fees Revenue		600

The accounts would appear as follows after this entry is posted:

Unearned Management Fees				Management Fees Revenue			
1/1 R.E.	600	12/31 A.E.	600	12/31 A.E.	600	12/1	900
				12/31 C.E.	300		
					900		900
						1/1 R.E.	600

Additional receipts for management fees in the next fiscal period are credited to the Management Fees Revenue account. This results in bookkeeping consistency as all receipts for management fees are recorded in this one account. The unearned fees are adjusted out at the end of the reporting period.

Reversing entries are not necessary for deferrals recorded initially in balance sheet accounts (the balance sheet method). When the balance sheet method is used, the adjusting process leaves the unexpired cost in an asset account and unearned revenue in the liability account. These balances are carried forward into the next period where a future cash payment for a prepaid expense is debited to the appropriate asset account; a cash receipt for service to be performed is credited to the appropriate liability account. As a result, all like transactions are recorded in the same account.

REVERSING ENTRIES RELATED TO ADJUSTMENTS FOR ACCRUALS

Adjusting entries for accruals of revenues and expenses are often reversed to permit the recording of a routine entry in the next accounting period when the cash is received or paid. To illustrate reversing entries for an accrued expense, we will use the same accrued salaries adjustment that was used in Chapter 6.

1. Salaries paid on December 23 were $2,500. The balance in the Salaries Expense account was $76,590 after this payment was posted.
2. Unpaid salaries of $1,250 were accrued on December 31.
3. Salaries earned for the period December 23 to January 6 in the amount of $2,300 were paid on January 6.

The journal entries to record the December 23 salary payment and the adjusting entry are:

Dec.	23	Salaries Expense	2,500	
		Cash		2,500
		To record payment of salaries.		
		Adjusting Entry		
	31	Salaries Expense	1,250	
		Salaries Payable		1,250
		To record unpaid salaries at the end of December.		

The accounts are shown below after these entries have been posted.

Salaries Payable			Salaries Expense		
	19X2		19X2		
	12/31 A.E.	1,250	Bal. 12/22	76,590	
			12/31 A.E.	1,250	
				77,840	

The next step in the process is to close the temporary account. The Salaries Expense account is closed along with the other expense accounts.

		Closing Entry		
Dec.	31	Income Summary	77,840	
		Salaries Expense		77,840
		To close the Salaries Expense		
		account.		

The account balances after closing are:

Salaries Payable			Salaries Expense			
	19X2		19X2		19X2	
	12/31 A.E.	1,250	Bal. 12/22	76,590	12/31 C.E.	77,840
			12/31 A.E.	1,250		
				77,840		77,840

REVERSING ENTRIES ARE NOT MADE

We will first assume that reversing entries are not made to demonstrate that (1) the process is optional, (2) the same results are obtained whether reversing entries are made or not, and (3) the reversing entry simplifies an entry made in the next period. The entry to record the salary payment on January 6 is:

19X3		(Reversing entry was not made on Jan. 1.)		
Jan.	6	Salaries Payable	1,250	
		Salaries Expense	1,050	
		Cash		2,300
		To record payment of salaries for the		
		period December 23 to January 6.		

Note that the entry to record the payment on January 6 requires two debits, a variation from the normal entry of one debit to the Salaries Expense account. Thus, a change from the normal procedure is necessary. The payment must be divided into two elements because the $2,300 payment is for salaries earned during two different accounting periods. The adjusting entry or the Salaries Payable account in the general ledger must be referred to in order to divide the payment between the two accounts. First, the $1,250 debit settles the liability for the salaries earned by employees in December that were reported as an expense in December. Second, the $1,050 debit to the expense account properly recognizes as an expense that portion of the payment made for salaries incurred in January.

After posting the entry, the Salaries Expense and Salaries Payable accounts appear as follows:

Salaries Payable					**Salaries Expense**			
19X3		19X2		19X2			19X2	
1/6	1,250	12/31 A.E.	1,250	Bal. 12/22	76,590		12/31 C.E.	77,840
				12/31 A.E.	1,250			
					77,840			77,840
				19X3				
				1/6	1,050			

REVERSING ENTRIES ARE MADE

To simplify the January 6 entry, a *reversing entry* may be made to reverse the effects of the adjusting entry as follows:

Jan.	1	Salaries Payable	1,250	
		Salaries Expense		1,250
		To reverse the adjusting entry to accrue unpaid salaries.		

This entry results in the following account balances.

Salaries Payable					**Salaries Expense**			
19X3		19X2		19X2			19X2	
1/1 R.E.	1,250	12/31 A.E.	1,250	Bal. 12/22	76,590		12/31 C.E.	77,840
				12/31 A.E.	1,250			
					77,840			77,840
				19X3				
				1/1 R.E.	1,250			

The reversing entry transfers the balance in the liability account to an expense account. This produces a temporary credit balance of $1,250 in the expense account on January 1 since it had a zero balance (as a result of the closing process) before the reversing entry. The credit balance of $1,250, however, is still a liability until the employees are paid. The reason for making the reversing entry is that it permits making the normal entry to record the payment, a debit to Salaries Expense, on January 6 as follows.

Jan.	6	(Assuming a reversing entry was made on Jan. 1.) Salaries Expense	2,300	
		Cash		2,300
		To record payments of salaries for the period December 23 to January 6.		

The accounts after this entry is posted are as follows:

Salaries Payable					Salaries Expense			
19X3		19X2			19X2		19X2	
1/1 R.E.	1,250	12/31 A.E.	1,250		Bal. 12/22	76,590	12/31 C.E.	77,840
					12/31 A.E.	1,250		
						77,840		77,840
					19X3		19X3	
					1/6	2,300	1/1 R.E.	1,250
					Bal.	1,050		

The debit of $2,300 to the Salaries Expense account is partially offset by the credit of $1,250 made in the reversing entry. This leaves a balance of $1,050 in the Salaries Expense account, which is the expense for January.

A comparison of these account balances to the account balances when a reversing entry was not made reveals that the two approaches produce identical results. Salaries expense for 19X2 and January 19X3 are $77,840 and $1,050, respectively, and a liability for $1,250 is reported in the December 31, 19X2, balance sheet.

Reversing entries are also useful when many similar transactions involve the computation of accruals. For example, a bank may have thousands of outstanding notes receivable. At the end of the period, interest earned but not received must be accrued in order to properly report interest revenue and interest receivable in the financial statements. If a reversing entry is not made, each time that an interest payment is received in the next period, an employee must refer back to the list of accruals. This is necessary in order to divide the amount of the payment between the reduction in the receivable balance and the interest earned in the current period. If the adjusting entry is reversed, the receipt of cash for interest is simply recorded as a debit to Cash and a credit to Interest Revenue. In this case, reversals will result in saving a great deal of time since an employee will not have to allocate each interest payment between two periods. An illustration of a reversing entry related to a revenue transaction is presented in Figure 8-3.

To illustrate the reversal of the accrual of revenue, assume that a company loaned a client $100,000 and that, at December 31, the fiscal year-end, unpaid interest of $2,000 had accrued on the note.

Without Reversing Entries	**With Reversing Entries**

1. December 31, 19X2 - Adjusting entry to accrue interest revenue and interest receivable.

Dec. 31	Interest Receivable	2,000			Interest Receivable	2,000	
	Interest Revenue		2,000		Interest Revenue		2,000

2. December 31, 19X2 - Closing entry assuming that the Interest Revenue account contained a $10,000 balance before the adjusting entry.

Dec. 31	Interest Revenue	12,000			Interest Revenue	12,000	
	Income Summary		12,000		Income Summary		12,000

3. January 1, 19X3 - Reversing entry is made if the company prepares reversing entries.

Jan. 1	No reversing entry				Interest Revenue	2,000	
	is made.				Interest Receivable		2,000

4. May 1, 19X3 - Record the receipt of the interest payment in the amount of $6,000.

May 1	Cash	6,000			Cash	6,000	
	Interest Receivable		2,000				
	Interest Revenue		4,000		Interest Revenue		6,000

```
                  Cash                                        Cash
5/1           6,000 |                            5/1      6,000 |


          Interest Receivable                         Interest Receivable
12/31 A.E.   2,000 | 5/1          2,000       12/31 A.E.  2,000 | 1/1 R.E.      2,000


           Interest Revenue                           Interest Revenue
12/31 C.E.  12,000 | Bal.       10,000        12/31 C.E. 12,000 | Bal.        10,000
                   | 12/31 A.E.  2,000                          | 12/31 A.E.   2,000
            12,000 |            12,000                   12,000 |             12,000
                   | 5/1         4,000        1/1 R.E.    2,000 | 5/1          6,000
```

FIGURE 8-3
ILLUSTRATION OF REVERSING ENTRY FOR REVENUE TRANSACTIONS

PRACTICE ACTIVITY 8-2

I. Rent was paid on October 1, 19X0, for one year, and the entry to record that payment was a debit to Rent Expense and a credit to Cash for $4,000. Prepare the adjusting entry needed on December 31, 19X0, the end of the company's fiscal year.

Prepare the reversing entry that would be made on January 1, 19X1.

II. At the end of 19X0, a company accrued salaries payable of $1,500. On January 4, the company paid employees $2,000. If the company made reversing entries, prepare the reversing entry made on January 1, 19X1, and the entry to record the payment on January 4.

What is the balance in the Salaries Expense account on January 4 after the payment is recorded? $_____

III. During the 19X0 fiscal year, Mystery Publishing Company received $82,500 for magazine subscriptions. The bookkeeper credits Subscriptions Revenue account for the full amount when cash is received. At December 31, 19X0, it is determined that $27,500 of the subscriptions relates to magazines to be published and delivered in future periods.

Required:
1. What amount should be reported in the 19X0 income statement for subscription revenue? $_____.
2. What amount should be reported in the December 31, 19X0, balance sheet for unearned subscriptions? $_____. What type of an account is this? _____
3. Prepare the adjusting entry needed as of December 31, 19X0.
4. Assuming that the company uses reversing entries, prepare the reversing entry, if any is needed, on January 1, 19X1.

SOLUTIONS TO PRACTICE ACTIVITIES

PRACTICE ACTIVITY 8-1
Part I.
1.

Unearned Subscriptions Revenue	Subscriptions Revenue
	465,000

2. $283,000 The portion of the $465,000 earned this period should be reported as revenue. In this case, $182,000 is computed to be the amount received for subscriptions to be provided in 19X3 and 19X4. The portion earned in 19X2 is then the remainder or $283,000 ($465,000 - $182,000).
3. $182,000 An amount received for services to be provided in the future is a liability of the firm. The liability is reduced as the subscriptions are provided.

4.

Dec. 31	Subscriptions Revenue			182,000	
	Unearned Subscriptions Revenue				182,000

Unearned Subscriptions Revenue		Subscriptions Revenue		
12/31	182,000	12/31	182,000	465,000
			Bal.	283,000

Part II.
1.

Unearned Subscriptions Revenue	Subscriptions Revenue
465,000	

2. $283,000
3. $182,000

4.

Dec. 31	Unearned Subscriptions Revenue		283,000	
	Subscriptions Revenue			283,000

Unearned Subscriptions Revenue			Subscriptions Revenue	
12/31	465,000		12/31	283,000
283,000				
Bal.	182,000			

Part III.

The amounts reported for subscriptions revenue in the income statement and the unearned portion in the balance sheet will be the same. The method of recording revenues received in advance does not affect how much is reported on the financial statements. The adjusting entry at year-end adjusts the account balances to reflect the proper amounts to be reported in the income statement and balance sheet.

PRACTICE ACTIVITY 8-2

I.   Adjusting entry

Dec. 31	Prepaid Rent		3,000	
	Rent Expense			3,000

Rent prepaid on 10/1/X0	$4,000	
Cost of rent expired for the period-10/1 - 12/31 ($4,000 X 3/12)	1,000	
Amount prepaid on 12/31/X0	$3,000	

Reversing entry on January 1, 19X1.

Jan. 1	Rent Expense		3,000	
	Prepaid Rent			3,000

II.   Reversing entry on January 1, 19X1

Jan. 1	Salaries Payable		1,500	
	Salaries Expense			1,500

Payment of salaries on January 4, 19X1.

Jan. 4	Salaries Expense		2,000	
	Cash			2,000

Salaries Expense account balance on January 4 is $500 ($2,000 debit – $1,500 credit)

III.   1. $55,000 ($82,500 cash received – $27,500 unearned in the current period.)
   2. $27,500, liability
   3.   Adjusting entry

Dec. 31	Subscriptions Revenue		27,500	
	Unearned Subscriptions Revenue			27,500

   4.   Reversing entry on January 1, 19X1

Jan. 1	Unearned Subscriptions Revenue		27,500	
	Subscriptions Revenue			27,500

CHAPTER 9

Accounting for Merchandising Operations–Perpetual Inventory System

CONTENTS

CHAPTER OVERVIEW AND OBJECTIVES

This chapter describes accounting procedures for businesses that buy and sell merchandise inventory. When you have completed the chapter, you should understand:

1. The nature of merchandise inventory.
2. The basic format of an income statement prepared for a merchandising firm.
3. How to record transactions related to the sale of inventory.
4. The various credit terms related to the sale of inventory.
5. Business practices as they relate to freight cost and the transfer of title to inventory.
6. The difference between perpetual and periodic inventory systems.
7. How to record inventory transactions for a firm using a perpetual inventory system.
8. How to prepare a worksheet and complete the closing process for a firm using a perpetual inventory system.

The preceding chapters used a service business to illustrate the accounting cycle. Service firms make up a significant part of our nation's economy. Service firms include law firms, accounting firms, motels, management consulting firms, equipment repair firms, photography studios. The primary business activity of many other firms centers on selling merchandise to earn revenue. *Manufacturing firms* purchase raw materials and component parts for conversion into finished products for sale to their customers. Accounting for these firms is covered in more advanced accounting courses. Merchandising or trading firms, which may distribute at the wholesale and/or retail levels, purchase goods in substantially the same form in which they are sold. A merchandising operation uses the term **merchandise inventory** or simply **inventory** to designate tangible assets held for sale in the normal course of business. Other assets held for future disposition but not normally sold as part of the regular business activities, such as unused office equipment, are not included in the inventory category.

This chapter discusses accounting for a merchandising firm. Although the accounting principles and methods described in earlier chapters apply to merchandising firms, a number of additional accounts and procedures are used to record inventory transactions. This chapter begins with a discussion of the operations of a merchandising firm with an emphasis on the accounting concepts involved in recording the operations. This is followed by an examination of an income statement prepared for a merchandising firm. Finally, accounting for the sale of inventory is described, along with the two inventory systems (perpetual and periodic) that are used to account for inventory costs. The perpetual inventory system is discussed in detail in this chapter, while the periodic inventory system is discussed in the next chapter.

MERCHANDISING FIRM OPERATIONS

As described in Chapter 1, the normal operating cycle for a merchandising firm is the average length of time it takes for the firm to acquire inventory, sell that inventory to its customers, and collect cash from the sale. At the time of purchase, inventory is recorded at its acquisition price in accordance with the cost principle. Cost is defined as all expenditures needed to acquire and prepare the inventory for sale to customers. Thus, inventory cost should include the invoice price plus such costs as freight charges paid on the goods purchased and costs incurred to assemble the product. The cost of inventory available for future sales is reported in the balance sheet as a current asset because it is expected to be sold within the normal operating cycle or one year, whichever is longer. Inventories are usually listed after receivables because they are one step further removed from cash.

When a sale is made, an asset account is debited and a revenue account is credited for an amount equal to the sales price. In the income statement, the cost of inventory sold is matched with the revenue received from selling it. Proper matching of costs and revenues is, in fact, a major objective of accounting for inventory. It involves determining the amount of the total inventory cost to be deducted from sales in the current period's income statement and the amount to be carried forward as an asset to be expensed in some future period.

Inventory-related transactions are among the most common transactions for a merchandising firm. Inventory is continually being acquired, sold, and replaced, and it makes up a significant part of a firm's total assets. The cost of goods sold for a given period is frequently the firm's largest expense, sometimes exceeding the sum of all operating expenses. For these reasons, the control and safeguarding of inventory are essential for efficient and profitable operations. The establishment of such controls is discussed in more advanced accounting courses.

INCOME STATEMENT FOR A MERCHANDISING FIRM

Figure 9-1 compares the major parts of an income statement for Scotch Records and Tapes, a merchandising firm, to the income statement of Quality Real Estate Office.

SCOTCH RECORDS AND TAPES Income Statement For the Year Ended December 31, 19X2			QUALITY REAL ESTATE OFFICE, INC. Income Statement For the Month Ended June 30, 19X2	
Net sales		$344,000	Revenues	$12,925
Less: Cost of goods sold		206,000	Less: Expenses*	11,175
Gross profit on sales		138,000	Income before income taxes	1,750
Less: Operating expenses			Less: Income tax expense	435
Selling expenses	$52,000		Net income	$ 1,315
Administrative expenses	36,000			
Total operating expenses		88,000	*Individual expenses are not listed.	
Income before income taxes		50,000		
Less: Income tax expense		20,000		
Net income		$ 30,000		

FIGURE 9-1
COMPARISON OF INCOME STATEMENTS

A comparison of the two income statements reveals several differences:

1. Revenue earned is the first item reported in both cases, but for a merchandising firm, revenue is called *sales*.

2. The income statement for Scotch Records and Tapes contains a cost of goods sold section that shows the total cost of the inventory ($206,000) that was sold during the period. The **cost of goods** sold is an expense that is subtracted from sales to arrive at an intermediate income amount called *gross profit* or *gross margin on sales*. The gross profit is calculated to show the amount of markup on the goods sold during this period. The relationship between gross profit and sales is of interest to statement users because companies must sell their inventory at an adequate markup if they are to cover operating expenses and produce a desirable profit.

3. Operating expenses and income taxes are subtracted from gross profit on sales to determine the net income (or net loss) for the period. Operating expenses, which are normally separated by function, are those expenses related to the major activities of the firm.

Although many of the operating expenses incurred by service firms are also incurred by merchandising firms, merchandising firms incur additional expenses that relate to buying and selling inventory. **Selling expenses** result from efforts to market the inventory and include advertising, sales salaries and commissions, and the cost of delivering goods to customers. **Administrative expenses** are management costs associated with the general administration of the company's operations. These expenses include those incurred to operate such subdivisions of the firm as the general office, accounting, personnel, and credit and collection departments. Income before income taxes for a merchandising firm results if the revenue from sales exceeds the cost of the goods sold and the operating expenses incurred.

ACCOUNTING FOR SALES TRANSACTIONS

In Figure 9-1, the first item in the income statement for Scotch Records and Tapes is net sales. Income statements prepared for use by parties outside the firm often begin with net sales because the details of the computation are not relevant to external users. Net sales is computed as follows and is included in the income statement in the format below when the detail is reported:

Revenue from sales:		
Gross sales		$363,000
Less: Sales returns and allowances	$14,000	
Sales discounts	5,000	19,000
Net sales		$344,000

The determination of these amounts is discussed in the following section.

RECORDING GROSS SALES

A sales transaction is generally recorded by the seller when the ownership of the inventory is transferred from the business to the customer. To record the sale, an asset account is debited and the Sales account is credited for an amount equal to the sales price. Usually, the asset recorded in exchange for the inventory is cash or accounts receivable. The entry to record a credit sale of $300 is as follows.

Oct.	10	Accounts Receivable	300	
		Sales		300
		Sold merchandise to John Reeves on account.		

The Cash account would be debited if this were a cash sale. At year end, the balance in the Sales account shows the total amount of cash and credit sales made during the accounting period.

CONTROL ACCOUNTS AND SUBSIDIARY LEDGERS

In the preceding entry, it was assumed that one Accounts Receivable account is used to record the sale of inventory on account. A firm that sells inventory on credit may have hundreds or even thousands of customers. In order to efficiently provide detailed information concerning the amount of sales to, the amount collected from, and the balance due from each customer, firms often establish a separate receivable account for each customer. However, rather than including a large number of individual receivable accounts in the general ledger, the firm establishes one Accounts Receivable account, called a **control account,** in the general ledger to summarize the transactions with all the customers.

The Accounts Receivable control account in the general ledger takes the place of the individual receivable accounts, which are contained in a separate record called the **subsidiary ledger**. The accounts receivable subsidiary ledger contains an individual account for each customer and provides the detailed information about the control account in the general ledger. The sum of the individual account balances in the subsidiary ledger should be equal to the balance in the general ledger control account.

A subsidiary ledger is established when a large amount of detailed information about a certain general ledger account must be kept. Companies often use a separate subsidiary ledger with a control account for a number of general ledger accounts–such as accounts receivable, accounts payable, merchandise inventory, marketable securities, plant assets, and operating expenses. Control accounts and subsidiary ledgers are discussed further in Chapter 11.

SALES RETURNS AND ALLOWANCES

To maintain good customer relations and honor warranty agreements, most businesses permit a customer to return unsatisfactory goods. Alternatively, the customer may agree to keep the goods in exchange for a reduction in the sales price. The return of goods (sales returns) or an adjustment to the sales price (sales allowances) is a reduction in the amount of recorded sales, and either a cash refund is made or the customer's account receivable is reduced. In either case, once a return or allowance is authorized, the seller issues a source document, called a **credit memorandum** or **credit memo**, to the customer and forwards a copy to the accounting department so that the transaction can be properly recorded. The document is called a credit memorandum because the seller is informing the customer that the customer's account is being reduced (credited) on the seller's books. [On the customer's (buyer's) books, the source document serves as a **debit memo** because the supplier's account payable is debited.]

Handling returned merchandise is time-consuming and results in increased costs. For these reasons, management must look for the cause of excessive returns and correct the problem whenever possible. To provide information on the volume of returns and allowances, a contra sales account called Sales Returns and Allowances is debited as follows:

| Oct. | 15 | Sales Returns and Allowances
    Accounts Receivable*
John Reeves returned, for credit,
unsatisfactory merchandise sold
on Oct. 10. (Making only one
entry at this time assumes use of
the periodic inventory system
discussed in a later section of this
chapter.) | 50 | 50 |

*Cash is credited if a cash refund is given.

As shown earlier, sales returns and allowances (a contra account) are subtracted from sales in the income statement.

CREDIT TERMS

The parties involved in a sale/purchase transaction may agree that payment is to be made immediately upon transfer of the goods (a cash sale). Sometimes the sale is made on credit, and payment is delayed for a specific length of time called the **credit period**. The length of the credit period varies among firms, but 30 to 60 days is typical.

When merchandise is sold on credit, the terms of payment, called the credit terms, should be clear as to the amount due and the credit period. The terms of payment normally appear in a source document called the **sales invoice** by the seller and the purchase invoice by the buyer. The credit period is usually abbreviated in the following form: "n/10 EOM" or "n/30." In the first case, the invoice price is due 10 days after the end of the month in which the sale occurred. In the second case, the invoice price is due within 30 days after the invoice date.

Cash Discounts

To provide an incentive for the buyer to make payment before the end of the credit period, the seller may grant a cash discount called a sales discount by the seller and a purchase discount by the buyer. A cash discount entitles the buyer to deduct a specified percentage of the sales price if payment is made within a given time period, called the discount period. The terms are normally quoted in a format such as "2/10, n/30" (verbally the terms are stated "two ten, net thirty"). This notation means that the buyer has two payment options. If payment is made within 10 days of the invoice date, the buyer may deduct 2% from the amount of the invoice. If payment is not made within the 10-day discount period, the full price is due 30 days from the invoice date.

To illustrate, assume that the credit terms were 2/10, n/30 on the $300 sale to John Reeves recorded earlier. The entry to record the collection within the discount period, net of the $50 return, is:

Oct.	20	Cash	245	
		Sales Discounts	5	
		Accounts Receivable		250
		Received payment from John Reeves		
		within the discount period.		

Note that the sales discount of $5 is computed on the sales price less the merchandise returned by the customer [($300 − $50) x 2% = $5].

Two methods, the net invoice method or the gross invoice method, may be used to record the purchase and sale of merchandise inventory. Entries in this text are based on use of the gross invoice method. The gross invoice method is illustrated because it is commonly used in practice and it avoids the problem of allocating the discount to individual units when a physical inventory is taken or when the amounts are entered on individual inventory cards. (The use of inventory cards is discussed later in the chapter.) In addition, the discount amounts are often immaterial.

Under the **gross invoice method** sales and accounts receivable are recorded at the gross invoice price (see the October 10 entry). In other words, under this method, sales discounts are not recorded unless the customer takes advantage of the cash discount as shown above in the October 20 transaction. If the customer pays within the discount period, the sales discount is recorded in a separate account in order to provide information to management on the amount of sales discounts taken. A sales discount is considered a reduction in the sales price of the goods. It is reported as a subtraction from gross sales (i.e., a contra sales account) in the income statement.

From the seller's point of view, the purpose of granting cash discounts is to induce the customer to pay the receivable earlier. Hence, the firm will have the cash available for use before the end of the credit period. The earlier payment also tends to reduce losses from uncollectible accounts receivable.

When a cash discount is included in the credit terms, the buyer must decide whether to pay the account payable within the discount period. Usually, the annual cost of forgoing cash discounts is quite high. This can be shown by converting the discount rate to an annual rate. For example, assume that an agreement for the purchase of $250 in goods contained the terms 2/10, n/30. To obtain the maximum benefit of the credit terms granted by the seller, the buyer should pay the invoice on the last possible date. Thus, the buyer will either (1) pay $245 within 10 days after the invoice date or (2) pay the full invoice price of $250 within 30 days after the invoice date. By not paying within the 10-day discount period, the buyer has the use of the $245 for an additional 20 days. The additional $5 that must be paid in 30 days is an interest charge for extending the credit period 20 days. The effective annual yield is computed as follows:

$$\text{Effective rate for the 20-day period} = \$5/\$245$$
$$= 2.04\%$$
$$\text{Effective annual rate} = (360 \text{ days}/20) \times 2.04\%$$
$$= 36.7\%$$

The effective rate of 36.7% is quite high. A company should compare this rate to the rate it would have to pay to other sources of credit–such as banks, savings and loans, or other lending institutions. The buyer should take advantage of the discount even if the firm has to borrow the money, provided that it can borrow the money at a lower interest rate.

Trade Discounts

A **trade discount** is a percentage reduction granted to a customer from a suggested list price. In contrast to a cash discount, a trade discount is not related to early payment. Instead, it is used to determine the actual invoice price to a particular class of customer. Trade discounts enable the firm to print one price list or catalog but still vary prices for different customer groups, such as retailers or wholesalers, or grant quantity discounts.

Trade discounts are not normally recorded in the accounts by either the buyer or the seller. For example, assume that a wholesaler quotes a list price of $350 per item but grants retailers a trade discount of 20% on the purchase of five or more items. The following entry is made to record the sale of 10 units:

June	16	Accounts Receivable	2,800	
		Sales		2,800
		To record the sale of inventory on credit subject to a 20% quantity discount.		

The computation is as follows:

List price ($350 x 10 units)	$3,500
Less: 20% quantity discount	700
Invoice price	$2,800

The buyer records a purchase of inventory in the amount of $2,800.

If included in the terms of the sale, a cash discount is computed on the $2,800 sales price less any subsequent returns or allowances. That is, if 3 of the 10 items are later returned, then the cash discount is computed on $1,960 (7 units x $280 per unit).

FREIGHT-OUT

The sales invoice will normally indicate which party to the transaction must pay the cost of shipping the goods. If the goods are sold **FOB (free on board) shipping point**, the buyer takes title at the seller's shipping dock. Therefore, freight costs incurred from the point of shipment are paid by the buyer. Conversely, the term **FOB destination** indicates that title passes when the goods reach the buyer's receiving dock. Hence, the seller is responsible for paying the freight cost. The point at which the title transfers and the party responsible for the freight cost are summarized below:

Shipping Terms	Point Title Transfers	Party Responsible for Freight Costs
FOB Shipping point	At shipping dock of seller	Buyer
FOB Destination	At receiving dock of buyer	Seller

When terms of the sale are FOB destination, the seller normally records the payment of freight costs as a debit to a **Freight-Out** or **Delivery Expense** account. The entry to record a $35 freight payment on goods sold is:

Aug.	10	Freight-out	35	
		Cash		35

Freight-out is an expense and should be reported in the selling expense category of the income statement. Freight charges *paid by the seller on goods sold* should not be confused with freight charges *paid on goods purchased*, which is discussed later in the next chapter.

PRACTICE ACTIVITY 9-1

Part I.
Complete the following statements by filling in the blanks.

1. Tangible assets held for sale in the normal course of business are called

    _____ _____.

2. A firm that buys and sells goods in a finished form is called a _____ firm.

3. In an income statement prepared for a merchandising firm, cost of goods sold is an _____ that is subtracted from net _____ to derive _____ _____ on sales.

4. Net sales is equal to revenue from sales minus _____ returns and _____ and sales _____.

5. A _____ _____ is a separate record that provides the detail for a _____ account in the general ledger.

6. A _____ _____ is a source document issued by a seller to inform the buyer that its account is being adjusted.

7. A _____ _____ is recorded when a payment from a customer is received within the discount period.

8. Goods shipped FOB shipping point indicate that the _____ must pay the freight.

9. Freight-out is reported as a _____ _____ in the income statement.

Part II.
The following transactions occurred between Joe's Wholesalers and Knotty Pine Furniture:

Mar. 2 Joe's Wholesalers sold merchandise with a total price of $60,000 to Knotty Pine Furniture. Terms 2/15, n/45; FOB destination; 20% trade discount.

Mar. 2 Joe's Wholesalers paid $3,100 in freight charges to ship the merchandise to Knotty Pine Furniture.

Mar. 8 Knotty Pine Furniture returned merchandise that had a list price (before trade discount) of $8,000.

Mar. 17 Knotty Pine paid for the merchandise.

Required:

Prepare entries for Joe's Wholesalers.

General Journal					Page 1
Date	Explanation	Post. Ref.	Debit	Credit	

METHODS OF ACCOUNTING FOR INVENTORY AND COST OF GOODS SOLD

As noted earlier, the cost of inventory sold during the year is matched against sales revenue. The cost of unsold inventory is reported as a current asset in the balance sheet. Two distinctly different inventory systems--perpetual and periodic--are used to determine the amounts reported for the ending inventory and the cost of goods sold. The system adopted by a firm is largely determined by the type of inventory held.

PERPETUAL INVENTORY SYSTEM

A **perpetual inventory system** involves keeping a current and continuous record of all increases and decreases of each item of inventory. Under this system, purchases are recorded in an asset account called the Merchandise Inventory account. As goods are sold, their cost is determined, and an entry is made to reduce the Merchandise Inventory account. A corresponding increase is made in an expense account called Cost of Goods Sold. That is, the cost of inventory purchased is accounted for as an asset until it is sold and produces revenue. The cost of sold inventory is transferred to an expense account to be matched against earned revenue. Thus, on any given date, the total dollar value of inventory held by the firm and the cost of goods sold to date can be determined from the two accounts.

A perpetual inventory system is used because it provides more timely information to management for use in planning and controlling inventory costs. Because the maintenance of perpetual inventory records involves more clerical work than the periodic system, it is usually used by firms that sell a limited number of items with a high unit cost (e.g., automobiles, heating and air-conditioning units, works of art, pianos, television sets, stereo equipment, computers, and home appliances). In recent years, however, the introduction of computers and other electronic business machines has made the perpetual inventory system feasible for many firms (e.g., drugstores, variety stores, hardware stores, and grocery stores) selling low unit-cost items.

The development of on-site computers, in particular, has been a real breakthrough for the perpetual inventory system. For example, many grocery stores now use optical scan cash registers that not only record the sales price of the item but also enter the item for inventory purposes. Firms that adopt the perpetual inventory system do so because they believe the benefits of improved managerial planning and control obtained from a current record of inventory on hand outweigh the additional cost of maintaining the system.

PERIODIC INVENTORY SYSTEM

Firms that sell a large number of items with a low cost per unit may find the maintenance of perpetual inventory records too costly and time-consuming. This type of business often uses the **periodic inventory system**, in which the cost of goods sold for the period is determined at the end of the accounting period. A store operating with a high volume of sales may conveniently record the amount of each sale, but it would find it difficult to trace the cost of each item sold back to the inventory records. Thus, a day-to-day record of goods on hand or cost of goods sold is not maintained.

ILLUSTRATION OF A PERPETUAL INVENTORY SYSTEM

When the perpetual inventory method is used, a single Merchandise Inventory account is maintained in the general ledger to record all inventory transactions. Supporting details are entered on individual inventory cards that serve as a subsidiary ledger. One card is maintained for each type of inventory item held. Each inventory card shows the quantity, unit cost, and total cost for each purchase, sale, and inventory balance. When every item is different, as with automobiles, where each unit has different options and cost, a separate inventory card is maintained for each item. The balance in the general ledger control account (the Merchandise Inventory account) should equal the sum of the dollar amounts shown on the inventory cards in the subsidiary ledger. Generally, the maintenance of such detailed inventory cards for each item of inventory requires a great deal of clerical effort. Consequently, most firms use some type of electronic equipment to process the data more efficiently and accurately than could be done in a manual system. The electronic processing of inventory records is very similar to the manual operations illustrated later in this chapter.

Figure 9-2 is an example of an inventory card kept for a (Model DP93) personal computer. The cost of the merchandise on hand at the beginning of the period ($2,400), called the **beginning inventory,** consists of two units at a unit cost of $1,200. The other data entered on the card are based on the following transactions:

1. July 12   Purchased six units of inventory for $1,200 per unit on account from Datapoint Inc.

2. July 14   Sold four units on account for $2,500 per unit, which cost $1,200 per unit.

3. July 17   Prepared a debit memo for a defective unit returned to Datapoint Inc., which cost $1,200.

4. July 18   A unit sold on July 14 is returned by a customer for credit on account. Because the unit was suitable for resale, it was returned to stock.

The entries to record the transactions above and the postings to the inventory related accounts for a perpetual inventory system are shown in Figure 9-3. The operations of the system may be summarized as follows:

1. The inventory on hand at the beginning of the period is reported in the Merchandise Inventory control account and on the inventory card.

2. Purchases of inventory are added to the beginning inventory balance in the Merchandise Inventory control account and to the inventory card.

3. When goods are sold, an entry is made to record the sale (the revenue aspect of the transaction) and another entry is made to reduce (credit) the Merchandise Inventory control account and increase (debit) Cost of Goods Sold (the expense aspect of the transaction). The number of units, unit cost, and total cost of those sold are also entered on the inventory card.

FIGURE 9-2
INVENTORY CARD

Item Personal Computer Code DP93			Location 1 Unit Showroom Remainder--Warehouse						Minimum Stock 2 Maximum Stock 10		
		Purchases			Cost of Goods Sold			Balance			
Date	Explanation	Units	Unit Cost	Total Cost	Units	Unit Cost	Total Cost	Units	Unit Cost	Total Cost
7/1	Beg. balance							2	1,200	2,400
7/12	Purchase	6	1,200	7,200				8	1,200	9,600
7/14	Sales				4	1,200	4,800	4	1,200	4,800
7/17	Purchase returns	(1)	1,200	(1,200)				3	1,200	3,600
7/18	Sales returns				(1)	1,200	(1,200)	4	1,200	4,800

FIGURE 9-3
ENTRIES TO RECORD INVENTORY TRANSACTIONS
UNDER THE PERPETUAL INVENTORY SYSTEM

Merchandise Inventory		
Beg. Bal. 2,400		

1. Purchased six computers on credit.

July	12	Merchandise Inventory	7,200	
		Accounts Payable		7,200

2. Sold four computers on account.

July	14	Accounts Receivable	10,000	
		Sales		10,000

	14	Cost of Goods Sold	4,800	
		Merchandise Inventory		4,800

3. Returned one computer to supplier for credit on account.

July	17	Accounts Payable	1,200	
		Merchandise Inventory		1,200

4. Customer returned one computer for credit on account.

July	18	Sales Returns and Allowances	2,500	
		Accounts Receivable		2,500

	18	Merchandise Inventory	1,200	
		Cost of Goods Sold		1,200

General ledger account balances at the end of the period.

Merchandise Inventory				Cost of Goods Sold			
Beg. Bal.	2,400	7/14	4,800	7/14	4,800	7/18	1,200
7/12	7,200	7/17	1,200	End Bal.	3,600		
7/18	1,200		———				
End Bal.	4,800						

4. To provide a continuous record of inventory on hand, units returned to the manufacturer and units suitable for resale that are returned by customers are recorded in the Merchandise Inventory control account, and they are either subtracted from or added to the balance on hand on the inventory card.

5. Assuming that this is the only item of inventory held, the cost of the ending inventory is the balance in the Merchandise Inventory control account ($4,800); the cost of goods sold for the period ($3,600) to be matched against revenues in the income statement is the balance in the Cost of Goods Sold account. The *ending inventory* is merchandise on hand at the end of the period that is available for sale in the next period, and it is reported as an asset in the balance sheet.

Note that every entry made to the Merchandise Inventory control account requires that the units, unit cost, and total cost also be entered on the appropriate inventory card in the subsidiary ledger, as shown in Figure 9-2.

PHYSICAL INVENTORY

Note that the balance in the Merchandise Inventory account agrees with the balance on the inventory card (see Figure 9-2). Keeping a continuous inventory record makes it unnecessary to take a physical count of the inventory on hand to determine the ending balance. Nevertheless, firms using a perpetual inventory system should take a physical inventory at least once a year to verify the accuracy of the inventory records.

A **physical inventory** involves (1) counting all inventory units on hand, (2) determining the unit cost of each type of item on hand from purchase invoices or inventory cards, and (3) multiplying the unit cost of each item by the appropriate number of units to determine the dollar cost of that particular item. The dollar cost of the entire inventory is the sum of the individual costs determined for each item.

Differences between the physical count and the inventory records could result from clerical error, theft of goods, breakage, and obsolescence. In some cases, the difference may result from natural causes such as evaporation or shrinkage. Causes of large discrepancies should be identified and eliminated if possible. Taking a physical inventory is discussed in more detail in Chapter 12.

When the physical inventory and the Merchandise Inventory account balance differ, a journal entry is made to bring the account balance into agreement with the physical count. For example, an entry to reduce the Merchandise Inventory account by $247 would be:

Dec.	31	Inventory Loss	247	
		Merchandise Inventory		247
		To adjust the inventory account to the physical count.		

The Inventory Loss account is for management information only. The account balance is normally included in cost of goods sold in the income statement.

PRACTICE ACTIVITY 9-2

Yolkhead distributes computer software. The beginning inventory on November 1 contained 11 units at a cost of $125 per unit. The following transactions relate to a spreadsheet package.

Nov. 2   Purchased 5 units for $125 each on account.

Nov. 11   Returned 2 units to the manufacturer for credit on account.

Nov. 13   Sold 10 units for $300 each on account. Terms: FOB shipping point, n/30.

Nov. 17   The customer returned 2 units. The units were not defective and were returned to stock.

Required:

Prepare journal entries for the above transactions.

	General Journal			Page 1
Date	Explanation	Post. Ref.	Debit	Credit

END-OF-PERIOD PROCESS

At the end of the accounting period, a worksheet can be used to organize the information needed to prepare financial statements, adjusting entries, and closing entries. Except for the new accounts introduced in this chapter, the preparation of the worksheet and the closing process for a merchandising business are similar to that illustrated for a service firm in Chapter 5.

When a perpetual inventory system is used to account for the flow of goods, the balance in the Merchandise Inventory account is the ending inventory amount. This balance is an asset, and accordingly, it is extended to the Balance Sheet debit column. The balance in the Cost of Goods Sold account is the cost of inventory sold this period. Since it is an expense account, it is extended to the Income Statement debit column and is closed along with the other expense accounts to the Income Summary account. A worksheet for Educational Software Company, a firm using the perpetual inventory system, is shown in Figure 9-4.

CLOSING ENTRIES – PERPETUAL INVENTORY SYSTEM

At the end of the accounting period, the worksheet prepared in Figure 9-4 is used to prepare the closing entries. The entries are similar to those discussed in Chapter 7 for a merchandising firm. There are several approaches that can be used in preparing closing entries. One common approach is illustrated below:

Closing entry 1: Reduce all revenue (Sales and Rent) and contra sales accounts to a zero balance, and credit the Income Summary account for an amount to balance the entry.

Dec.	31	Sales	638,860	
		Rent Revenue	2,160	
		Income Summary		618,830
		Sales Returns and Allowances		19,250
		Sales Discounts		2,940
		To close revenue and contra revenue accounts and record the net balance in the Income Summary account.		

EDUCATIONAL SOFTWARE COMPANY
Worksheet
For the Year Ended December 31, 19X2

Account Titles	Unadjusted Trial Balance Debit	Credit	Adjustments Debit	Credit	Adjusted Trial Balance Debit	Credit	Income Statement Debit	Credit	Balance Sheet Debit	Credit
Cash	47,050				47,050				47,050	
Accounts Receivable	91,620				91,620				91,620	
Merchandise Inventory	57,480				57,480				57,480	
Prepaid Insurance	1,720			d) 550	1,170				1,170	
Store Equipment	64,800				64,800				64,800	
Acc.Depr.–StoreEquip.		41,940		b) 6,840		48,780				48,780
Office Equipment	23,760				23,760				23,760	
Acc. Depr.–Off. Equip.		11,970		c) 2,880		14,850				14,850
Accounts Payable		59,630				59,630				59,630
Salaries Payable		-0-		a) 3,300		3,300				3,300
Income Taxes Payable		-0-		e) 1,100		1,100				1,100
Notes Payables		50,000				50,000				50,000
Capital Stock		45,000				45,000				45,000
Retained Earnings		32,400				32,400				32,400
Dividends Declared	9,000				9,000				9,000	
Sales		638,860				638,860		638,860		
Sales Ret. & Allow.	19,250				19,250		19,250			
Sales Discount	2,940				2,940		2,940			
Cost of Goods Sold	*410,860*				*410,860*		*410,860*			
Advertising Expense	9,980				9,980		9,980			
Bad Debt Expense	6,380				6,380		6,380			
Delivery Expense	6,060				6,060		6,060			
Depr. Exp.–Off. Equip.	-0-		c) 2,880		2,880		2,880			
Depr. Exp.–Store Equp.	-0-		b) 6,840		6,840		6,840			
Income Tax Expense	8,100		e) 1,100		9,200		9,200			
Insurance Expense	-0-		d) 550		550		550			
Rent Expense	26,100				26,100		26,100			
Salaries Expense	95,960		a)3,300		99,260		99,260			
Rent Revenue		2,160				2,160		2,160		
Interest Expense	900				900		900			
Totals	881,960	881,960	14,670	14,670	896,080	896,080	601,200	641,020	294,880	255,060
Net inc. for the period							39,820			39,820
Totals							641,020	641,020	294,880	294,880

FIGURE 9-4
WORKSHEET–PERPETUAL INVENTORY SYSTEM

Closing entry 2: Reduce all expense accounts to a zero balance, and debit the Income Summary account for an amount to balance the entry.

Dec.	31	Income Summary	579,010	
		Cost of Goods Sold		410,860
		Advertising Expense		9,980
		Bad Debt Expense		6,380
		Delivery Expense		6,060
		Depreciation Expense-Office Equip.		2,880
		Depreciation Expense-Store Equip.		6,840
		Income Tax Expense		9,200
		Insurance Expense		550
		Rent Expense		26,100
		Salaries Expense		99,260
		Interest Expense		900
		To close all expense accounts and record the total in the Income Summary account.		

Closing entry 3: Transfer the balance in the Income Summary account to the Retained Earnings account.

Dec.	31	Income Summary	39,820	
		Retained Earnings		39,820
		To close net income to retained earnings.		

Closing entry 4: Close the Dividends Declared account to the Retained Earnings account.

Dec.	31	Retained Earnings	9,000	
		Dividends Declared		9,000
		To close dividends declared to retained earnings.		

PRACTICE ACTIVITY 9-3

The unadjusted trial balance for Marcia's Fashion Source is shown on the following page.
Required:
A. Complete the worksheet for the year ended January 31, 19X2. The following
    information is available to make the year-end adjustments. Use only the accounts
    listed in the trial balance for making adjustments.
    a. Insurance expired during the year is $4,400.
    b. The store equipment has an estimated useful life of 10 years with no residual
        value.
    c. The income tax expense for the year is $3,200.
    d. The ending merchandise inventory, as determined by a physical count of the
        goods on hand, is $66,600.
B. Prepare closing entries.

General Journal				Page 1
Date	Explanation	Post. Ref.	Debit	Credit
19X2				

Part A.

MARCIA'S FASHION SOURCE
Worksheet
For the Year Ended December 31, 19X2

Account Titles	Unadjusted Trial Balance Debit	Unadjusted Trial Balance Credit	Adjustments Debit	Adjustments Credit	Adjusted Trial Balance Debit	Adjusted Trial Balance Credit	Income Statement Debit	Income Statement Credit	Balance Sheet Debit	Balance Sheet Credit
Cash	25,200									
Merchandise Inventory	66,600									
Prepaid Insurance	5,500									
Store Equipment	31,500									
Acc. Depr.—Store Equip.		18,900								
Payables		21,730								
Capital Stock		25,000								
Retained Earnings		55,150								
Dividends Declared	10,000									
Sales		212,600								
Sales Ret. & Allow.	4,080									
Cost of Goods Sold	98,400									
Expenses	92,100									
Totals	333,380	333,380								

SOLUTIONS TO PRACTICE ACTIVITIES

PRACTICE ACTIVITY 9-1

Part I

1.	merchandise inventory	6.	Credit memorandum
2.	merchandising	7.	sales discounts
3.	expenses, sales, gross profit or margin	8.	buyer
4.	sales, allowances, discounts	9.	selling expense
5.	subsidiary ledger, control		

Part II

	General Journal			**Page 1**
Date	Explanation	Post. Ref.	Debit	Credit
Mar. 2	Accounts Receivable		48,000	
	Sales ($60,000 X 80%)			48,000
2	Freight-out		3,100	
	Cash			3,100
8	Sales Returns and Allowances ($8,000 X 80%)		6,400	
	Accounts Receivable			6,400
17	Cash		40,768	
	Sales Discounts ($41,600 X 2%)		832	
	Accounts Receivable ($48,000 – $6,400)			41,600

PRACTICE ACTIVITY 9-2

	General Journal			**Page 1**
Date	Explanation	Post. Ref.	Debit	Credit
Nov. 2	Merchandise Inventory		625	
	Accounts Payable			625
11	Accounts Payable		250	
	Merchandise Inventory			250
13	Accounts Receivable		3,000	
	Sales			3,000
13	Cost of Goods Sold		1,250	
	Merchandise Inventory			1,250

			Debit	Credit
17	Sales Returns and Allowances		600	
	Accounts Receivable			600
17	Merchandise Inventory		250	
	Cost of Goods Sold			250

PRACTICE ACTIVITY 9-3

The solution to Part A is on the next page.

Part B.

General Journal				Page 1
Date	Explanation	Post. Ref.	Debit	Credit
19X2				
Dec. 31	Sales		212,600	
	Income Summary			208,520
	Sales Returns and Allowances			4,080
31	Income Summary		201,250	
	Cost of Goods Sold			98,400
	Expenses			102,850
31	Income Summary		7,270	
	Retained Earnings			7,270
31	Retained Earnings		10,000	
	Dividends Declared			10,000

PRACTICE ACTIVITY 9-3

Part A.

MARCIA'S FASHION SOURCE
Worksheet
For the Year Ended December 31, 19X2

Account Titles	Unadjusted Trial Balance		Adjustments		Adjusted Trial Balance		Income Statement		Balance Sheet	
	Debit	Credit	Debit	Credit	Debit	Credit	Debit	Credit	Debit	Credit
Cash	25,200				25,200				25,200	
Merchandise Inventory	66,600				66,600				66,600	
Prepaid Insurance	5,500			a) 4,400	1,100				1,100	
Store Equipment	31,500				31,500				31,500	
Acc. Depr. — Store Equip.		18,900		b) 3,150		22,050				22,050
Payables		21,730		c) 3,200		24,930				24,930
Capital Stock		25,000				25,000				25,000
Retained Earnings		55,150				55,150				55,150
Dividends Declared	10,000				10,000				10,000	
Sales		212,600				212,600		212,600		
Sales Ret. & Allow.	4,080				4,080		4,080			
Cost of Goods Sold	98,400				98,400		98,400			
Expenses	92,100		a) 4,400		102,850		102,850			
			b) 3,150							
			c) 3,200							
Totals	333,380	333,380	10,750	10,750	339,730	339,730	205,330	212,600	134,400	127,130
Net income for the year							7,270			7,270
Totals							212,600	212,600	134,400	134,400

CHAPTER 10

Accounting for Merchandising Operations–Periodic Inventory System

CONTENTS

- Chapter Overview and Objectives
- Illustration of a Periodic Inventory System
- Determining the Cost of Inventory
- End-of-Period Process – Periodic Inventory System
- Illustration of a Worksheet for a Merchandising Firm
- Income Statement for a Merchandising Firm
- An Alternative Method for Closing Accounts – Periodic Inventory System
- Perpetual and Periodic Inventory Systems Contrasted

CHAPTER OVERVIEW AND OBJECTIVES

The periodic inventory system is discussed in this chapter. When you have completed this chapter, you will be able to:

1. Record transactions for a firm using a periodic inventory system.
2. Prepare a worksheet, and complete the closing process for a firm using a periodic inventory system.
3. Prepare a multiple-step income statement.
4. Use an alternative method for closing inventory-related accounts

The perpetual inventory system was covered in the last chapter. Although it provides more timely information to management, it may be too costly to operate for a firm that sells a large number of items with a low unit cost. This type of business often uses the *periodic inventory system*. Such businesses will record the amount of each sale, but will not maintain an up-to-date record of goods on hand and will defer the computation of cost of goods sold until the end of the period. This chapter discusses accounting for a merchandising firm using a periodic inventory system.

ILLUSTRATION OF A PERIODIC INVENTORY SYSTEM

In a periodic inventory system, the cost of the merchandise on hand at the beginning of the period is reported in the Merchandise Inventory account. The balance in the account is not changed, except to correct errors, until the end of the accounting period.

Inventory purchases made during the period are recorded in a Purchases account. At the end of the period, the balance in the Purchases account is added to the beginning inventory balance to determine the cost of goods available for sale during the period. The goods available for sale either were sold during the period or should still be on hand.

When inventory is sold, an entry is made to record the sale only. Unlike the perpetual inventory system, no record of the cost of goods on hand or the cost of goods sold is maintained during the period. Instead, they are computed at the end of each accounting period. The cost of goods on hand is determined by taking a physical inventory. Cost of goods sold is then computed by subtracting the cost of goods on hand (i.e., the ending inventory) from the cost of goods available for sale, as shown below, based on the data shown in Figure 10-1:

Cost of beginning merchandise inventory	$2,400
Add: Cost of goods purchased during the current period	6,000
Cost of goods available for sale	8,400
Less: Cost of ending merchandise inventory (per physical count)	4,800
Cost of goods sold	$3,600

The cost of the ending inventory for the current period of $4,800 becomes the beginning inventory amount for the next period. The process of adjusting the inventory account to its end-of-year balance is discussed later in this chapter.

A periodic inventory system is illustrated below. To facilitate a comparison between a periodic system and a perpetual system, the illustration is based on the same data used in the perpetual illustration in Chapter 9 (see Figure 9-3). In practice, remember, the periodic system would normally be used when selling a high volume of low-priced items. The Merchandise Inventory account at the beginning of the period is:

Merchandise Inventory

7/1 Beg. Bal.	
(2 units @ $1,200) 2,400	

The beginning inventory of $2,400 is the ending inventory determined by a physical inventory conducted on the last day of the preceding period.

July 12 Purchased 6 units of inventory at $1,200 per unit on account from Datapoint, Inc. Terms of the transaction were 2/10, n/30, FOB destination.

July	12	Purchases	7,200	
		Accounts Payable		7,200

The Purchases account is a temporary account used to accumulate the cost of all inventory acquired for resale during the period. This account is used to record inventory purchases only. (Acquisitions of other assets are recorded in appropriate asset accounts.) Because the balance in the Purchases account is closed at the end of each accounting period, the accumulated account balance reflects the purchases for the current period only.

July 14 Sold 4 units for $2,500 per unit to customers on account.

July	14	Accounts Receivable	10,000	
		Sales		10,000

At the time of sale, one entry is made to record the revenue earned from the sale of merchandise. A second entry to record the cost of goods sold is not made.

July 17 Returned a defective unit that cost $1,200 to the manufacturer for credit on account.

The buyer and seller may agree that an item is to be returned or that the item is to be kept and an adjustment made to the purchase price for a number of reasons, such as that the goods were damaged when received. A source document that contains the information needed to record the transaction, called a **debit memorandum** or **debit memo,** is prepared. It is called a debit memorandum because the supplier's account payable is debited on the buyer's books. The return of goods to Datapoint, Inc., is recorded as follows:

July	17	Accounts payable	1,200	
		Purchases Returns and		
		Allowances		1,200

There is a cost to the firm to order merchandise, to receive and inspect the merchandise, and to re-pack it for return to the manufacturer. To provide relevant information to management concerning the total amount of goods returned, the return is recorded in a contra purchases account, called Purchases Returns and Allowances, rather than directly as a credit to the Purchases account. The entry is the same if the goods are kept by the buyer and an adjustment is made to the invoice price.

July 18 A unit that was sold for $2,500 was returned by a customer for credit on account.

July	18	Sales Returns and Allowances	2,500	
		Accounts Receivable		2,500

When a periodic inventory system is used, only one entry is needed to record the merchandise returned. A second entry, to credit the cost of goods sold, is not needed here because the cost of goods sold was not recorded on the date of sale.

July 22 Paid for the purchase made on July 12 within the discount period.

Accounting for cash discounts by the seller and the notation 2/10, n/30 were discussed in Chapter 9. Recall that a cash discount entitles the buyer to deduct a specified amount from the invoice price if payment is made within the discount period. When such payment is made, a purchase discount is recorded by the buyer. The entry to record the payment is:

July	22	Accounts Payable	6,000	
		Cash		5,880
		Purchase Discounts		120

The amount of the cash payment and discount are computed as follows:

Total cost of goods purchased	$7,200
Less: Cost of goods returned on July 17	1,200
Cost of goods being paid for	6,000
Less: Cash discount ($6,000 X .02)	120
Cash payment	$5,880

The Purchase Discounts account is reported as a contra account to Purchases in the buyer's income statement.

Based on these transactions, a partial income statement is prepared in Figure 10-1. It is assumed that a physical inventory count taken at the end of the period confirmed that four units were on hand. The dollar amount is computed to be $4,800 (4 units x $1,200).

You should compare results reported in Figure 10-1 to the ending inventory and the cost of goods sold computed in the last chapter when the perpetual inventory system was illustrated (see Figure 9-3). The results would be the same except that in this illustration the company qualified for a cash discount of $120. Thus, cost of goods sold is less by $120 ($3,600 perpetual − $3,480 periodic). This raises an interesting issue as to how the discount should be reported. When the full discount is subtracted from purchases, as is usually done in practice because the amount is considered immaterial, the discount reduces cost of goods sold in the period taken. However, theoretically, the discount should be allocated $24 ($120 / 5 units purchased) to each unit that qualified for the discount.

Some relationships shown in statement format for the periodic inventory system are summarized below:

1. Gross profit on sales = Net sales - Cost of goods sold

2. Cost of goods purchased = Purchases - Purchases returns and allowances

3. Cost of goods available for sale = Cost of beginning inventory + Cost of goods purchased

4. Cost of goods sold = Cost of goods available for sale - Cost of ending inventory;

or

Cost of goods sold = Cost of beginning inventory + Cost of goods purchased - Cost of ending inventory

Familiarity with these relationships will aid in understanding the characteristics of the periodic inventory system and make it easier to determine the effect of inventory errors.

Note that under the periodic inventory system, the cost of goods sold is a residual amount that is left after deducting the ending inventory from the cost of goods available for sale. As a result, losses of inventory from causes—such as theft, shrinkage, breakage, and clerical error—are difficult to identify.

FIGURE 10-1
PARTIAL INCOME STATEMENT–PERIODIC INVENTORY SYSTEM

CAMPUS COMPUTERS			
Income Statement			
For the Month Ended July 31, 19X2			
Sales			$10,000
Less: Sales returns and allowances			2,500
Net sales			7,500
Cost of goods sold:			
Cost of beginning merchandise inventory		$2,400	
Add: Purchases	$7,200		
Less: Purchases returns and allowances	1,200		
Purchases discounts	120		
Cost of goods purchased		5,880	
Cost of goods available for sale		8,280	
Less: Cost of ending merchandise inventory		4,800	
Cost of goods sold			3,480
Gross profit on sales			$ 4,020

PRACTICE ACTIVITY 10-1

Track Company completed the following transactions. Track Company uses a periodic inventory system, and there were no units on hand at the beginning of the period.

March   6   Purchased 60 units at $50 per unit, terms n/30, FOB destination.
           11   Returned 5 of the units purchased on March 6 because they were defective. Credit of $50 per unit was granted by the seller.
           15   Sold 20 units on account to Corso Company for $85 per unit. Terms, n/30.
April   5   Paid supplier for the units purchased in March.

Required:

Prepare journal entries to record the transactions.

General Journal				Page 1
Date	Explanation	Post. Ref.	Debit	Credit

2.   For each of the following independent cases, compute the missing amounts.

Cases	1	2	3
Sales	$87,400	$64,320	$ (g)
Beginning inventory	(a)	15,900	55,000
Purchases	58,600	(d)	79,120
Ending inventory	39,240	17,600	(h)
Cost of goods sold	(b)	39,500	73,430
Gross profit on sales	42,750	(e)	(i)
Operating expenses	(c)	28,480	47,550
Net income (loss)	10,380	(f)	15,300

DETERMINING THE COST OF INVENTORY

As with accounting for other assets, cost is the primary basis of accounting for inventory. Applied to inventory, cost means the sum of all direct and indirect expenditures incurred to acquire the inventory and bring it to its existing location in salable condition.

Conceptually, the invoice price, freight charges, insurance on the goods while in transit, special handling costs, adjustments and assembly costs incurred in preparing the goods for sale, costs incurred to operate a purchasing department, costs associated with receiving and inspecting the goods, and storage costs incurred before the goods are sold are among the costs that may be properly identified and allocated to inventory. For example, this means that freight costs incurred on a shipment of merchandise should be allocated to each unit and recorded as a cost of the inventory. Under the periodic system, such costs should be included in the cost of goods available for sale and, at the end of the period, should be allocated between the units of the ending inventory and the units sold during the period. If a perpetual inventory system is in use, freight charges should be debited to the inventory account. The invoice price plus the freight cost should be expensed as each unit is sold to be matched against revenue as part of the cost of goods sold.

In practice, however, freight costs *are normally not allocated* between units on hand and units sold because of the practical problem of allocating the cost to individual units when several types of inventory are acquired in one shipment. Furthermore, in most cases the allocation of freight costs does not significantly change the firm's financial statements. If not allocated, freight costs become an expense in the period incurred rather than added to the cost of inventory, which is the conceptually preferred treatment.

If the seller includes the freight charges in the list price, it is not separated on the invoice and becomes a part of the inventory cost when the entry is made to record the purchase transaction. If the seller pays the freight and charges the buyer, it will normally be listed separately on the invoice and is generally debited to an account called either Freight-in or Transportation-in. This account is also used to record freight costs paid by the buyer when the terms of the sale are FOB shipping point. For example, assume that the terms of a purchase of inventory were FOB shipping point and freight costs of $825 were incurred. The entry to record payment of the freight is:

July	15	Freight-in	825	
		Cash		825
		Paid freight cost on merchandise		
		purchased FOB shipping point.		

In the income statement, freight-in is added to purchases (periodic inventory system) or is combined with the amount reported for the cost of goods sold (perpetual inventory system). The result is that freight costs incurred during the period are expensed in full as part of cost of goods sold.

Other costs related to the purchase of merchandise, such as storage costs and costs of operating a purchasing and receiving department, also are usually expensed in the period incurred. Such a procedure is supported on the basis that it avoids making arbitrary allocations and allocation does not produce enough benefits to justify the additional cost of making the allocation. Thus, many inventory costs are expensed in the period incurred rather than added to the cost of inventory. As a result, only the invoice price is normally used in computing a unit cost of goods purchased.

END-OF-PERIOD PROCESS--PERIODIC INVENTORY SYSTEM

At the end of the accounting period, a worksheet may be used to organize the information for completing the accounting cycle for a merchandising firm. The preparation of a worksheet, along with financial statements, and the completion of the adjusting and the closing process for a merchandising business are similar to those given for a service firm in Chapter 7, except for a few differences associated with inventory-related accounts.

For a merchandising firm using the periodic inventory system, the accounts that enter into the determination of cost of goods purchased and both the beginning and ending inventory balances are needed to compute the cost of goods sold. Thus, in addition to recording such adjusting and closing entries as illustrated in previous chapters, it is necessary to do the following:

1. Remove the beginning inventory balance from the Merchandise Inventory account, and transfer it to the Income Summary account.

2. Enter the ending inventory balance in the Merchandise Inventory account and the Income Summary account.

3. Close the balances in the accounts that enter into the cost of goods purchased, and transfer the balances to the Income Summary account.

Several approaches can be used to accomplish the three steps above. Some accountants prefer to do this as part of the adjusting process. Others adjust the Inventory account and close the purchases-related accounts as part of the closing process. The first approach is illustrated in the next section. The second approach is illustrated in a later section of this chapter. Although the preparation of the worksheet and the adjusting and closing entries differ with the various approaches, the end results are the same. Selecting which approach to use is just a matter of personal preference.

ILLUSTRATION OF A WORKSHEET FOR A MERCHANDISING FIRM

A worksheet for Educational Software, Inc., a firm that has adopted the periodic inventory system, is presented in Figure 10-2. In the figure, the Unadjusted Trial Balance columns contain a listing of the account balances taken from the general ledger of the company. The next two columns are for the end-of-year adjustments based on the following information:

(a) Accrued salaries: Sales		$1,980
	Administrative	1,320
(b) Depreciation – Store equipment		6,840
(c) Depreciation – Office equipment		2,880
(d) Prepaid insurance expired during the year		550
(e) Unpaid income taxes at the end of the period		1,100

Based on a physical inventory taken December 31 of each year, the ending merchandise inventory was determined to be $57,480 at the end of the current period and was $52,560 at the end of the prior period. Completion of the worksheet proceeds as illustrated in Chapter 7.

Merchandise Inventory in the Worksheet

When the adjusting entry approach is used to determine the cost of goods sold for the period, an additional adjustment is required. The entry removes the beginning balance in the Merchandise Inventory account, records the ending balance in the Merchandise Inventory account per the physical count, and reduces the purchases-related accounts to a zero balance. This entry contains elements of an adjusting entry and some of a closing entry. For Educational Software, Inc., the adjusting entry is:

Dec.	31	Merchandise Inventory (12/31)	57,480	
		Purchases Returns and Allowances	12,130	
		Purchases Discounts	2,570	
		Cost of Goods Sold	410,860	
		Merchandise Inventory (1/1)		52,560
		Purchases		425,360
		Freight-in*		5,120

*Again note that the total Freight-in becomes a part of cost of goods sold.

The debit to the Cost of Goods Sold account for $410,860 is a balancing amount in the above entry. The amount can be verified by checking the cost of goods sold reported in the income statement prepared in Figure 10-3. In the worksheet, the balance reported for the cost of goods sold is extended to the Income Statement debit column as shown in Figure 10-2. The credit to the Merchandise Inventory account reduces the account to a zero balance. The debit to Merchandise Inventory establishes the ending inventory balance, which is extended to the Balance Sheet debit column. The entries for the closing process become:

Closing Entries

Dec.	31	Sales	638,860	
		Rent Revenue	2,160	
		Income Summary		618,830
		Sales Returns and Allowances		19,250
		Sales Discounts		2,940
		To close revenue and contra revenue		
		accounts.		

EDUCATIONAL SOFTWARE COMPANY
Worksheet
For the Year Ended December 31, 19X2

Account Titles	Unadjusted Trial Balance Debit	Credit	Adjustments Debit	Credit	Adjusted Trial Balance Debit	Credit	Income Statement Debit	Credit	Balance Sheet Debit	Credit
Cash	47,050				47,050				47,050	
Accounts Receivable	91,620				91,620				91,620	
Merchandise Inventory	52,560		f) 57,480	f) 52,560	57,480				57,480	
Prepaid Insurance	1,720			d) 550	1,170				1,170	
Store Equipment	64,800				64,800				64,800	
Acc. Depr. -StoreEquip.		41,940		b) 6,840		48,780				48,780
Office Equipment	23,760				23,760				23,760	
Acc. Depr. -Off. Equip.		11,970		c) 2,880		14,850				14,850
Accounts Payable		59,630				59,630				59,630
Salaries Payable		-0-		a) 3,300		3,300				3,300
Income Taxes Payable		-0-		e) 1,100		1,100				1,100
Notes Payables		50,000				50,000				50,000
Capital Stock		45,000				45,000				45,000
Retained Earnings		32,400				32,400				32,400
Dividends Declared	9,000				9,000				9,000	
Sales		638,860				638,860		638,860		
Sales Ret. & Allow.	19,250				19,250		19,250			
Sales Discount	2,940				2,940		2,940			
Purchases	425,360			f)425,360						
Purch. Ret. & Allow.		12,130	f) 12,130							
Purch. Discounts		2,570	f) 2,570							
Freight-in	5,120			f) 5,120						
Cost of Goods Sold	-0-		f)410,860		410,860		410,860			
Advertising Expense	9,980				9,980		9,980			
Bad Debt Expense	6,380				6,380		6,380			
Delivery Expense	6,060				6,060		6,060			
Depr. Exp.-Off. Equip.	-0-		c) 2,880		2,880		2,880			
Depr. Exp.-Store Equp.	-0-		b) 6,840		6,840		6,840			
Income Tax Expense	8,100		e) 1,100		9,200		9,200			
Insurance Expense	-0-		d) 550		550		550			
Office Salaries Exp.	43,010		a) 1,320		44,330		44,330			
Rent Expense	26,100				26,100		26,100			
Sales Sal. & Comm.	52,950		a)1,980		54,930		54,930			
Rent Revenue		2,160				2,160		2,160		
Interest Expense	900				900		900			
Totals	896,660	896,660	497,710	497,710	896,080	896,080	601,200	641,020	294,880	255,060
Net inc. for the period							39,820			39,820
Totals							641,020	641,020	294,880	294,880

FIGURE 10-2

WORKSHEET -- PERIODIC INVENTORY SYSTEM
COST OF GOODS SOLD DETERMINED AS PART OF ADJUSTMENT PROCESS

	31	Income Summary		579,010	
		Cost of Goods Sold			410,860
		Advertising Expense			9,980
		Bad Debt Expense			6,380
		Delivery Expense			6,060
		Depreciation Expense--Office Equipment			2,880
		Depreciation Expense--Store Equipment			6,840
		Insurance Expense			550
		Income Tax Expense			9,200
		Office Salaries Expense			44,330
		Rent Expense			26,100
		Sales Salaries and Commissions			54,930
		Interest Expense			900
		To close expense accounts.			
	31	Income Summary		39,820	
		Retained Earnings			39,820
		To close net income to retained earnings.			
	31	Retained Earnings		9,000	
		Dividends Declared			9,000
		To close dividends declared to retained earnings.			

Note that the balance in the Income Summary account ($39,820) that is transferred to the Retained Earnings is the net income determined in the worksheet developed in Figure 10-2. This is the net increase in owners' equity during the period from operating activities.

PRACTICE ACTIVITY 10-2

The unadjusted trial balance for Shelly's Shoe, Inc., is shown on the following page. The following information is available to make the year-end adjustments. Use only the accounts listed in the trial balance for making adjustments.
a. Sixty percent of the prepaid insurance has expired.
b. The store equipment has an estimated useful life of 10 years with no residual value.
c. The unpaid income tax expense for the period is $520.
d. The ending merchandise inventory, as determined by a physical count of the goods on hand, is $38,300. Assume that cost of goods sold is determined as part of the adjustments process.
Complete the worksheet for the year ended January 31, 19X2.

SHELLY'S SHOE COMPANY
Worksheet
For the Year Ended January 31, 19X2

Account Titles	Unadjusted Trial Balance Debit	Unadjusted Trial Balance Credit	Adjustments Debit	Adjustments Credit	Adjusted Trial Balance Debit	Adjusted Trial Balance Credit	Income Statement Debit	Income Statement Credit	Balance Sheet Debit	Balance Sheet Credit
Cash	15,700									
Merchandise Inventory	42,900									
Prepaid Insurance	4,800									
Store Equipment	26,000									
Acc. Depr.–StoreEquip.		6,000								
Payables		6,300								
Capital Stock		50,000								
Retained Earnings		13,830								
Sales		151,870								
Sales Ret. & Allow.	3,890									
Purchases	70,680									
Purch. Ret. & Allow.		3,250								
Purch. Discounts		1,040								
Freight-in	3,800									
Cost of Goods Sold	-0-									
Expenses	64,520									
Totals	232,290	232,290								

INCOME STATEMENT FOR A MERCHANDISING FIRM

Although not shown here, the worksheet is used as a basis for preparing the balance sheet and the retained earnings statement, and for entering the adjusting entries and the closing entries in the general journal. An income statement for Educational Software, Inc., is presented in Figure 10-3 to show how a merchandiser's income statement accounts are reported. The company uses a periodic inventory system and reports a detailed cost of goods sold section. In practice, there is considerable variation in income statement formats. As a general rule, only the net sales and cost of goods sold amounts are reported in annual reports.

The format shown in Figure 10-3 is called a *multiple-step income statement* because it shows several subtotals to highlight significant relationships, such as gross profit on sales. Note that in this format, items that do not result from regular operations of the firm are reported near the bottom of the statement in a section called Other Revenue and Expense. In other words, other revenues and expenses result from transactions related to secondary or miscellaneous activities of the firm. Included in this category are items such as interest expense, dividend revenue, interest revenue, miscellaneous earnings from rentals, and gains and losses from the sale of non-merchandise assets.

Also note that in this format, the expenses are classified by function, such as cost of goods sold, selling expenses, and administrative expenses. Operating expenses, which are often separated into selling expenses and administrative expenses, exclude cost of goods sold and other expenses. Some expenses, such as the rent expense of $26,100, may need to be allocated between selling expenses ($18,200) and administrative expenses ($7,900). Several methods can be used to allocate an expense. The allocation should be based on a logical relationship between the expense to be allocated and the benefits from the expense. For example, rent could be allocated on the basis of the number of square feet occupied by each department. Allocation methods are covered in more detail in a managerial accounting course.

FIGURE 10-3
INCOME STATEMENT FOR A MERCHANDISING FIRM

EDUCATIONAL SOFTWARE, INC.
Income Statement
For the Year Ended December 31, 19X2

Gross sales			$638,860
Less: Sales returns and allowances		$ 19,250	
Sales discounts		2,940	22,190
Net sales			616,670
Cost of goods sold:			
Merchandise inventory—1/1		52,560	
Add: Purchases	$425,360		
Less: Purchases returns and allowances	$12,130		
Purchases discounts	2,570	14,700	
Net purchases		410,660	
Add: Freight-in		5,120	
Cost of goods purchased		415,780	
Cost of goods available for sale		468,340	
Less: Merchandise inventory—12/31		57,480	
Cost of goods sold			410,860
Gross profit on sales			205,810
Operating expenses:			
Selling expenses:			
Advertising expense		9,980	
Bad debt expense		6,380	
Delivery expense		6,060	
Depreciation expense—store equipment		6,840	
Rent expense—store space		18,200	
Sales salaries and commissions expense		54,930	
Total selling expense		102,390	
Administrative expenses:			
Depreciation expense—office equipment		2,880	
Insurance expense		550	
Office salaries expense		44,330	
Rent expense—office space		7,900	
Total administrative expense		55,660	
Total operating expenses			158,050
Income from operations			47,760
Other revenue and expense:			
Add: Rent revenue		2,160	
Less: Interest expense		900	1,260
Income before income taxes			49,020
Income tax expense			9,200
Net income for the year			$ 39,820
Earnings per share			$.40

AN ALTERNATIVE METHOD FOR CLOSING ACCOUNTS--PERIODIC INVENTORY SYSTEM

As noted earlier, the adjustments to the Merchandise Inventory account and the reduction of the purchases-related accounts to zero may be completed as part of the closing process. Under this approach, the beginning merchandise inventory balance of $52,560 listed in the Unadjusted Trial Balance Debit column is extended to the Income Statement Debit column (see Figure 10-4). The accounts that enter into the cost of goods purchased-- Purchases ($425,360 debit), Freight-in ($5,120 debit), Purchases Returns and Allowances ($12,130 credit), and Purchases Discounts ($2,570 credit)--are also extended to the appropriate Income Statement columns. The sum of the balances is equal to the cost of purchases for the period. The beginning inventory plus the cost of purchases have now all been extended to the Income Statement columns and are equal to the cost of goods available for sale.

The ending merchandise inventory of $57,480 does not appear in the accounts and must be entered on the worksheet. The $57,480 is entered directly in the Income Statement Credit column since it is a deduction from the cost of goods available for sale when computing the cost of goods sold. The ending inventory amount is also entered in the Balance Sheet Debit column because the ending inventory is on hand and, thus, is an asset to the firm at year-end, and it is necessary to enter an equal debit to maintain the equality of debits and credits in the worksheet. In other words, the ending inventory is reported in two statements: (1) in the income statement (a credit balance) as a subtraction from cost of goods available for sale, and (2) in the balance sheet (a debit balance) as a current asset. Journal entries made to enter the balances in the general ledger Merchandise Inventory account are discussed in the next section. The inventory balances, purchases, and purchases-related accounts enter into the computation of cost of goods sold for Educational Software, Inc., as shown in the income statement in Figure 10-3.

Information needed to prepare the closing entries is available in the Income Statement columns of the worksheet. As shown in Figure 10-5, closing entries are made (1) to close the temporary accounts with debit balances, (2) to close the temporary accounts with credit balances, (3) to close the balance in the Income Summary account, and (4) to close the balance in the Dividends Declared account. In addition, it is necessary to remove the beginning inventory balance and record the ending inventory in the Merchandise Inventory account. Thus, when using this approach, the inventory account is included with revenue and expense accounts in the closing process because when a periodic inventory system is used, the beginning and ending inventory balances are part of the cost of goods sold computation.

EDUCATIONAL SOFTWARE, INC.
Worksheet
For the Year Ended December 31, 19X2

FIGURE 10-4
WORKSHEET-PERIODIC INVENTORY SYSTEM

Beginning Inventory Balance

Enter Ending Inventory Balance

Net Purchases

Account Titles	Unadjusted Trial Balance Debit	Credit	Adjustments Debit	Credit	Adjusted Trial Balance Debit	Credit	Income Statement Debit	Credit	Balance Sheet Debit	Credit
Cash	47,050				47,050				47,050	
Accounts Receivable	91,620				91,620				91,620	
Merchandise Inventory	**52,560**			d)550	**52,560**		**52,560**	**57,480**	**57,480**	
Prepaid Insurance	1,720				1,170				1,170	
Store Equipment	64,800				64,800				64,800	
Acc. Depr.-Store Equip.		41,940		b)6,840		48,780				48,780
Office Equipment	23,760				23,760				23,760	
Acc. Depr.-Off. Equip.		11,970		2,880		14,850				14,850
Accounts Payable		59,630				59,630				59,630
Salaries Payable		-0-		a) 3,300		3,300				3,300
Income Taxes Payable		-0-		e) 1,100		1,100				1,100
Notes Payables		50,000				50,000				50,000
Capital Stock		45,000				45,000				45,000
Retained Earnings		32,400				32,400				32,400
Dividends Declared	9,000				9,000				9,000	
Sales		638,860				638,860		638,860		
Sales Ret. & Allow.	19,250				19,250		19,250			
Sales Discount	2,940				2,940		2,940			
Purchases	**425,360**				**425,360**		**425,360**			
Purch. Ret. & Allow.		**12,130**				**12,130**		**12,130**		
Purch. Discounts		**2,570**				**2,570**		**2,570**		
Freight-in	**5,120**				**5,120**		**5,120**			
Advertising Expense	9,980				9,980		9,980			
Bad Debt Expense	6,380				6,380		6,380			
Delivery Expense	6,060				6,060		6,060			
Depr. Exp.-Off. Equip.	-0-		c) 2,880		2,880		2,880			
Depr. Exp.-Store Equp.	-0-		b) 6,840		6,840		6,840			
Income Tax Expense	8,100		e) 1,100		9,200		9,200			
Insurance Expense	-0-		d) 550		550		550			
Office Salaries Exp.	43,010		a) 1,320		44,330		44,330			
Rent Expense	26,100				26,100		26,100			
Sales Sal. & Comm.	52,950		a) 1,980		54,930		54,930			
Rent Revenue		2,160				2,160		2,160		
Interest Expense	900				900		900			
Totals	896,660	896,660	14,670	14,670	910,780	910,780	673,380	713,200	294,880	255,060
Net inc. for the period							39,820			39,820
Totals							713,200	713,200	294,880	294,880

FIGURE 10-5
CLOSING ENTRIES FOR THE PERIODIC INVENTORY SYSTEM

Dec.	31	Income Summary		673,380	
		Merchandise Inventory (Beg. Balance)			52,560
		Sales Returns and Allowances			19,250
		Sales Discounts			2,940
		Purchases			425,360
		Freight-in			5,120
		Advertising Expense			9,980
		Bad Debt Expense			6,380
		Delivery Expense			6,060
		Depreciation Expense--Office Equipment			2,880
		Depreciation Expense--Store Equipment			6,840
		Income Tax Expense			9,200
		Insurance Expense			550
		Office Salaries Expense			44,330
		Rent Expense			26,100
		Sales Salaries and Commissions			54,930
		Interest Expense			900
		To remove the beginning balance from the inventory account, close all temporary accounts with a debit balance, and record the total in the Income Summary account.			
	31	Merchandise Inventory (Ending Balance)		57,480	
		Sales		638,860	
		Purchases Returns and Allowances		12,130	
		Purchases Discounts		2,570	
		Rent Revenue		2,160	
		Income Summary			713,200
		To close the ending inventory balance, close all temporary accounts with a credit balance, and record the total in the Income Summary account.			
	31	Income Summary		39,820	
		Retained Earnings			39,820
		To close net income to retained earnings.			
	31	Retained Earnings		9,000	
		Dividends Declared			9,000
		To close dividends declared to retained earnings.			

Note that in the sequence illustrated here, the temporary accounts with debit balances are closed before temporary accounts with credit balances. This is the reverse of what was done in previous chapters. The sequence of making entries one and two could be reversed, but this sequence shown here is commonly used for pedagogical reasons because it more clearly shows the adjustment to the inventory account. That is, the beginning inventory amount is first removed and then the ending inventory is entered in the account. If the sequence is reversed, the ending inventory is added before the beginning amount has been removed. Which approach to use is simply a matter of personal preference rather than based on conceptual merit. The objective of making closing entries is the same regardless of which order the entries are made or whether the cost of goods sold accounts are closed as part of the adjusting or closing process. The objective is to reduce all temporary accounts to a zero balance and transfer the net income or net loss to retained earnings.

The closing entries reduce all the temporary accounts to a zero balance. In addition, the entries accomplish the following:

1. The credit of $52,560 to the Merchandise Inventory account in the first closing entry removes the beginning balance from the account, and this amount plus the balances in the temporary accounts with debit balances (includes expense accounts and contra sales account) is debited to the Income Summary account. After this entry is posted, the balance in the Merchandise Inventory account is zero as shown here.

Merchandise Inventory

1/1 Beg. Bal.	52,560	12/31 Clos. Ent.	52,560

2. In the second closing entry, the ending inventory balance of $57,480 is recorded as a debit to the Merchandise Inventory account, and this amount plus the balances in the temporary accounts with credit balances is credited to the Income Summary account. Before the second closing entry is made and posted, the ending inventory is not reported in any ledger account. Note that temporary accounts with credit balances include all revenue accounts and contra purchases accounts. The effect of these two closing entries on the Merchandise Inventory account is shown here.

Merchandise Inventory

1/1 Beg. Bal.	52,560	12/31 Clos. Ent.	52,560
12/31 Clos. Ent.	57,480		
Bal.	57,480		

Although both a debit and a credit are made to the Merchandise Inventory account as part of the closing process, the account is not closed because the account balance is an asset (a permanent account).

3. The balances in the accounts that enter into the computation of cost of goods purchased are reduced to zero balances, and the net effect is debited to the Income Summary account.

4. The net effect of including all the purchases-related accounts in the closing process is that the cost of goods sold for the period is included as a debit balance in the Income Summary account. Although the total debit of entry 1 and the total credit of entry 2 are posted to the Income Summary account, it may be helpful to understand the purpose of the entries and confirm the cost of goods sold amount by separating the inventory and purchases-related accounts from the total debit and the total credit as follows:

Income Summary

[From closing entry (1)]		[From closing entry (2)]	
12/31 Beg. Inv.	52,560	12/31 End. Inv.	57,480
Purchases	425,360	Purchased Ret.	
		and Allow.	12,130
Freight-in	5,120	Purchases Disc.	2,570
Balance	410,860		

Cost of goods sold is $410,860.
See computation in Figure 10-3.

Compare the credit made to retained earnings in this approach (entry 3) with the credit made using the adjusting entry approach illustrated earlier. Note that the results are identical with a net income of $39,820 closed to retained earnings. This is as expected since the objective of making closing entries is the same regardless of which approach is used.

PRACTICE ACTIVITY 10-3

The unadjusted trial balance for Shelly's Shoe, Inc., is shown on the following page. Complete the worksheet for the year ended January 31, 19X2. The company follows the approach of adjusting the inventory balance and closing the inventory-related accounts as part of the closing process. The following information is available to make the year-end adjustments. Use only the accounts listed in the trial balance for making adjustments.
a. Sixty percent of the prepaid insurance has expired.
b. The store equipment has an estimated useful life of 10 years with no residual value.
c. The unpaid income tax expense for the period is $520.
d. The ending merchandise inventory, as determined by a physical count of the goods on hand, is $38,300. Assume that cost of goods sold is determined as part of the adjustments process.

PERPETUAL AND PERIODIC
INVENTORY SYSTEMS CONTRASTED

Chapters 9 and 10 focused on the accounting for and the reporting of transactions of a merchandising firm. A merchandising firm is one that purchases finished products (called merchandise inventory) for sale to its customers as a means of earning revenue. Accounting for inventory involves measuring the cost of the inventory and allocating the cost between the inventory on hand and the inventory that was sold during the accounting period. The cost of inventory on hand is reported as a current asset, whereas the cost of goods sold is an expense matched against sales in the income statement.

SHELLY'S SHOE COMPANY
Worksheet
For the Year ended January 31, 19X2

Account Titles	Adjusted Trial Balance		Adjustments		Unadjusted Trial Balance		Income Statement		Balance Sheet	
	Debit	Credit	Debit	Credit	Debit	Credit	Debit	Credit	Debit	Credit
Cash	15,700									
Merchandise Inventory	42,900									
Prepaid Insurance	4,800									
Store Equipment	26,000									
Acc. Depr.—StoreEquip.		6,000								
Payables		6,300								
Capital Stock		50,000								
Retained Earnings		13,830								
Sales		151,870								
Sales Ret. & Allow.	3,890									
Purchases	70,680									
Purch. Ret. & Allow.		3,250								
Purch. Discounts		1,040								
Freight-in	3,800									
Cost of Goods Sold	-0-									
Expenses	64,520									
Totals	232,290	232,290								

Either the perpetual or the periodic inventory system is used to account for inventory costs. The perpetual and periodic inventory systems are contrasted with the entries shown in Figure 10-6. There are several basic differences between the two systems.

1. Under the perpetual inventory system, inventory purchases are recorded in the Merchandise Inventory account. Each time a sale is made, two entries are made: one to record the sale and another one to reduce the Merchandise Inventory account and record the cost of goods sold. Thus, the perpetual inventory system provides a current record of goods on hand and cost of goods sold. This system provides useful information to management for controlling inventory costs, but it requires more clerical effort to operate than the periodic system. The periodic inventory system does not provide this useful information to management.

2. A perpetual system provides for an accumulation of the cost of goods sold during the period. When a periodic inventory system is used, a physical inventory must be taken to determine the inventory on hand and the cost of goods sold. A physical count is taken under the perpetual system only to verify the accuracy of the ending inventory.

3. In contrast, under the periodic inventory system, the cost of inventory purchases is recorded in the Purchases account. A physical count must be taken to determine the goods on hand. The cost of goods can then be determined as follows:

Cost of beginning inventory	+	Cost of purchases	=	Cost of goods available for sale
Cost of goods available for sale	-	Cost of ending inventory	=	Cost of goods sold

4. A Purchases account is maintained with a periodic system, where as a Cost of Goods Sold account is maintained with a perpetual system.

As shown in Figure 10-6, the two systems should produce approximately the same financial statements.

FIGURE 10-6
COMPARISON OF PERPETUAL AND PERIODIC INVENTORY SYSTEMS

DATA:	Unit cost	$500
	Unit sales price	$800
	Beginning inventory	4 units @ $500 per unit = $2,000
	Ending inventory	8 units @ $500 per unit = $4,000

Perpetual Merchandise Inventory	Periodic Merchandise Inventory
Beg. Bal. 2,000		Beg. Bal. 2,000	

Transaction 1: Purchased six units on credit

Merchandise Inventory	3,000		Purchases	3,000	
Accounts Payable		3,000	Accounts Payable		3,000

Transaction 2: Sold two units to customers on account

Accounts Receivable	1,600		Accounts Receivable	1,600	
Sales		1,600	Sales		1,600
Cost of Goods Sold	1,000		(No entry required to record the		
Merchandise Inventory		1,000	cost of units sold.)		

Transaction 3: Returned one unit to supplier for credit on account.

Accounts Payable	500		Accounts Payable	500	
Merchandise Inventory		500	Purchases Returns and		
			Allowances		500

Transaction 4: Customer returned one unit for credit on account. Returned unit was suitable for resale and was returned to stock.

Sales Returns and Allowances	800		Sales Returns and Allowances	800	
Accounts Receivable		800	Accounts Receivable		800
Merchandise Inventory	500		(No entry required to record the		
Cost of Goods Sold		500	cost of returned units.)		

General ledger account balances at the end of the period:

Merchandise Inventory

Beg. Bal.	2,000		(2)	1,000
(1)	3,000		(3)	500
(4)	500			
End. Bal.	4,000			

Merchandise Inventory

Beg. Bal. 2,000	

Cost of Goods Sold

(2)	1,000		(4)	500
End. Bal.	500			

Purchases

(1)	3,000

Purchases Returns and Allowances

	(3)	500

Computation of cost of goods sold.

Balance in the Cost of Goods Sold account, $500.

Beginning Inventory		$2,000
Add: Purchases	$3,000	
Less : Purchases returns and allowances	500	
Cost of goods purchased		2,500
Cost of goods available for sales		4,500
Less: Ending inventory		4,000
Cost of goods sold		$ 500

THE NET INVOICE METHOD OF RECORDING INVENTORY TRANSACTIONS

As briefly discussed in Chapter 9, there are two methods of recording inventory transactions: the gross invoice method and the net invoice method. All transactions in Chapter 9 were recorded using the gross invoice method. When the gross invoice method is used, the cost of the inventory and account payable is recorded at the full invoice price, and purchase discounts are not recorded unless payment is made within the discount period. The net invoice method is an alternative approach to recording the cost of inventory.

As the name implies, the net invoice method records all inventory transactions at their **NET** amount (invoice price - cash discount). In other words the transaction is initially recorded as if the sales or purchases discount has been taken. The net invoice method is based on the accounting theory that transactions should be recorded at the "cash equivalent price." For example, assume that a company makes a $2,000 purchase and is granted terms of 2/10, n/30. A payment of only $1,960 is required if the company pays within the discount period. Therefore, at the time the transaction occurred, its cash equivalent price is only $1,960. The same theory is used to justify recording sales at the net invoice amount.

There are also practical benefits from using the net invoice method. As discussed in Chapter 9, failure to take advantage of purchase discounts equates to an annual financing charge of 36.7%. As such, it is important to provide management with information regarding discounts that are not being taken. Under the gross invoice method management is provided no information regarding lost discounts. In contrast, the net invoice method provides management with lost discount information because an account "Purchase Discounts Lost" is established and management can easily determine the cost of not taking purchase discounts. Accordingly, managers have information that can be useful in managing cash flows. Furthermore, the disclosure of lost discounts provides external parties with information about the quality of cash management within the company.

The different entries required under the net invoice method are illustrated in the following sections. Purchase transactions, including purchase returns, will be described first. Sales transactions will be described second. Finally, the entry required when discount periods have expired and the accounting period has ended is illustrated.

PURCHASE TRANSACTIONS

Assume that on June 15, 19X2, Pear Computer Inc. makes a $5,000 purchase with credit terms of 2/10, n/30. On the invoice the sales price will be listed as $5,000; however, Pear Computer will record the purchase as follows:

| June | 15 | Purchases ($5,000 X .98) | 4,900 | |
| | | Accounts Payable | | 4,900 |

If the company pays for the purchase on June 25, 19X2, they will remit a $4,900 check and the journal entry will be:

June	25	Accounts Payable	4,900	
		Cash		4,900

However, if the company allows the discount period to expire, they will be required to remit the full $5,000. Therefore, if the company pays for the purchase on July 24, 19X2, the journal entry will be:

June	24	Accounts Payable	4,900	
		Purchase Discounts Lost	100	
		Cash		5,000

Extending the Pear Computer example, assume that on July 18, 19X2, the company makes a $4,000 purchase, with terms of 2/10, n/30, and then on July 20, 19X2, the company returns $200 of the merchandise purchased. The entry will be:

July	20	Accounts Payable ($200 X .98)	196	
		Purchase Returns & Allowances		196

SALES TRANSACTIONS

Sales transactions are recorded using the same procedures as for purchase transactions. The only difference is the accounts involved. Assume that on May 18, 19X2, Eastbrook Distributors makes a $2,000 sales with credit terms of 2/10, n/30. The entry to record the transaction will be:

May	18	Accounts Receivable ($2,000 X .98)	1,960	
		Sales		1,960

If the company receives payment on May 28, 19X2, the entry will be:

May	28	Cash	1,960	
		Accounts Receivable		1,960

However, if payment is received after the discount period expires (May 28, 19X2), the full purchase price will be due. Assuming that payment is received on June 17, 19X2, the entry will be:

June	17	Cash	2,000	
		Accounts Receivable		1,960
		Interest Revenue		40

The discount not taken by a customer is recorded in Interest Revenue because it represents the additional revenue a firm receives by financing its customers purchases.

END-OF-THE-PERIOD ADJUSTMENTS

An accounting problem arises when the discount period for a purchase or sale has expired, cash has not yet been exchanged, and the accounting period ends. Accrual accounting requires that revenues and expenses be recorded in the period earned or incurred. Therefore, an adjusting entry is required when the above scenario occurs. For example, assume that on December 15, 19X2, Matrix, LTD, a calendar year company, made a $3,000 purchase with terms of 2/10, n/30. The journal entry to record the purchase would be:

| Dec. | 15 | Purchases ($3,000 X .98) | 2,940 | |
| | | Accounts Payable | | 2,940 |

Assuming that payment has not been made before the accounting period ends, and no other transactions have occurred, the balance in Accounts Payable will be $2,940. However, the company is now obligated to remit $3,000 rather than $2,940. Therefore, the balance in Accounts Payable is understated. Furthermore, the balance in the expense account Purchase Discounts Lost will be understated. As such, liabilities will be understated and net income will be overstated. Accordingly, the following adjusting entry is made to achieve a proper matching of revenues and expenses:

| Dec. | 31 | Purchase Discounts Lost | 60 | |
| | | Accounts Payable | | 60 |

The above illustration is from the perspective of the purchasing company. The procedure is essentially the same for a selling company. The only difference is that Accounts Receivable will be debited for the discount not taken and Interest Revenue will be credited an equal amount.

PRACTICE ACTIVITY 10-4

Wilson Company purchased merchandise for $800 on June 15. The credit terms were 2/15, n/30, and the goods were shipped FOB destination. Wilson Company uses a periodic inventory system and the net invoice method is used to record purchases.
Required:
1. Prepare the journal entry to record the purchase on June 15.
2. Prepare the journal entry to record the payment assuming that Wilson paid for the goods on June 25 within the discount period.
3. Assume now that Wilson paid for the goods on July 15. Prepare the journal entry to record the payment.
4. Discuss how the purchases discounts loss would be reported in the firm's financial statements.

1., 2., and 3.

	General Journal			Page 1
Date	Explanation	Post. Ref.	Debit	Credit

4.

_____

_____

_____

_____

SOLUTIONS TO PRACTICE ACTIVITIES

PRACTICE ACTIVITY 10-1

1.

	General Journal			Page 1
Date	Explanation	Post. Ref.	Debit	Credit
19X1				
Mar. 6	Purchases ($50 X 60 units)		3,000	
	Accounts Payable			3,000
11	Accounts Payable ($50 X 5 units)		250	
	Purchases Returns and Allowances			250
15	Accounts Receivable		1,700	
	Sales (85 units X 20 units)			1,700
Apr. 5	Accounts Payable		2,750	
	Cash ($3,000 − $250)			2,750

2.   Solution to Part 2 is on page 30.

SHELLY'S SHOE COMPANY
Worksheet
For the Year Ended January 31, 19X2

Account Titles	Unadjusted Trial Balance Debit	Unadjusted Trial Balance Credit	Adjustments Debit	Adjustments Credit	Adjusted Trial Balance Debit	Adjusted Trial Balance Credit	Income Statement Debit	Income Statement Credit	Balance Sheet Debit	Balance Sheet Credit
Cash	15,700				15,700				15,700	
Merchandise Inventory	42,900		d) 38,300	d) 42,900	38,300				38,300	
Prepaid Insurance	4,800			a) 2,880	1,920				1,920	
Store Equipment	26,000				26,000				26,000	
Acc. Depr. —Store Equip.		6,000		b) 2,600		8,600				8,600
Payables		6,300		c) 520		6,820				6,820
Capital Stock		50,000				50,000				50,000
Retained Earnings		13,830				13,830				13,830
Sales		151,870				151,870		151,870		
Sales Ret. & Allow.	3,890				3,890		3,890			
Purchases	70,680			d) 70,680						
Purch. Ret. & Allow.		3,250	d) 3,250							
Purch. Discounts		1,040	d) 1,040							
Freight-in	3,800			d) 3,800						
Cost of Goods Sold			d) 74,790		74,790		74,790			
Expenses	64,520		a) 2,880		70,520		70,520			
			b) 2,600							
			c) 520							
Totals	232,290	232,290	123,380	123,380	231,120	231,120	149,200	151,870	81,920	79,250
Net income for period							2,670			2,670
Totals							151,870	151,870	81,920	81,920

SHELLY'S SHOE COMPANY
Worksheet
For the Year Ended January 31, 19X2

Account Titles	Unadjusted Trial Balance Debit	Credit	Adjustments Debit	Credit	Adjusted Trial Balance Debit	Credit	Income Statement Debit	Credit	Balance Sheet Debit	Credit
Cash	15,700				15,700				15,700	
Merchandise Inventory	42,900				42,900		42,900	38,300	38,300	
Prepaid Insurance	4,800			a) 2,880	1,920				1,920	
Store Equipment	26,000				26,000				26,000	
Acc. Depr. —Store Equip.		6,000		b) 2,600		8,600				8,600
Payables		6,300		c) 520		6,820				6,820
Capital Stock		50,000				50,000				50,000
Retained Earnings		13,830				13,830				13,830
Sales		151,870				151,870		151,870		
Sales Ret. & Allow.	3,890				3,890		3,890			
Purchases	70,680				70,680		70,680			
Purch. Ret. & Allow.		3,250				3,250		3,250		
Purch. Discounts		1,040				1,040		1,040		
Freight-in	3,800				3,800		3,800			
Expenses	64,520		a) 2,880		70,520		70,520			
			b) 2,600							
			c) 520							
Totals	232,290	232,290	6,000	6,000	235,410	235,410	191,790	194,460	81,920	79,250
Net income for period							2,670			2,670
Totals							194,460	194,460	81,920	81,920

PRACTICE ACTIVITY 10-1 PART 2.

2. (a) + 58,600 - $39,240 = 44,650 (b)   (a)   25,290
    87,400 - (b) = 42,750   (b)   44,650
    42,750 - (c) = 10,380   (c)   32,370
    15,900 + (d) - 17,600 = 39,500   (d)   41,200
    64,320 - 39,500 = (e)   (e)   24,820
    24,820 - 28,480 = (f)   (f)   (3,660)
    (g) - 73,430 = 62,850 (i)   (g)   136,280
    55,000 + 79,120 - (h) = 73,430   (h)   60,690
    (i) - 47,550 = 15,300   (i)   62,850

PRACTICE ACTIVITY 10-4

	General Journal			Page 1
Date	Explanation	Post. Ref.	Debit	Credit
June 15	Purchases		784	
	Accounts Payable ($800 X .98)			784
June 25	Accounts Payable		784	
	Cash			784
July 15	Accounts Payable		784	
	Purchase Discounts Lost		16	
	Cash			800

4. Purchase discounts lost is generally reported as interest expense in the other revenues and expense sections of a multiple-step income statement.

CHAPTER 11

Subsidiary Ledgers and Special Journals

CONTENTS

- Chapter Overview and Objectives
- Control Accounts and Subsidiary Ledgers
- Processing of Repetitive Transactions in a Manual System
- Special Journals
- Sales Journal
- Purchases Journal
- Cash Receipts Journal
- Cash Disbursements Journal
- Controlling Liabilities and Cash Disbursements with a Voucher System
- The Voucher Register
- The Check Register

CHAPTER OVERVIEW AND OBJECTIVES

This chapter describes accounting systems that are designed for more efficient and dependable processing of financial data. When you have completed this chapter, you will be able to:

1. Explain how control accounts and subsidiary ledgers are used in a manual accounting system.
2. Explain the advantages of special journals.
3. Describe the formats of and procedures used with a sales journal, purchases journal, cash receipts journal, and cash disbursements journal.
4. Describe the purpose and operation of a voucher system to control cash disbursements.

In earlier chapters, we saw that the effects of various business transactions are collected, processed, and reported with a firm's accounting system. Accounting systems can take many forms, ranging from simple manual systems to sophisticated computerized ones. Regardless of its form, the dual purpose of any accounting system is to keep track of a firm's business transactions and report their effects on the operating performance and financial position of the firm to interested parties.

The accounting system illustrated in previous chapters was both simple and manually operated so as to introduce and focus on basic accounting procedures. As the name suggests, a manual accounting system is operated by human effort. Clerical personnel or bookkeepers prepare business forms, make journal entries, post to ledger accounts, and prepare financial reports. Many small businesses are able to satisfy their information requirements with a manual system, although the number has decreased significantly in recent years because of the increasing popularity and decreasing cost of computers. In most cases, even relatively small businesses require a more sophisticated accounting system for two reasons:

1. The procedures described earlier may be too time-consuming for rapid data processing and timely reporting. The volume of transactions may be so great that the accounting staff cannot process the data manually at a reasonable cost and on a sufficiently prompt basis.

2. Many transactions will be so repetitive that they can be handled more efficiently with more specialized treatment than the general procedures so far discussed.

This chapter begins with a discussion of the use of subsidiary ledgers. It also covers special journals, which are used to record such repetitive transactions as sales, purchases, cash receipts, and cash disbursements more efficiently than the general journal.

CONTROL ACCOUNTS AND SUBSIDIARY LEDGERS

So far, the discussion of a ledger as an essential part of an accounting system has been limited to a general ledger. For more timely and efficient processing, we need to examine the use of control accounts and subsidiary ledgers. Before doing so, assume that a business sells merchandise on credit to 5,000 customers. If the firm used only one Accounts Receivable account--as we have done until now--it would not provide adequate detail concerning the amount of merchandise sold to individual customers, the amount of money received from them, and the amount still owed by them. Consequently, the firm will want to establish a separate Accounts Receivable account for each customer. If this were done in the general ledger, 5,000 accounts would have to be established and combined with the other assets, liabilities, owners' equity, revenues, and expenses. As a result, the general ledger would be unwieldy, and the likelihood of errors would be high. The trial balance prepared from such a large general ledger would also be very long and difficult to work with. This situation is complicated further by the fact that other general ledger accounts, such as Accounts Payable and Merchandise Inventory, require similar detailed information.

When a large amount of detailed information about a certain general ledger account must be kept, a separate record called a **subsidiary ledger** is used. Thus, the detailed information is recorded outside the general ledger. For example, one Accounts Receivable account can be used in the general ledger and a separate Accounts Receivable account can be established for each customer (5,000 in the case above) in the subsidiary ledger. The Accounts Receivable account in the general ledger is called a **control account,** a general ledger account supported by the detail of a subsidiary ledger. A subsidiary ledger consists of a group of individual accounts, whose total should equal the balance of the related control account in the general ledger after all accounting is finished. Control accounts and subsidiary ledgers are used for a number of general ledger accounts —such as Accounts Receivable, Accounts Payable, Merchandise Inventory, and Plant Assets.

To illustrate the relationship between Accounts Receivable as a control account and its subsidiary ledger, consider the simplified illustration in Figure 11-1. In this illustration, the November sales and cash receipts activities are summarized for a firm with three customers. The account balances at the beginning of the month are assumed.

General Ledger Accounts Receivable			
Date	Debit	Credit	Balance
Nov. 1			6,500
30	5,100		11,600
30		6,900	4,700

Proof of Agreement between Control Account and Subsidiary Ledger:

Beginning balances:
  $6,500 = $3,200 + $1,100 + $2,200$
Ending balances:
  $4,700 = $1,800 + $2,400 + 500

Debits to accounts:
  $5,100 = $1,800 + $2,400 + 900
Credits to accounts:
  $6,900 = $3,200 + $1,100 + 2,600$

Subsidiary Ledger P. Able			
Date	Debit	Credit	Balance
Nov. 1			3,200
8	1,800		5,000
16		3,200	1,800

R. Baker			
Date	Debit	Credit	Balance
Nov. 1			1,100
3		1,100	-0-
20	2,400		2,400

D. Cane			
Date	Debit	Credit	Balance
Nov. 1			2,200
12	900		3,100
28		2,600	500

FIGURE 11-1
RELATIONSHIP OF SUBSIDIARY LEDGER TO CONTROL ACCOUNT

The accounts receivable subsidiary ledger is an alphabetical file with a separate account for each customer. Note that at the beginning and end of November, the total of the subsidiary ledger accounts is in agreement with the Accounts Receivable control account in the general ledger. The use of a subsidiary ledger has three major advantages:

1. It relieves the general ledger of a mass of detail.
2. It allows a division of labor in maintaining the ledgers.
3. It provides effective internal control for the dollar amounts involved.

PRACTICE ACTIVITY 11-1

Ebbets Company maintains an accounts receivable subsidiary ledger and an Accounts Receivable control account. The subsidiary ledger account balances on March 1 were as follows:

	Balance
C. Furrillo	$820
G. Hodges	360
C. Labine	180
J. Robinson	425
D. Snider	670

Sales and cash receipts for the month of March were as follows:

	Sales	Cash Receipts
C. Furrillo	$160	$780
G. Hodges	460	360
C. Labine	740	840
J. Robinson	475	480
D. Snider	210	770

Required:

A. Compute the balance in the Accounts Receivable control account on March 1.
B. Set up T accounts for each customer in a subsidiary ledger and an Accounts Receivable control account, and enter the beginning balances in the accounts.
C. Prepare a journal entry to record the total sales. Post the proper sale to the individual accounts in the subsidiary ledger.
D. Prepare a journal entry to record the total cash receipts. Post the proper cash receipt to the individual accounts in the subsidiary ledger.
E. Post the two entries to the Accounts Receivable control account.
F. Verify the ending balance in the Accounts Receivable control account.

Part A.

Customer	Balance

Parts C and D.

	General Journal			Page 1
Date	Explanation	Post. Ref.	Debit	Credit

Parts B, C, D, and E.

General Ledger

Accounts Receivable

Subsidiary Ledger

C. Furrillo

G. Hodges

C. Labine

J. Robinson

D. Snider

Part F.

	Balance
C. Furrillo	
G. Hodges	
C. Labine	
J. Robinson	
D. Snider	
Total	

PROCESSING OF REPETITIVE TRANSACTIONS IN A MANUAL SYSTEM

In earlier chapters, we illustrated basic accounting procedures by recording each transaction with an entry in a general journal and later posting each debit and credit to an appropriate account in the general ledger. For most firms, many of the transactions are so repetitive that they can be handled more efficiently with more specialized treatment than the general procedures discussed so far. To process a large number of repetitive transactions, the basic version of a manual accounting system can be streamlined and made more efficient by incorporating subsidiary ledgers and special journals into the accounting system. Special journals and subsidiary ledgers similar to those discussed below are also used in computer accounting systems. It is important that you learn how they function in a manual system where it is easier to visualize their use.

SPECIAL JOURNALS

The general journal described in earlier chapters can be used to record all types of transactions--sales, purchases, cash receipts, cash disbursements, sales returns and allowances, and purchase returns and allowances. The universal nature of the general journal imposes some limitations that adversely affect the efficiency of processing data.

- Each debit and credit recorded in the general journal must be posted individually to the general ledger, requiring a large amount of posting time. As the number of transactions increases, this inefficiency can make it difficult to provide accounting information on a timely basis.

- Only one person at a time can record the effects of transactions and post debits and credits to the ledger accounts, since all of the entries are recorded in one journal.

To avoid the limitations of using only a general journal, transactions are grouped into like categories and a **special journal** is set up for each category. Most of a typical firm's transactions fall into four categories, which in turn require four special journals.

Category of Transaction	Special Journal
Sales of merchandise on credit	Sales journal
Purchases of merchandise on credit	Purchases journal
Receipts of cash	Cash receipts journal
Disbursements of cash	Cash disbursements journal

The general journal is retained for recording transactions other than those recorded in these four categories. For example, sales returns and allowances, purchase returns and allowances, adjusting entries, and closing entries are recorded in the general journal. If the sales returns and allowances or the purchase returns and allowances occur frequently, special journals may also be designed for them. The combination of the five journals represents a much more efficient way to process data than the use of a general journal alone. As will be seen later, the time required to journalize entries under this system will be less, and totals, rather than individual entries, can be posted to ledger accounts in many cases. Also, an efficient division of labor can be achieved by assigning different journals to different employees so that work can be performed concurrently at a reduced cost of accounting labor.

Several selected transactions involving the Baldwin Video Equipment Store during the month of January illustrate the four special journals. The formats used for the four special journals are typical. The nature of a given business determines the exact formats required. Additional columns can be added to each of the special journals to accommodate other repetitive transactions that are not illustrated here.

SALES JOURNAL

A **sales journal**, such as the one shown in Figure 11-2, is used solely for recording *sales of merchandise on credit.* (Cash sales are recorded in the cash receipts journal, as will be shown later.) As each credit sale occurs, several copies of a sales invoice are prepared to document the transaction. The information shown on a sales invoice includes the customer's name, date of sale, invoice number (usually prenumbered), amount of sale, and credit terms. One copy of the sales invoice is used by the seller to record the sale in the sales journal.

In Figure 11-2, eight sales to five different customers have been recorded. All credit sales in this example are made on the basis of 2/10, n/30 terms. Other columns can be added to the sales journal to satisfy the needs of a specific business. If credit terms vary among customers, an additional column can be added to the sales journal to identify the terms of each sale. In addition, a sales tax payable column can be used to record the amount of sales tax to be collected from customers when a business is required to do so for state or local taxing authorities. To observe how a sales tax payable column is used, refer to Figure 11-3 (it shows a sales journal with a single entry made to record a sale of $100 to M. Wright, subject to a 6% sales tax, or $6).

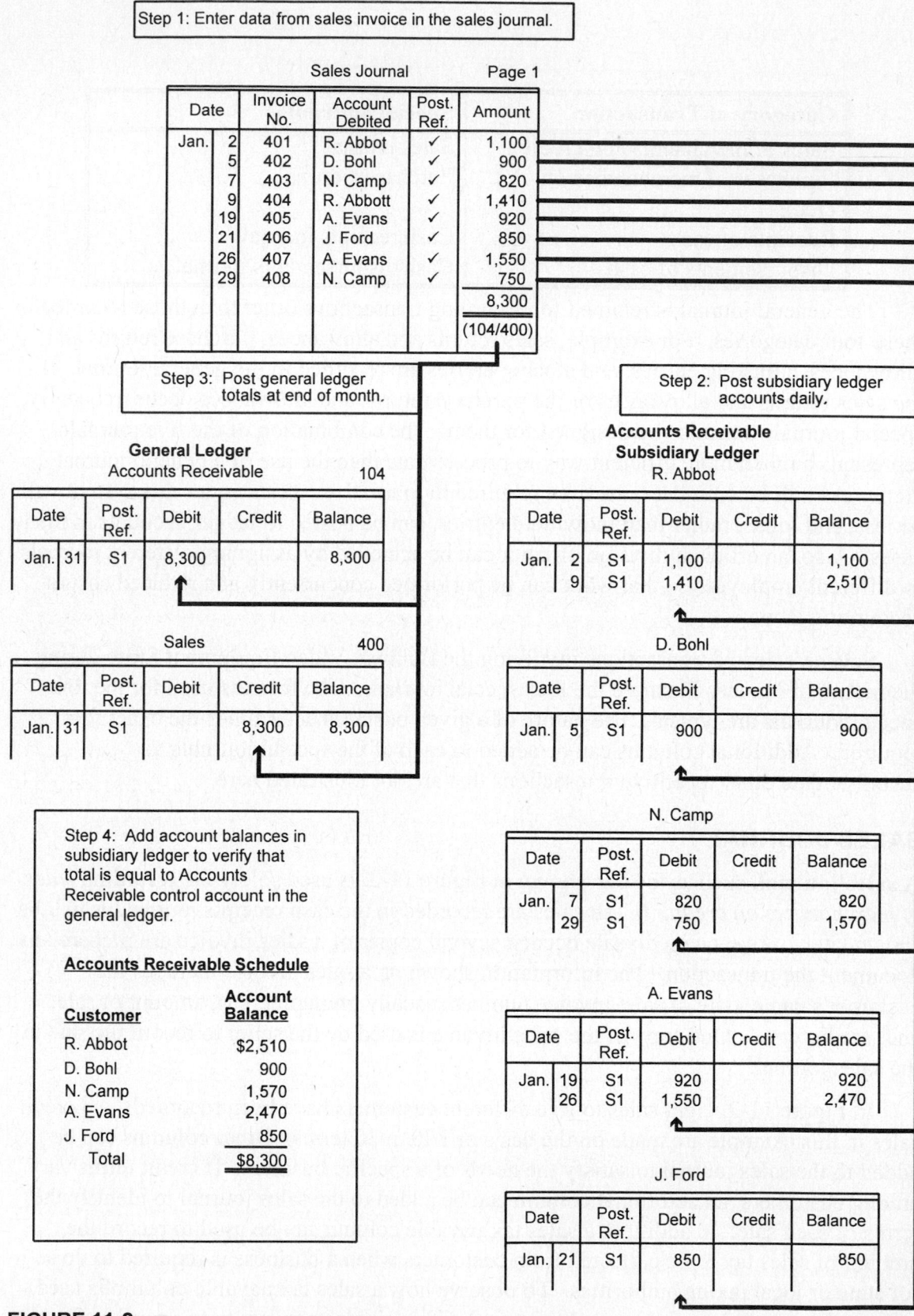

FIGURE 11-2
RELATIONSHIP OF SALES JOURNAL TO LEDGER ACCOUNTS

Date	Invoice No.	Account Debited	Post. Ref.	Debit	Credits	
				Accounts Receivable	Sales Taxes Payable	Sales
Feb. 10	230	M. Wright		106.00	6.00	100.00

FIGURE 11-3
MULTICOLUMN SALES JOURNAL

The total of the sales tax payable column is posted to the Sales Tax Payable account at the end of the month, and the other totals are posted, as discussed later, for the sales journal in Figure 11-2.

Advantages of a Sales Journal

The sales journal shown in Figure 11-2 has these time-saving advantages:

1. Each sales transaction is recorded on a single line. All credit sales are alike in that they result in a debit to Accounts Receivable and a credit to Sales. Record keeping efficiency is achieved by simply identifying the customer who is the debtor instead of entering the account titles--Accounts Receivable and Sales--for each transaction.

2. The entries in the sales journal do not require an explanation because (a) all the transactions involved are the same, as previously discussed, and (b) the detailed information related to each sale is documented on a sales invoice that is referenced in the second column of the sales journal. If additional information concerning a particular sale is required, the interested party can simply identify the invoice number and refer to the details of the sales invoice.

3. Posting efficiency is achieved with the sales journal since only one amount, the total credit sales for the month, is posted to the general ledger. Note that in Figure 11-2, the total sales on account ($8,300) is posted twice--once to the Accounts Receivable control account and once to the Sales account. This procedure eliminates posting separate debits and credits during the month. In addition, the sales information needed for each customer in the accounts receivable subsidiary ledger is posted daily from the line items of the sales journal.

A check mark is recorded in the Post. Ref. (Posting Reference) column to indicate that each sale has been posted to the subsidiary ledger. The account numbers for Accounts Receivable (104) and Sales (400) are entered below the total credit sales for the month to show that the general ledger accounts have been posted. A Posting Reference column is also included in both the general and subsidiary ledger accounts to indicate the source of the entries posted for cross-referencing purposes. S1 refers to the first page of the sales journal. Note that we can use the Posting Reference columns of the journal and the ledger to go back and forth easily between the two accounting records.

Summary of Sales Journal Procedures

The procedures used with the sales journal illustrated in Figure 11-2 can be summarized as follows:

1. From each sales invoice, enter the date of the sale, invoice number, customer's name, and amount of sale on a line of the sales journal.

2. *At the end of each day*, post each sale to the related customer's account in the subsidiary ledger. Place a check mark in the Posting Reference column of the sales journal and S1 (indicating page one of the sales journal) in the Posting Reference column of the customer's account. These posting reference marks indicate that the journal entry has been posted and identify the source of the entry.

3. *At the end of each month*, total the Amount column of the sales journal and post the total amount as a debit and credit to the two general ledger accounts, Accounts Receivable and Sales, respectively. Place the general ledger account numbers involved (104/400) below the Amount column total and S1 in the Posting Reference columns of the two general ledger accounts.

4. Add the account balances of the accounts receivable subsidiary ledger to verify that the total is equal to the Accounts Receivable control account balance in the general ledger. In Figure 11-2, the amount involved is $8,300 (the same as the balance of the Accounts Receivable control account), as shown in the following accounts receivable schedule:

Accounts Receivable Schedule	
Customer	**Amount**
R. Abbot	$2,510
D. Bohl	900
N. Camp	1,570
A. Evans	2,470
J. Ford	850
Total	$8,300

PURCHASES JOURNAL

The **purchases journal** can be set up as either a single-column or a multicolumn journal. In either case, the purchases of merchandise must be recorded separately from the acquisition of other assets because, as seen earlier, the total purchases of merchandise for a period are used to compute cost of goods sold. A single-column purchases journal, such as that shown in Figure 11-4, is used solely for recording the purchases of merchandise on credit with a periodic inventory system. Cash purchases of merchandise are recorded in the cash disbursements journal, as discussed later. Other purchases, such as the acquisition of an automobile or an office machine, will be recorded in some other journal, determined by the means of payment involved. If such assets are acquired for cash, the transactions are recorded in the cash disbursements journal; if purchased on credit, they are recorded in the general journal.

Advantages of a Purchases Journal

The advantages of and procedures required for a single-column purchases journal are similar to those described earlier for a sales journal. Recall from the discussion in Chapter 10 that the purchase of merchandise on credit with a periodic inventory system (as we are assuming here) is recorded with a debit to Purchases and a credit to Accounts Payable. If a perpetual inventory system is used, the debit is to the Merchandise Inventory account. The account credited on each line item of a purchases journal is an account payable with a particular creditor to whom the business has an obligation. A subsidiary ledger is maintained to provide the detailed information concerning each individual account payable. An Accounts Payable control account is established in the general ledger. The procedures used with a single-column purchases journal, as illustrated in Figure 11-4, can be summarized as follows:

1. From each purchase invoice, enter the recording date, invoice date, name of the supplier, credit terms, if applicable, and dollar amount of purchase on a line of the purchases journal.

2. *At the end of each day*, post each purchase to the related supplier's account in the subsidiary ledger. Place a check mark in the Posting Reference column of the purchases journal and Pl (indicating page one of the purchases journal) in the Posting Reference column of the creditor's account.

3. *At the end of each month*, total the Amount column of the purchases journal and post the total amount as a debit and credit to the two general ledger accounts, Purchases and Accounts Payable, respectively. Place the general ledger account numbers involved (510/210) below the Amount column total and Pl in the Posting Reference columns of the two general ledger accounts.

Step 1: Enter data from purchase invoice in the purchases journal.

Purchases Journal — Page 1

Date Recorded		Date of Invoice		Account	Terms	Post. Ref.	Amount
Jan.	3	Jan.	2	Kirby Company	n/30	✓	1,900
	6	Jan.	4	Risk Company	n/30	✓	1,200
	8	Jan.	8	Dunn Supply	n/30	✓	1,410
	13	Jan.	12	Dunn Supply	n/30	✓	1,820
	20	Jan.	18	CSR Inc.	2/10,n/30	✓	820
	24	Jan.	24	Cooper Company	2/10,n/30	✓	900
	27	Jan.	26	Risk Company	2/10,n/30	✓	2,810
	30	Jan.	29	CSR Inc.	n/30	✓	900
							11,760
							(510/210)

Step 3: Post general ledger totals at end of month.

Step 2: Post subsidiary ledger accounts daily.

General Ledger
Accounts Payable — 210

Date		Post. Ref.	Debit	Credit	Balance
Jan.	31	P1		11,760	11,760

Purchases — 510

Date		Post. Ref.	Debit	Credit	Balance
Jan.	31	P1	11,760		11,760

Accounts Payable Subsidiary Ledger
Cooper Company

Date		Post. Ref.	Debit	Credit	Balance
Jan.	24	P1		900	900

CSR Inc.

Date		Post. Ref.	Debit	Credit	Balance
Jan.	20	P1		820	820
	30	P1		900	1,720

Dunn Supply

Date		Post. Ref.	Debit	Credit	Balance
Jan.	8	P1		1,410	1,410
	13	P1		1,820	3,230

Kirby Company

Date		Post. Ref.	Debit	Credit	Balance
Jan.	3	P1		1,900	1,900

Risk Company

Date		Post. Ref.	Debit	Credit	Balance
Jan.	6	P1		1,200	1,200
	27	P1		2,810	4,010

Step 4: Add account balances in subsidiary ledger to verify that total is equal to Accounts Payable control account in the general ledger.

Accounts Payable Schedule

Creditor	Account Balance
Cooper Company	$ 900
CSR Inc.	1,720
Dunn Supply	3,230
Kirby Company	1,900
Risk Company	4,010
Total	$11,760

**FIGURE 11-4
RELATIONSHIP OF PURCHASES JOURNAL
AND LEDGER ACCOUNTS**

4. Add the account balances of the accounts payable subsidiary ledger to verify that the total is equal to the Accounts Payable control account balance in the general ledger. In Figure 11-4, the amount involved is $11,760 (the same as the balance of the Accounts Payable control account), as verified by the following accounts payable schedule:

Accounts Payable Schedule	
Supplier	**Amount**
Cooper Co.	$ 900
CSR Inc.	1,720
Dunn Supply	3,230
Kirby Co.	1,900
Risk Co.	4,010
Total	$11,760

A single-column purchases journal can be expanded to a multicolumn format such as the one shown in Figure 11-5. This journal has a single credit column for accounts payable and several debit columns for purchases of merchandise, purchases of store supplies, purchases of office supplies, and other debits. The other debits column can be used to record such transactions as the acquisition of equipment or the incurrence of freight-in charges. All transactions recorded in this journal will involve credit, rather than cash, because of the single accounts payable credit column. The recording and posting procedures with a multicolumn purchases journal are similar to those described next for the cash receipts journal.

Date	Account	Post. Ref.	Purchases Debit	Store Supplies Debit	Office Supplies Debit	Other Debits Account	Other Debits Post. Ref.	Other Debits Amount	Accounts Payable Credit
Jan. 3	Hull Co.	√	1,900						1,900
10	Kirk, Inc.	√	2,800						2,800
14	Decker Inc.	√		810					810
19	Short, Co.	√			465				465
24	Zinn Co.	√				Office Equip.	170	1,155	1,155

FIGURE 11-5
MULTICOLUMN PURCHASES JOURNAL

CASH RECEIPTS JOURNAL

The **cash receipts journal** is used to record all transactions involving the receipt of cash (a debit to Cash). Typical sources of cash are the sale of merchandise for cash, the collection of accounts receivable from customers, investments by owners, and bank loans. A multicolumn cash receipts journal is necessary because of the numerous sources of cash. Two debit columns are required—one for the actual cash collected and another one for sales discounts. To keep the required number of columns manageable but, at the same time, achieve efficient processing, three credit columns often are used to separate the sources of cash in the journal. The headings on the three credit columns as shown in Figure 11-6 are Sales, Accounts Receivable, and Other Accounts. The first two credit columns are used to record collections from cash sales and accounts receivable. All other sources of cash are entered in the third credit column.

The following cash receipts transactions for the Baldwin Video Equipment Store provide the basis for the entries in Figure 11-6:

1. The owner of the business, Betty Baldwin, invested $10,000 of her own cash on January 3 through the purchase of capital stock.
2. Video equipment was sold for $285 cash on January 8.
3. Received payment from Robert Abbot for an eight-day-old account receivable of $1,100 less a 2% sales discount of $22 on January 10. Therefore, $1,078 cash was received. Credit terms are 2/10, n/30, and the cash was received within 10 days.
4. Received payment from Don Bohl for a 15-day-old account receivable of $900 on January 20. No discount was involved since the cash was not received within 10 days.
5. Video equipment was sold for $220 cash on January 21.
6. A bank loan of $2,500 was received on January 31.

The two debit columns and three credit columns of the cash receipts journal shown in Figure 11-6 are used as follows:

Debits

Cash. The Cash column is used in *every* entry because only cash receipt transactions are recorded in the cash receipts journal.

Sales Discounts. This column is used to record all sales discounts allowed customers for prompt payment. Note that on January 10, the 2% discount (2% x $1,100 = $22) given to R. Abbot was recorded because the payment was made within 10 days. The total debits to Cash ($1,078) and Sales Discounts ($22) are equal to the $1,100 credit to Accounts Receivable, all of which are recorded on one line.

Credits

Sales. All cash sales are recorded in the Sales column. Most firms use cash registers to account for daily cash sales. At the end of a day, a sales tape showing the total cash sales is removed from the cash register and used to make the entry in the Sales column.

Accounts Receivable. This column is used to record the collections on accounts from customers. The name of the customer is written in the Account Credited column to identify the proper account to be credited in the subsidiary ledger.

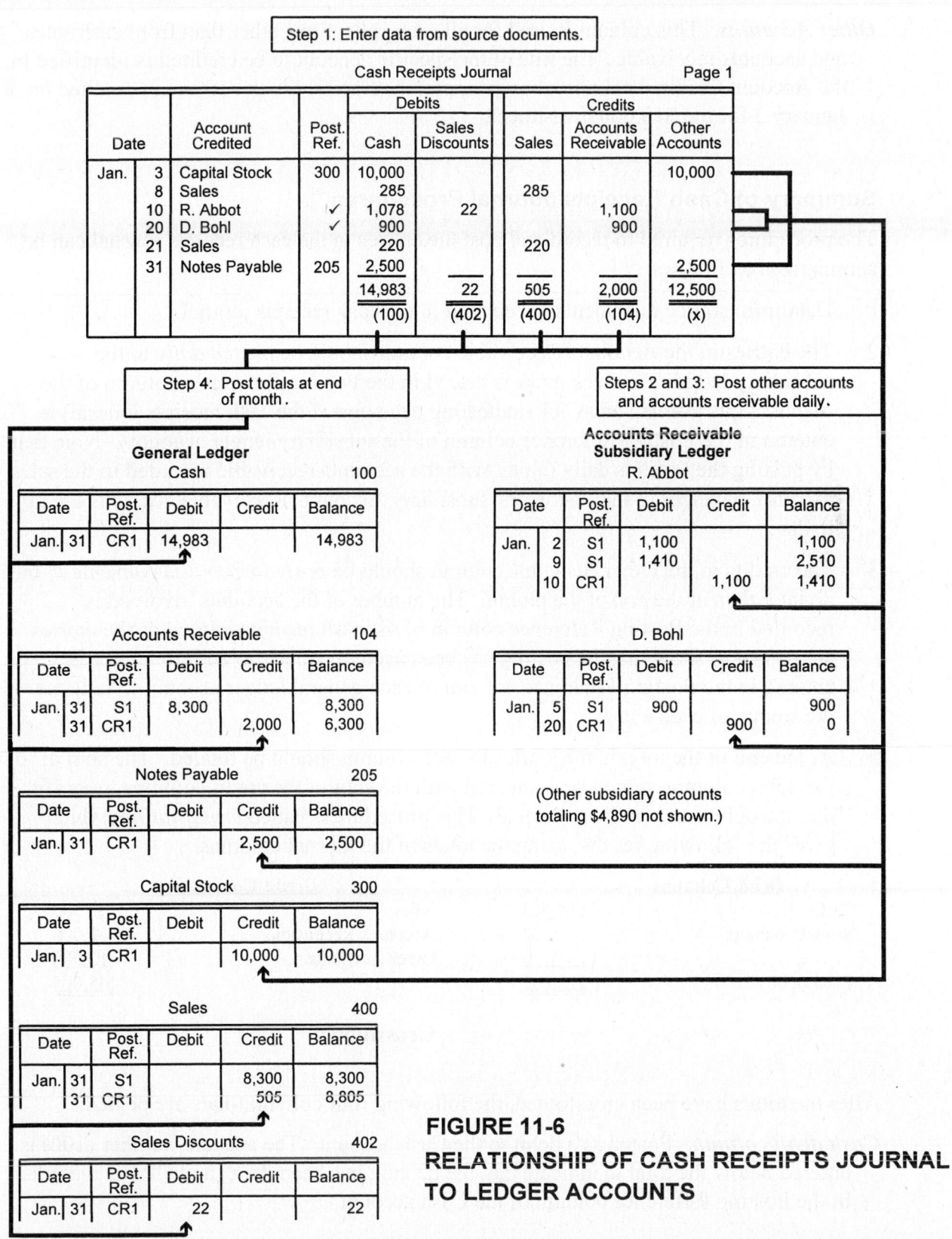

FIGURE 11-6

RELATIONSHIP OF CASH RECEIPTS JOURNAL TO LEDGER ACCOUNTS

Other Accounts. This column is used for all cash collections other than from cash sales and accounts receivable. The title of the specific account to be credited is identified in the Account Credited column. For example, the Capital Stock account is credited on January 3 for the $10,000 investment.

Summary of Cash Receipts Journal Procedures

The procedures required to record and post the entries in the cash receipts journal can be summarized as follows:

1. Data from source documents are entered in the cash receipts journal.

2. The entries in the Accounts Receivable column should be *posted daily* to the subsidiary ledger. A check mark is placed in the Posting Reference column of the cash receipts journal, and CR1 (indicating page one of the cash receipts journal) is entered in the Posting Reference column of the subsidiary ledger accounts. Note that by posting the receipts daily (along with the accounts receivable recorded in the sales journal), balances in the customers' subsidiary Accounts Receivable accounts are up to date.

3. The credits in the Other Accounts column should be *posted when it is convenient,* but no later than at the end of the month. The number of the accounts involved is recorded in the Posting Reference column of the cash receipts journal as the entries are posted to show that the posting has been accomplished. In addition, CR1 is entered in the Posting Reference column of each general ledger account to indicate the source of each entry.

4. At the end of the month, the entries in each column should be totaled. The sum of the debit columns should be compared with the sum of the credit columns to verify that the debits and credits are equal. This procedure is called *crossfooting,* which gives the following results, using the totals of the journal columns.

Debit Columns		Credit Columns	
Cash	$14,983	Sales	$ 505
Sales Discounts	22	Accounts Receivable	2,000
		Other Accounts	12,500
Total debits	$15,005		$15,005

Crossfooted

After the totals have been crossfooted, the following four column totals are posted:

Cash debit column. Posted as a debit to the Cash account. The account number (100) is entered below the total to indicate that the posting has been done, and CR1 is recorded in the Posting Reference column of the Cash account.

Sales Discounts debit column. Posted as a debit to the Sales Discounts account. The account number (402) is placed below the total to show that the posting has been accomplished, and CR1 is entered in the Sales Discounts account.

Sales credit column. Posted as a credit to the Sales account. The account number (400) is entered below the total as an indication that the posting has taken place, and CR1 is recorded in the Sales account.

Accounts Receivable credit column. Posted as a credit to the Accounts Receivable control account. The account number (104) is recorded below the total, and CR1 is entered in the control account.

The total of the Other Accounts column is *not posted at the end of the month* because each entry is posted individually. Some accountants use a special symbol--such as (x) at the bottom of the column--to indicate that it is not posted as a total.

CASH DISBURSEMENTS JOURNAL

The **cash disbursements journal,** also called the **cash payments journal,** is used to record all transactions involving payments of cash--cash purchases of merchandise, payment of accounts payable to creditors, disbursements for operating expenses, and payment of bank loans. The multicolumn format of the cash disbursements journal is similar to the one described earlier for the cash receipts journal. Three debit columns (Purchases, Accounts Payable, and Other Accounts) are used along with two credit columns (Cash and Purchases Discounts), as illustrated in Figure 11-7. The following transactions for Baldwin Video Equipment Store illustrate the cash disbursements journal:

1. Merchandise costing $680 was purchased for cash on January 4.
2. Store rent of $325 was paid on January 7.
3. Store equipment costing $410 was purchased for cash on January 14.
4. Merchandise costing $840 was purchased for cash on January 28.
5. A one-year premium for an insurance policy amounting to $510 was paid on January 29.
6. The $1,900 account payable to the Kirby Company was paid on January 30.
7. The $900 account payable to Cooper Company was paid, less a 2% discount of $18, on January 30. Therefore, $882 cash was paid.

The three debit columns and two credit columns of the cash disbursements journal are shown in Figure 11-7.

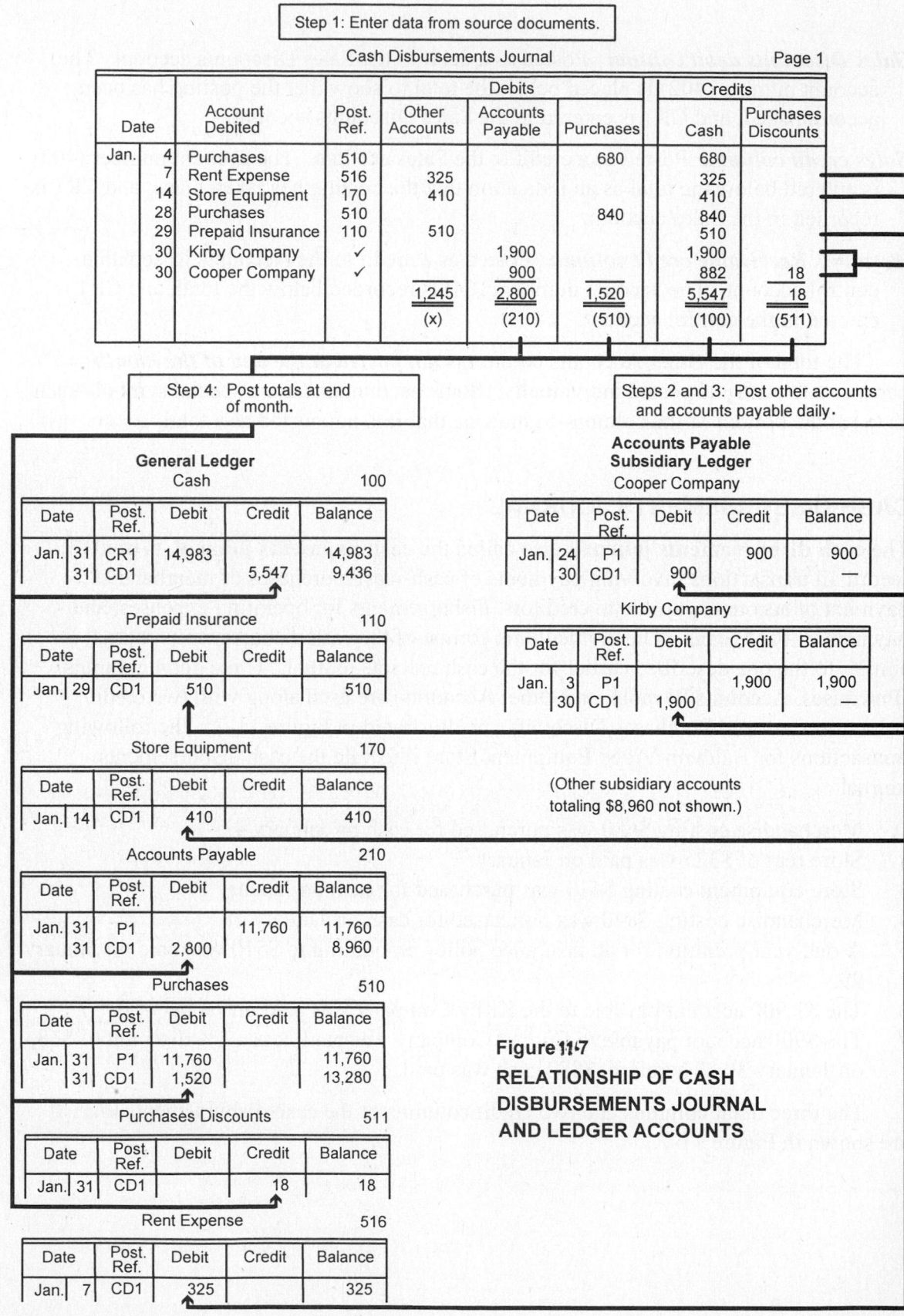

Step 1: Enter data from source documents.

Cash Disbursements Journal — Page 1

Date	Account Debited	Post. Ref.	Debits Other Accounts	Debits Accounts Payable	Debits Purchases	Credits Cash	Credits Purchases Discounts
Jan. 4	Purchases	510			680	680	
7	Rent Expense	516	325			325	
14	Store Equipment	170	410			410	
28	Purchases	510			840	840	
29	Prepaid Insurance	110	510			510	
30	Kirby Company	✓		1,900		1,900	
30	Cooper Company	✓		900		882	18
			1,245	2,800	1,520	5,547	18
			(x)	(210)	(510)	(100)	(511)

Step 4: Post totals at end of month.

Steps 2 and 3: Post other accounts and accounts payable daily.

General Ledger

Cash — 100

Date	Post. Ref.	Debit	Credit	Balance
Jan. 31	CR1	14,983		14,983
31	CD1		5,547	9,436

Prepaid Insurance — 110

Date	Post. Ref.	Debit	Credit	Balance
Jan. 29	CD1	510		510

Store Equipment — 170

Date	Post. Ref.	Debit	Credit	Balance
Jan. 14	CD1	410		410

Accounts Payable — 210

Date	Post. Ref.	Debit	Credit	Balance
Jan. 31	P1		11,760	11,760
31	CD1	2,800		8,960

Purchases — 510

Date	Post. Ref.	Debit	Credit	Balance
Jan. 31	P1	11,760		11,760
31	CD1	1,520		13,280

Purchases Discounts — 511

Date	Post. Ref.	Debit	Credit	Balance
Jan. 31	CD1		18	18

Rent Expense — 516

Date	Post. Ref.	Debit	Credit	Balance
Jan. 7	CD1	325		325

Accounts Payable Subsidiary Ledger

Cooper Company

Date	Post. Ref.	Debit	Credit	Balance
Jan. 24	P1		900	900
30	CD1	900		—

Kirby Company

Date	Post. Ref.	Debit	Credit	Balance
Jan. 3	P1		1,900	1,900
30	CD1	1,900		—

(Other subsidiary accounts totaling $8,960 not shown.)

Figure 11-7

RELATIONSHIP OF CASH DISBURSEMENTS JOURNAL AND LEDGER ACCOUNTS

Debits

Purchases. The Purchases column is used to record all cash purchases of merchandise. The total of this column is posted to the Purchases account in the general ledger. When posted, the amount is added to the purchases made on credit, posted from the purchases journal, to determine the total purchases for the period.

Accounts Payable. Payments of accounts payable are entered in this column. The name of the supplier is written in the Account Debited column, so that the entry can be posted to the appropriate subsidiary ledger account.

Other Accounts. This column is used for all cash disbursements *except* cash purchases and payments of accounts payable. The title of the account to be debited is entered in the Account Debited column to identify the specific type of cash disbursement. In Figure 11-7, rent expense and prepaid insurance were paid, along with the acquisition of store equipment.

Credits

Cash. The Cash column must be used for *each* transaction because *only* cash payments are recorded in this journal.

Purchases Discounts. Any purchases discounts taken for prompt payment are recorded in this column. We are assuming that the gross invoice price method is used in this illustration.

Summary of Cash Disbursements Journal Procedures

The recording and posting procedures required with the cash disbursements journal are the two types discussed earlier for the cash receipts journal: *postings during the month* and postings *at the end of the month.* The procedures can be summarized as follows:

1. Data from source documents are entered in the cash disbursements journal.

2. The entries in the Accounts Payable column should be posted *daily* to the subsidiary ledger. A check mark is placed in the Posting Reference column of the cash disbursements journal, and CD1 (representing page one of the cash disbursements journal) is entered in the Posting Reference column of the subsidiary ledger accounts. By combining the daily postings of both the cash payments and the accounts payable recorded in the purchases journal, we have up-to-date balances of the amounts owed to suppliers.

3. The debits in the Other Accounts column should *be posted when convenient,* but no later than at the end of the month. The number of each account involved is recorded in the Posting Reference column, as the entries are posted, to indicate that the posting has been done. CD1 is entered in the Posting Reference column of each account to show the source of each entry.

4. *At the end of the month,* the dollar amounts entered in each column should be totaled and crossfooted to verify that the debits and credits are equal as follows:

Debit Columns		Credit Columns	
Other Accounts	$1,245	Cash	$5,547
Accounts Payable	2,800	Purchase Discounts	18
Purchases	1,520		
Total debits	$5,565	Total credits	$5,565

Crossfooted

5. The column totals for Accounts Payable, Purchases, Cash, and Purchases Discounts are posted at the end of the month to their respective accounts in the general ledger. The account numbers are entered below the column totals, and CD1 is recorded in the Posting Reference column of the general ledger accounts. The total of the Other Accounts column is *not posted at the end of the month* because each entry is posted individually. An (x) can be placed below the column total to indicate that it is not posted as a total.

PRACTICE ACTIVITY 11-2

The New River Company uses a sales journal, purchases journal, cash receipts journal, cash disbursements journal, and a general journal. The firm also maintains subsidiary accounts receivable and accounts payable ledgers in addition to the control accounts. The relevant account balances as of August 1, 19X2, were as follows:

Acct. No.	Account Title	Account Balance Debit	Account Balance Credit
100	Cash	$ 7,500	
110	Accounts Receivable	4,100	
135	Merchandise Inventory	25,000	
210	Plant and Equipment	72,000	
300	Accounts Payable		$ 5,300
320	Notes Payable		45,000
400	Capital Stock		62,000
500	Sales		10,300
510	Sales Discounts	200	
520	Sales Returns and Allowances	100	
600	Purchases	8,000	
610	Purchases Discounts		300
700	Selling and Administrative Exp.	6,000	
	Totals	$122,900	$122,900

The accounts receivable and accounts payable subsidiary ledger balances were as follows:

Accounts Receivable	
C. Clark	$1,400
P. Hills	600
R. Kennison	900
B. Murray	1,200
Total	$4,100

Accounts Payable	
Miller Company	$ 800
Royal, Inc.	3,500
Sterling Co.	1,000
Total	$5,300

The following transactions occurred during August:

Aug. 2   Purchased merchandise from Sterling Co. for $1,800 on account with terms, 2/10, n/30.

3   Received $600 from P. Hills as payment on account.

6   Paid $1,000 to Sterling Co. on its previous balance. No discount was taken.

9   Sold merchandise to B. Murray on account for $500, Invoice 201.

12   Paid $1,764 to Sterling Co., taking advantage of the 2% discount.

13   Sold $1,500 of merchandise to P. Hills on account with terms 1/10, n60, Invoice 202.

14   Received $300 from R. Kennison as payment on account.

15   Paid $2,000 on the Royal Inc., account.

17   Purchased inventory for $1,000 from Miller Company on account with terms n/30.

19   Sold merchandise for $500 cash.

21   Purchased equipment for $8,000 by issuing a 14% note due in two years.

22   Borrowed $10,000 from United Bank by issuing a 12% note payable.

23   Received $1,000 from C. Clark as payment on account. There was no discount.

29   Purchased merchandise for $100 cash.

30   Made a $1,000 principal payment on note payable. (Ignore interest for this transaction.)

Required:

A.   Journalize the August transactions in the appropriate journals.

B.   Post the journal entries to the appropriate general ledger and subsidiary ledger accounts.

C.   Prepare a schedule of accounts receivable and accounts payable as of August 31, 19X2, to confirm the balance in each control account.

D.   Prepare a trial balance of the general ledger.

Part A.

General Journal				Page 1
Date	Explanation	Post. Ref.	Debit	Credit

		Sales Journal		Page 1
Date	Invoice No.	Account Debited	Post. Ref.	Amount

	Purchases Journal			Page 1
Date	Account Credited	Terms	Post. Ref.	Amount

			Debits		Credits		
Date	Account Credited	Post. Ref.	Cash	Sales Discounts	Sales	Accts. Receiv.	Other Accounts

Cash Receipts Journal — Page 1

			Debits			Credits	
Date	Account Debited	Post. Ref.	Other Accounts	Accounts Payable	Purchases	Cash	Purch. Discounts

Cash Disbursements Journal — Page 1

Part B.

General Ledger Accounts

Cash		100
8/1 Bal.	7,500	

Accounts Receivable		110
8/1 Bal.	4,100	

Merchandise Inventory		135
8/1 Bal.	25,000	

Plant and Equipment		210
8/1 Bal.	72,000	

Accounts Payable		300
	8/1 Bal.	5,300

Notes Payable		320
	8/1 Bal.	45,000

Capital Stock		400
	8/1 Bal.	62,000

Sales		500
	8/1 Bal.	10,300

Sales Discount		510
8/1 Bal.	200	

Sales Returns and Allowances		520
8/1 Bal.	100	

Purchases		600
8/1 Bal.	8,000	

Purchases Discounts		610
	8/1 Bal.	300

Selling and Administrative Expenses		700
8/1 Bal.	6,000	

Accounts Receivable Subsidiary Ledger

C. Clark	
8/1 Bal.	1,400

P. Hills	
8/1 Bal.	600

R. Kennison	
8/1 Bal.	900

B. Murray	
8/1 Bal.	1,200

Accounts Payable Subsidiary Ledger

Miller Company		
	8/1 Bal.	800

Royal, Inc.		
	8/1 Bal.	3,500

Sterling Company		
	8/1 Bal.	1,000

Part C.

Accounts Receivable	
C. Clark	
P. Hills	
R. Kennison	
B. Murray	
Total	

Accounts Payable	
Miller Company	
Royal, Inc.	
Sterling Co.	
Total	

Part D.

NEW RIVER COMPANY
Unadjusted Trial Balance
August 31, 19X2

Acct. No.	Account Title	Account Balance	
		Debit	Credit
100	Cash		
110	Accounts Receivable		
135	Merchandise Inventory		
210	Plant and Equipment		
300	Accounts Payable		
320	Notes Payable		
400	Capital Stock		
530	Sales		
510	Sales Discounts		
520	Sales Returns and Allowances		
600	Purchases		
610	Purchases Discounts		
700	Selling and Administrative Exp.		
	Totals		

CONTROLLING LIABILITIES AND CASH DISBURSEMENTS WITH A VOUCHER SYSTEM

A **voucher system** consists of the procedures used to obtain control over liabilities and cash expenditures from the time an obligation is incurred for goods or services received until the obligation is settled by the payment of cash. Under a voucher system, the incurrence of a liability and the payment of cash to settle the liability are considered separate independent transactions. Four relatively distinct steps make up the cycle involved in ordering, receiving, and paying for goods and services:

1. Orders are placed.
2. Goods or services are received.
3. The accuracy of invoices is verified, and the invoices are approved for payment.
4. Checks are written in payment of approved invoices.

A major ingredient of control with a voucher system is assigning responsibility for these steps to specific individuals or departments. One or more source documents are prepared at each step to provide verification that the step was completed properly. Although the same general procedures are followed for the acquisition of both goods and services, the following description concentrates on the acquisition of goods, that is, merchandise or other physical assets.

PLACING ORDERS

Operating department managers are normally prohibited from placing orders directly with suppliers; to permit them to do so would prohibit effective centralization of the control of the total goods ordered and the resulting liabilities. Operating managers, who have responsibility for determining the goods needed by their departments, prepare a **purchase requisition** (Figure 11-8) that lists the items needed by the department. The purchase requisition is sent to a central purchasing department (which has responsibility for placing orders), and a copy is forwarded to the accounting department. Purchasing department personnel determine the appropriate source of supply, negotiate the terms of the purchase with the supplier, and place the order by preparing a **purchase order.** The purchase order is a business form that authorizes a supplier to ship specific goods (Figure 11-9). The original copy of the purchase order is sent to the supplier, a copy is sent to the requisitioning department to inform the manager that the order has been placed, and another copy is forwarded to the accounting department, which will eventually approve payment for the order.

PURCHASE REQUISITION

No. ___269___
DATE: ___8/6/19X2___

DATA COMPANY
NEW YORK, NEW YORK

From: Assembly Department
To: Purchasing Department

Please place the following order.

Quantity	Number	Description
200	142 JX	J-Type Gear Boxes
400	142 JY	Gear Box Brackets

For Purchasing Department Use:
Date ordered ___August 9, 19X2___   Approved
Purchase Order No. ___348___   by ___Betty Wallace___

FIGURE 11-8
A PURCHASE REQUISITION

PURCHASE ORDER

No. ___348___

DATA COMPANY
1842 Elm Street
New York, New York 10059

Sold to: Croyden Gear Supply Company   Date   August 9, 19X2
1478 Sundown Avenue   Ship Via.   Acme Trucking
Los Angeles, CA   Terms   2/10, n/30
94412

Quantity	Description	Price	Amount
200	142 JX J-Type Gear Boxes	$4.95	$ 990.00
400	142 JY Gear Box Brackets	.78	312.00
			$1,302.00

Data Company
Approved by P. Powell

FIGURE 11-9
A PURCHASE ORDER

RECEIPT OF GOODS

When goods are shipped, the supplier prepares a document called an **invoice** or **bill** (Figure 11-10) that itemizes the goods shipped, the price charged for each item, the terms of the sale, and the total amount of the invoice. A copy of the invoice is mailed to the purchaser. When the invoice is received, it is sent to the accounting department, where it is held until the goods are received and inspected by the receiving department. The receiving department prepares a receiving report (Figure 11-11), which lists the type and quantity of goods received. Copies are sent to the requisitioning department and the purchasing department to serve as notification that the goods have been received, and a copy is sent to the accounting department for comparison with the purchase requisition, purchase order, and invoice.

INVOICE

Invoice No. ___2416___

Croyden Gear Supply Company
1478 Sundown Avenue
Los Angeles, California 94412

Sold to: Data Company
1842 Elm Street
New York, NY 10059

Invoice Date	8/15/19X2
Order No.	348
Date Shipped	8/15/X2
Terms	2/10, n/30

Quantity	Description	Price	Amount
200	142 JX J-Type Gear Boxes	$4.95	$ 990.00
400	142 JY Gear Box Brackets	.78	312.00
			$1,302.00

FIGURE 11-10
AN INVOICE

RECEIVING REPORT			
DATA COMPANY **NEW YORK, NEW YORK**		No. 694	
To: Accounting Department		Date Received	8/19/19X2
From: Receiving Department		Purchase Order No.	348
		Supplier	Croyden Gear Supply Co.
The following items were received.			
Description		Quantity	Condition
142 JX J-Type Gear Boxes		200	*Good*
142 JY Gear Box Brackets		400	*Good*
		Received by	*S. B. Franklin*

FIGURE 11-11
A RECEIVING REPORT

The flow of documents in the acquisition of goods is depicted as follows:

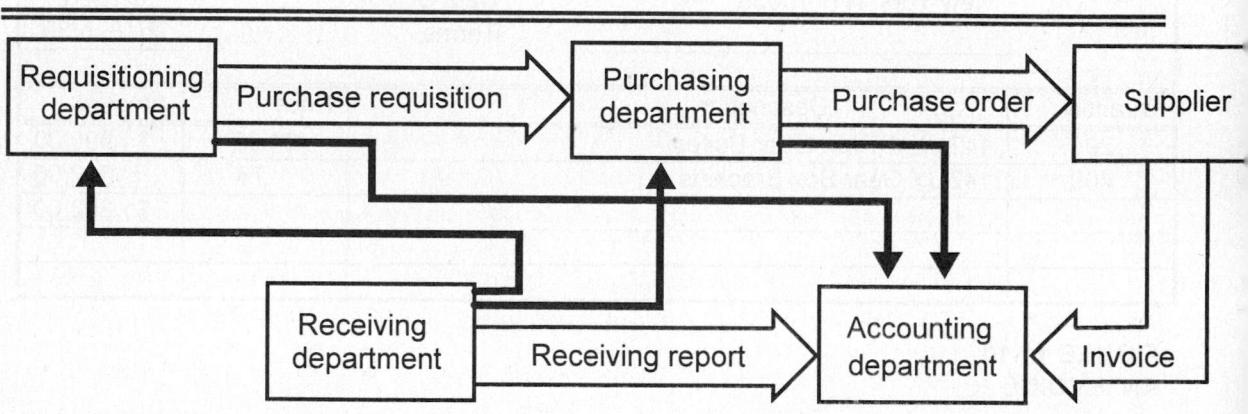

FIGURE 11-12
FLOW OF DOCUMENTS

The large arrows represent the transfer of the original documents; the single lines show the transfer of copies of the various documents.

VERIFICATION OF THE ACCURACY OF INVOICES AND APPROVAL OF PAYMENT

The accounting department receives copies of all the source documents relating to each specific purchase--the purchase requisition, purchase order, purchase invoice, and receiving report. Accounting department personnel then perform the following verification procedures, after which the invoice is approved for entry into the accounting records and for payment:

1. Items on the purchase order are compared with those listed on the purchase requisition to verify that the goods ordered were properly requisitioned.

2. Items on the invoice are compared with those listed on the purchase order to verify that the goods shipped are the same as those ordered.

3. Items listed on the invoice are compared with those listed on the receiving report to verify that the goods billed by the supplier were actually received.

4. Additional verification is performed on the invoice to ensure that prices charged and credit terms are those agreed upon, and that computations and price extensions are accurate.

The Voucher

A document, called a **voucher** (Figure 11-13), is attached to each purchase order when it is received by the accounting department. As the other related documents (purchase requisition, receiving report, and invoice) are received, they too are attached to the voucher. A voucher typically contains the types of information shown in the sample voucher in Figure 11-13.

The voucher contains the following categories of information:

1. The name of the creditor, the date the voucher is prepared, and the last date on which payment can be made to obtain cash discounts, or the date on which payment is otherwise due.

2. General invoice data--such as the date of the invoice, payment terms, the amount of the invoice, and the net amount due after allowing for cash discounts, if any.

3. The initials of the person performing the verification steps and of the employee authorized to approve payment of the invoice.

4. Amounts to be debited to identified general ledger accounts by the accounting department and the total amount to be credited to Vouchers Payable.

5. Payment data identifying the date paid, the check number, and the amount of the check.

Every cash payment, including reimbursement of the petty cash fund, requires a voucher regardless of whether the payment is for services, merchandise, equipment, or a mortgage payment. Even the receipt of a bill that is to be paid immediately (such as a utility bill) must first be entered on a voucher. Probably the greatest benefit received from use of a voucher system is the assurance that every cash expenditure has been thoroughly reviewed and amounts verified before payment is made.

		VOUCHER NO.		341
	DATA COMPANY **NEW YORK, NEW YORK**			
Pay to:	Reardon Wholesale 224 W. Oak Phoenix, AZ 85042	Date Due Date		Sept. 1, 1992 Sept. 11, 1992
Date of Invoice	Sept. 1, 19X2	Invoice Amount		$2,147.80
Invoice Number	2163	Cash Discount		42.97
Payment Terms	2/10, n/30	Net Amount		2,104.83

Verification of:

	Approved by
Proper purchase requisition	R. S.
Quantities on purchase order with invoice	R. S.
Quantities on receiving report with invoice	R. S.
Prices on purchase order with invoice	R. S.
Credit terms in agreement with purchase order	R. S.
Invoice extensions and footings	R. S.
Approved for payment	J. Abren

Account Distribution	Amount
Advertising	
Freight-in	
Office Salaries	
Office Supplies	
Purchases	$2,147.80
Sales Salaries	
Utilities	
Miscellaneous Expense	
Total Vouchers Payable Credit	$2,147.80

Payment record
Date Paid __9/10/X2__   Check No. __260__   Amount $2,104.83

FIGURE 11-13
VOUCHER

THE VOUCHER REGISTER

After the voucher is prepared, it is recorded in a **voucher register,** a book of original entry that takes the place of the purchases journal. It is used in combination with a check register, which, under the voucher system, takes the place of the cash disbursements journal. The function of the check register is described later in this chapter. An example of a voucher register is shown in Figure 11-14.

Under the voucher system, a Vouchers Payable account replaces the Accounts Payable account. Every voucher is entered in the voucher register with a debit to various asset, expense, liability, or owners' equity accounts and a credit to Vouchers Payable. All information in the voucher register is entered from the voucher at the time it is approved for recording, with the exception of the payment information, which is entered as each voucher is paid.

The posting of the voucher register follows the same general procedures used to post to the other special journals. Columns are totaled and crossfooted at the end of the month to verify the equality of debits and credits. The total of all debit columns, including the Other Debits column, must equal the total of the Vouchers Payable column. The total of each column, with the exception of the Other Debits column, is posted as a debit or credit to the appropriate account listed in the column heading. Evidence of the posting is indicated by placing the general ledger account number in parentheses just below the column total. Entries in the Other Debits column are posted individually as debits to the account listed, and the account number is entered in the Posting Reference column.

VOUCHER REGISTER

Date 19X2	Voucher No.	Payee	Payment Date	Check No.	Vouchers Payable Credit	Purchases Debit	Freight-in Debit	Advertising Debit	Sales Salaries Debit	Office Salaries Debit	Other Debits Account	P/R	Amount
Sept. 1	341	Reardon Wholesale	9/10	260	2,147.80	2,147.80							
1	342	Daly Freight Co.	9/3	251	122.50		122.50						
4	343	Haried Insurance Co.	9/5	253	347.80						Prepaid Insurance	136	347.80
6	344	Acme Office Supply	9/12	263	89.40						Office Supp. on Hand	124	89.40
6	345	The Leader	9/11	261	138.00			138.00					
7	346	Doug Johnson	9/7	256	236.50				236.50				
7	347	Rick Burdick	9/7	257	149.30					149.30			
7	348	Chuck Myler	9/7	258	220.00				220.00				
8	349	Zylon Equipment Co.	9/20	284	370.00						Office Equipment	158	370.00

The middle part of the statement is deleted for this illustration.

Date 19X2	Voucher No.	Payee	Payment Date	Check No.	Vouchers Payable Credit	Purchases Debit	Freight-in Debit	Advertising Debit	Sales Salaries Debit	Office Salaries Debit	Other Debits Account	P/R	Amount
30	382	United Bank	9/30	349	2,060.00						Notes Payable	210	2,000.00
											Interest Expense	535	60.00
30	383	Turner Supply Co.			896.22	896.22							
30	384	Adventure Travel	9/30	350	384.50						Travel Expense	574	384.50
30	385	The Leader			74.90			74.90					
					18,249.24	6,483.94	286.89	399.40	1,839.42	597.20			8,642.39
					(202)	(533)	(520)	(504)	(562)	(572)			(x)

FIGURE 11-14
A VOUCHER REGISTER

The Unpaid Vouchers File

Some vouchers, particularly those prepared for the payment of ongoing expenses–such as sales salaries, office salaries, and utilities – are often paid on the date they are recorded in the voucher register. With other payments, however, there may be a time lag between the receipt of an invoice and its due date. In those cases, the voucher is prepared and filed in an *unpaid vouchers file*. To protect the company's credit rating and to ensure the payment of invoices in time to obtain cash discounts, the vouchers are filed under the dates on which payment is due. The unpaid vouchers file constitutes a subsidiary ledger of vouchers payable and, under a voucher system, takes the place of the accounts payable subsidiary ledger. The elimination of the accounts payable subsidiary ledger often results in a considerable cost savings to the business. At the end of the month, after month-end posting has taken place, the total of all vouchers in the unpaid vouchers file should be equal to the balance in the Vouchers Payable account in the general ledger.

THE CHECK REGISTER

On each business day, the vouchers in the unpaid vouchers file under that date are removed and sent to the employee authorized to approve vouchers for payment. The employee reviews the vouchers to ensure that all verification steps have been completed, initials the voucher to signify approval for payment, prepares a check, fills in the payment-record section of the voucher, and forwards the check and voucher to the person authorized to sign checks, usually the company's treasurer. The treasurer then reviews the voucher for proper authorization of payment, signs the check and mails it to the creditor, and sends the voucher to the accounting department.

When the voucher is received by the accounting department, an entry is made in the Payment column of the voucher register to indicate that the voucher has been paid. The check is then recorded in a **check register** (Figure 11-15), which serves as a record of all cash disbursements, and the paid voucher is filed in numerical order in a *paid vouchers file*.

Because checks are written only in payment of specific vouchers, every check drawn is recorded as a debit to Vouchers Payable and a credit to Cash, with the exception of cases where a check is drawn in payment of a voucher on which a cash discount is taken. In those cases, the entry in the check register results in a debit to Vouchers Payable for the gross amount, a credit to Purchase Discounts for the discount, and a credit to Cash for the net amount paid. At the end of the month, the columns of the check register are footed and crossfooted, and the column totals are posted to the general ledger accounts specified by the column headings. As with the posting of other special journals, the general ledger account numbers are written in parentheses at the bottom of each column to indicate that the total has been posted.

After the voucher register and check register have been posted, the general ledger Vouchers Payable account has a balance of $971.12.

Vouchers Payable

9/30 C12	18,629.90	9/1 Balance (assumed)	1,351.78
		9/30 VR17	18,249.24
		9/30 Balance	971.12

Reference to the voucher register and vouchers in the unpaid vouchers file shows that there are two unpaid vouchers on September 30 as follows:

Payee	Amount
Turner Supply Co.	$896.22
The Leader	74.90
Total	$971.12

Thus, the list of unpaid vouchers reconciles with the balance in the Vouchers Payable account as of September 30.

CHECK REGISTER							Page 12
Date 19X2	Check No.	Payee	Voucher No.	Vouchers Payable Debit	Purchases Discounts Credit	Cash Credit	
Sept. 3	251	Daly Freight Co.	342	122.50		122.50	
5	253	Haried Insurance	343	347.80		347.80	
5	254	Reardon Wholesale	335	1,246.00	24.92	1,221.08	
6	255	Batho Company	334	1,322.80	26.46	1,296.34	
7	256	Doug Johnson	346	236.50		236.50	
		Middle part of the register is deleted for illustration					
30	349	United Bank	382	2,060.00		2,060.00	
30	350	Adventure Travel	384	384.50		384.50	
				18,629.90	193.48	18,436.42	
				(202)	(534)	(101)	

FIGURE 11-15
A CHECK REGISTER

PRACTICE ACTIVITY 11-3

Collins Company completed the following transactions during February 19X2. Collins uses a voucher system and records merchandise purchases using the gross invoice method.

Feb. 4   Prepared voucher No. 104 payable to Sebac Co. for merchandise purchased, $485; invoice dated February 3; terms 2/10, n/60.

6   Prepared voucher No. 105 payable to High Country Realty for February rent, $1,600.

10   Prepared voucher No. 106 payable to Drummond Company for office equipment, $2,550; invoice dated February 9; terms, n/20.

10   Prepared voucher No. 107 for employee wages, $1,480.

11   Issued check No. 346 to payroll bank account in payment of voucher No. 107.

13   Issued check No. 347 in payment of voucher No. 104.

16   Issued check No. 348 in payment of voucher No. 105.

17   Prepared voucher No. 108 payable to Brock Company for merchandise purchased, $1,764; invoice dated February 16; terms 2/10, n/30.

20   Prepared voucher No. 109 payable to Gothic Press for advertising $710; invoice dated February 16; terms, n/30.

20   Prepared voucher No. 110 payable to Southern Power Company, $327 for monthly utility bill.

23   Issued check No. 349 in payment of voucher No. 110.

24   Prepared voucher No. 111 for employee wages, $1,810.

24   Issued check No. 350 to payroll bank account in payment of voucher No. 111.

26   Issued check No. 351 in payment of voucher No. 108.

27   Prepared voucher No. 112 payable to Brown Company for merchandise purchased, $931; invoice dated February 25; terms, 2/10, n/30.

27   Issued check No. 352 in payment of voucher No. 106.

Required:

A. Enter the transactions in the voucher and check register given on the next page. Set up separate accounts for Purchases, Wages Expense, and Utilities Expense.

B. Foot the voucher register and check register, and post the appropriate amounts from both registers to the Vouchers Payable general ledger account (No. 222).

C. Reconcile the Vouchers Payable general ledger account balance with the unpaid vouchers file at the end of February. No vouchers payable were outstanding at the end of January.

Part B.

Vouchers Payable   222

Part C.

Voucher No.	Payee	Amount

Part A.

VOUCHER REGISTER

Page 10

Date 19X2	Voucher No.	Payee	Payment Date	Payment Check No.	Vouchers Payable Credit	Pur-chases Debit	Wages Debit	Utilities Debit	Other Debits Account	Other Debits P/R	Other Debits Amount

CHECK REGISTER

Page 9

Date 19X2	Check No.	Payee	Voucher No.	Vouchers Payable Debit	Purchases Discounts Credit	Cash Credit

SOLUTIONS TO PRACTICE ACTIVITIES

PRACTICE ACTIVITY 11-1

Part A. The March 1 balance in the Accounts Receivable control account should be equal to the sum of the March 1 balances in the subsidiary ledger.

	Balance
C. Furrillo	$ 820
G. Hodges	360
C. Labine	180
J. Robinson	425
D. Snider	670
	$2,455

Parts C and D.

General Journal				Page 1
Date	Explanation	Post. Ref.	Debit	Credit
	Accounts Receivable		2,045	
	Sales			2,045
	$160 + $460 + $740 + $475 + $210			
	Cash		3,230	
	Accounts Receivable			3,230
	$780 + $360 + $840 + $480 + $770			

Parts B, C, D and E.

General Ledger

Accounts Receivable

3/1	2,455	Cash Receipts	3,230
Sales	2,045		
3/31	1,270		

Subsidiary Ledger

C. Furrillo

3/1 Bal.	820	CR	780
Sales	160		—
3/31	200		

G. Hodges

3/1 Bal.	360	CR	360
Sales	460		—
3/31	460		

C. Labine

3/1 Bal.	180	CR	840
Sales	740		—
3/31	80		

J. Robinson

3/1 Bal.	425	CR	480
Sales	475		—
3/31	420		

D. Snider

3/1 Bal.	670	CR	770
Sales	210		—
3/31	110		

Part F.

	Balance
C. Furrillo	$ 200
G. Hodges	460
C. Labine	80
J. Robinson	420
D. Snider	110
Total	$1,270

PRACTICE ACTIVITY 11-2

Part A.

	General Journal				**Page 1**
Date	Explanation	Post. Ref.	Debit		Credit
Aug. 21	Plant and Equipment	210	8,000		
	Notes Payable	320			8,000
	Purchased equipment by issuing a 14%				
	note payable.				

		Sales Journal		**Page 1**
Date	Invoice No.	Account Debited	Post. Ref.	Amount
Aug. 9	201	B. Murray	√	500
13	202	P. Hills	√	1,500
				2,000
				(110/500)

	Purchases Journal			**Page 1**
Date	Account Credited	Terms	Post. Ref.	Amount
Aug. 2	Sterling Co.	2/10,n30	√	1,800
17	Miller Co.	n/30	√	1,000
				2,800
				(600/300)

	Cash Receipts Journal						**Page 1**
			Debits		Credits		
Date	Account Credited	Post. Ref.	Cash	Sales Discounts	Sales	Accts. Receiv.	Other Accounts
Aug. 3	P. Hills	√	600			600	
14	R. Kennison	√	300			300	
19	Sales		500		500		
22	Notes Payable	320	10,000				10,000
23	C. Clark	√	1,000			1,000	
			12,400		500	1,900	10,000
			(100)		(500)	(110)	(x)

Cash Disbursements Journal							Page 1
			Debits			Credits	
Date	Account Debited	Post. Ref.	Other Accounts	Accounts Payable	Purchases	Cash	Purch. Discounts
Aug. 6	Sterling Co.	√		1,000		1,000	
12	Sterling Co.	√		1,800		1,764	36
15	Royal, Inc.	√		2,000		2,000	
29	Purchases				100	100	
30	Notes Payable	320	1,000			1,000	
			1,000	4,800	100	5,864	36
			(x)	(300)	(600)	(100)	(610)

Part B.

General Ledger Accounts

	Cash			100
8/1 Bal.	7,500	8/31CD1	5,864	
8/31 CR1	12,400			
8/31 Bal.	14,036			

	Accounts Receivable			110
8/1 Bal.	4,100	8/31 CR1	1,900	
8/31 SJ1	2,000			
8/31 Bal.	4,200			

	Merchandise Inventory		135
8/1 Bal.	25,000		

	Plant and Equipment		210
8/1 Bal.	72,000		
8/31 GJ1	8,000		
8/31 Bal.	80,000		

	Accounts Payable			300
8/31 CD1	4,800	8/1 Bal.	5,300	
		8/31 P1	2,800	
		8/31 Bal.	3,300	

	Notes Payable			320
8/30 CD1	1,000	8/1 Bal.	45,000	
		8/21 GJ1	8,000	
		8/31 CD1	10,000	
		8/31 Bal.	62,000	

	Capital Stock		400
		8/1 Bal.	62,000

	Sales		500
		8/1 Bal.	10,300
		8/31 S1	2,000
		8/31 CR1	500
		8/31 Bal.	12,800

	Sales Discount		510
8/1 Bal.	200		

	Sales Returns and Allowances		520
8/1 Bal.	100		

	Purchases		600
8/1 Bal.	8,000		
8/31 P1	2,800		
8/31 CD1	100		
8/31 Bal.	10,900		

	Purchases Discounts		610
		8/1 Bal.	300
		8/31 CD1	36
		8/31 Bal.	336

Selling and Administrative Expenses			700
8/1 Bal.	6,000		

Accounts Receivable Subsidiary Ledger

C. Clark					P. Hills			
8/1 Bal.	1,400	8/23 CR1	1,000		8/1 Bal.	600	8/3 CR1	600
8/31 Bal.	400				8/13 S1	1,500		
					8/31 Bal.	1,500		

R. Kennison					B. Murray			
8/1 Bal.	900	8/14 CR1	300		8/1 Bal.	1,200		
8/31 Bal.	600				8/9 S1	500		
					8/31 Bal.	1,700		

Accounts Payable Subsidiary Ledger

Miller Company					Royal, Inc.			
		8/1 Bal.	800		8/15 CD1	2,000	8/1 Bal.	3,500
		8/17 P1	1,000				8/31 Bal.	1,500
		8/31 Bal.	1,800					

Sterling Company			
8/6 CD1	1,000	8/1 Bal.	1,000
8/12 CD1	1,800	8/17 P1	1,800
		8/31 Bal.	-0-

Part C.

Accounts Receivable	
C. Clark	$ 400
P. Hills	1,500
R. Kennison	600
B. Murray	1,700
Total	$4,200

Accounts Payable	
Miller Company	$1,800
Royal, Inc.	1,500
Sterling Co.	-0-
Total	$3,300

Part D.

NEW RIVER COMPANY Unadjusted Trial Balance August 31, 19X2			
Acct. No.	Account Title	Account Balance	
		Debit	Credit
100	Cash	$ 14,036	
110	Accounts Receivable	4,200	
135	Merchandise Inventory	25,000	
210	Plant and Equipment	80,000	
300	Accounts Payable		$ 3,300
320	Notes Payable		62,000
400	Capital Stock		62,000
500	Sales		12,800
510	Sales Discounts	200	
520	Sales Returns and Allowances	100	
600	Purchases	10,900	
610	Purchases Discounts		336
700	Selling and Administrative Exp.	6,000	
	Totals	$140,436	$140,436

PRACTICE ACTIVITY 11-3

Part B.

Vouchers Payable   222

Feb.	28	C9	10,016.00	Feb.	1	Balance	-0-
					28	VR10	11,657.00
					28	Balance	1,641.00

Part C.

Voucher No.	Payee	Amount
109	Gothic Press	$ 710.00
110	Brown Company	931.00
Total		$1,641.00

PART A.

VOUCHER REGISTER
Page 10

Date 19X2	Voucher No.	Payee	Payment Date	Check No.	Vouchers Payable Credit	Purchases Debit	Wages Debit	Utilities Debit	Other Debits Account	P/R	Other Debits Amount
Feb. 4	104	Sebac Company	2/13	347	485	485					
6	105	High Country Realty	2/16	348	1,600				Rent Expense		1,600
10	106	Drummond Company	2/27	352	2,550				Office Equipment		2,550
10	107	Payroll	2/11	346	1,480		1,480				
17	108	Brock Company	2/26	351	1,764	1,764					
20	109	Gothic Press			710				Advertising Expense		710
20	110	Southern Power Co.	2/23	349	327			327			
24	111	Payroll	2/24	350	1,810		1,810				
27	112	Brown Company			931	931					
					11,657	3,180	3290	327			4,860
					(222)						

CHECK REGISTER
Page 9

Date 19X2	Check No.	Payee	Voucher No.	Vouchers Payable Debit	Purchases Discounts Credit	Cash Credit
Feb. 11	346	Payroll	107	1,480.00		1,480.00
13	347	Sebac Company	104	485.00	9.70	475.30
16	348	High Country Realty	105	1,600.00		1,600.00
23	349	Southern Power Co.	110	327.00		327.00
24	350	Payroll	111	1,810.00		1,810.00
26	351	Brock Company	108	1,764.00	35.28	1,728.72
27	352	Drummond Company	106	2,550.00		2,550.00
				10,016.00	44.98	9,971.02
				(222)		

CHAPTER 12

Inventory
Costing Methods

Contents

- Chapter Overview and Objectives
- Determining the Inventory on Hand
- Allocation of Inventory Cost between Ending Inventory and Cost of Goods Sold
- Periodic Inventory System
  - Specific Identification Method
  - First-in, First-out (FIFO) Method
  - Last-in, First-out (LIFO) Method
  - Weighted Average Method
- Comparison of Costing Methods
- Which Method to Select?
- Consistency in Using a Costing Method
- The Lower of Cost or Market Rule
- Net Realizable Value
- Perpetual Inventory Systems
  - Specific Identification Method
  - First-in, First-out Method
  - Last-in, First-out Method
  - Moving Average Method
- Comparison of the Perpetual and Periodic Inventory Systems

CHAPTER OVERVIEW AND OBJECTIVES

This chapter describes various methods used to assign cost to ending inventory and cost of goods sold. When this chapter is completed, you will be able to:

1. Determine when the title to inventory transfers.
2. Allocate the total inventory cost between ending inventory and cost of goods sold using four different costing methods when the periodic inventory system is used.
3. Determine inventory values by applying the lower of cost or market rule.
4. Compute the net realizable value of an inventory item.

5.   Allocate the total inventory cost between ending inventory and cost of goods sold using four different costing methods when the perpetual inventory system is used.

The term *inventory* is used to describe the tangible assets of a firm that (1) are held for sale in the normal course of business, (2) are in the process of being produced for sale, but not yet completed, or (3) are materials being held for future use in producing goods or services. The accounts used to record inventory costs depend upon the firm's normal activity:

- For a merchandising firm, the term *merchandise inventory* is used to designate all goods owned and held for future sale to the firm's customers in the normal course of business.

- For a manufacturing firm, the term *finished goods inventory* designates units that are completed and ready for sale, the term *raw materials inventory* designates materials and component parts that are to be used in the manufacturing process, and the term *work-in-process inventory* refers to units that are in the course of production, but not yet completed.

This chapter begins with a discussion of how to identify the units to be included in inventory. The perpetual and periodic inventory systems described and illustrated in Chapters 9 and 10 assumed that the cost per unit was the same for both the beginning inventory and all purchases made during the year. However, in today's markets, the prices of most goods change frequently during the accounting period. When prices change, the firm is confronted with an accounting problem of determining what portion of the total cost of goods available for sale should be assigned to ending inventory and what portion to cost of goods sold. This chapter considers four alternative methods used to assign the cost of goods available for sale to ending inventory and cost of goods sold when prices are changing.

Although cost is the primary basis for measuring inventory values, there are circumstances under which it is appropriate to value inventory at less than its historical cost. Several of these situations are discussed in this chapter. In addition, the effects of inventory errors on the company's financial statements are discussed. The chapter concludes with a discussion of two methods that are used to estimate ending inventory values.

DETERMINING THE INVENTORY ON HAND
TAKING A PHYSICAL INVENTORY

When a periodic inventory system is used, the cost of inventory purchased during the period is recorded in the Purchases account, as seen in Chapter 10. The balance in the Merchandise Inventory account is the cost of the inventory on hand at the beginning of the period. To determine the cost of the ending inventory, the units on hand must be counted and priced. The ending inventory is then reported as a current asset in the balance sheet. It is also deducted from the cost of goods available for sale in the income statement to determine the cost of goods sold. Although the inventory on hand and the cost of goods sold balances are available in the accounts when a perpetual inventory system is used, a physical inventory is also taken at least once a year to verify the balances reported.

Before conducting the actual physical count of units on hand, commonly referred to as *taking an inventory,* and pricing the units, the entire process must be carefully planned. The procedures established for the counting process must be supervised to ensure that all units owned by the firm are properly counted. Although the specific details vary from firm to firm, the following is a typical approach:

1. A prenumbered inventory ticket is issued for each type of item in stock and distributed to each department. The ticket provides space to record (a) a description or code number of the item, (b) the number of units counted, (c) the initials of the person making the count, and (d) the initials of the person verifying the count.
2. An employee counts the units, enters the number of units on hand on the inventory ticket, and initials the ticket to identify the person performing the count. The inventory ticket is then attached to the units counted.
3. A supervisor recounts a sufficient number of items to verify the recorded count and initials the inventory ticket.
4. A supervisor examines the inventory in each department to be sure that an inventory ticket has been attached to all items. Any group of like items without a ticket attached has not been counted.
5. The inventory tickets are collected and forwarded to the accounting department, where the prenumbered tickets are all accounted for. The information on the inventory tickets is summarized on an inventory summary sheet.
6. The unit cost of each individual item in stock is determined from purchase invoices or other supplementary records.
7. The number of units of the various individual items is multiplied by their unit cost and added together to compute the total ending inventory value.

Because conducting the physical count is often difficult, this step is frequently performed outside of business hours.

TRANSFER OF OWNERSHIP

During an inventory count, care must be exercised to ensure that all goods legally owned by the firm on the inventory date are counted and included in the ending inventory, regardless of where the inventory is located. Transfer of ownership normally depends on the terms of the shipment. When goods are sold *FOB (free on board) shipping point,* freight is paid by the buyer. Title ordinarily transfers when the goods are delivered to the transportation company by the seller. If the terms are *FOB destination*, the seller is responsible for paying the freight, and title usually does not transfer until delivery is made to the buyer.

From an accounting point of view, the seller should record a sale and the buyer should record a purchase when title to the goods transfers. In practice, however, sales are normally recorded when shipment is made and purchases are recorded when the inventory is received irrespective of the shipping terms.

To increase the accuracy of the financial statements at year-end, purchases and sales invoices for both the last week or two of the current accounting period and the first week or two of the next period should be reviewed to determine whether there were units in transit on the date of the physical inventory count that should be included with the units counted. For example, goods purchased with the terms FOB shipping point and in transit at year-end should be recorded as a purchase and included in the physical count, even though they were not physically there when the actual count was made. Although exclusion of this inventory will have no effect on net income (purchases, goods available for sale, and ending inventory will each be understated by an equal amount), total assets and total liabilities will each be understated if the purchase is not recorded. Similarly, goods sold with the terms FOB destination should be included in the seller's ending inventory if in transit at year-end, since title to the goods has not transferred. The sale and related cost of goods sold are transactions to be recorded in the succeeding period.

In some cases, the seller may have received orders for goods, but shipment may not have been made. In such situations, a sale is *not* recorded because the revenue has not been earned. However, an exception is made when (1) an order for goods has been received, (2) the goods are ready for shipment, and (3) the buyer has requested that the goods be held for later delivery. Such items should be excluded from the seller's inventory and included in the buyer's inventory. In some cases, however, it may not be clear whether title has transferred. The accountant must then use his or her best judgment to assess when the parties to the transaction intended the title to transfer.

GOODS ON CONSIGNMENT

Another problem sometimes encountered in taking an inventory is the treatment of goods held on *consignment*. A consignment is a marketing arrangement whereby a business (the *consignor*) ships goods to a dealer (*the consignee*) who agrees to sell the goods for a commission. Although a physical transfer of goods has taken place, title to the goods remains with the consignor. It does not transfer.

Since title to the goods has not transferred, the shipment of consigned goods is not considered a sale/purchase transaction. Therefore, goods out on consignment are part of the consignor's inventory, even though physical possession of the goods is with the consignee. The goods are excluded from the consignee's inventory since they remain the consignor's property.

PRACTICE ACTIVITY 12-1

Complete the following statements by entering a word or words in the blank space(s) that will make the statement a valid statement.

1. Goods in transit at year-end should be included in the inventory of the _____ if terms of the sale were FOB shipping point.

2. Goods shipped from Evans Co. to Delta Co. on consignment should be included in the inventory of _____ Co. Evans Co. is called the _____.

3. When the terms are _____, title to the goods usually remains with the seller until the goods are delivered to the buyer.

4. FOB destination is a shipping term that means the _____ pays the freight charges.

ALLOCATION OF INVENTORY COST BETWEEN ENDING INVENTORY AND COST OF GOODS SOLD

In Chapter 6, it was assumed that the unit cost was the same for all units acquired. However, units purchased on different dates often have different unit costs. When this happens, management is confronted with the problem of selecting the unit costs to be matched against sales. Assume that the following purchases of the same model of personal computer were made:

January 15	$480
February 10	560
March 8	600

If one unit is sold for $900 on March 25, which unit cost is charged to cost of goods sold to be matched against the revenue of $900? Whichever unit is selected means that the other two units will be reported as the inventory on hand. Gross profit could vary by as much as $120, depending on which item is assumed sold.

To implement the matching principle, the allocation of total inventory cost between ending merchandise inventory and cost of goods sold is based on some cost-flow assumption. The flow of inventory cost through a firm refers to the assignment of cost to the units that were sold and to those on hand. Intuitively, we may expect to be able to match precisely the identified cost of specific units with the revenues derived from their sale. However, there are limited cases in which this is practical. These include situations in which each item in inventory is unique, such as automobiles on a car dealer's lot and works of art held by an art gallery. In many instances, it is impossible, or it may not be practical because of the clerical cost involved, to identify each unit in inventory -with its original cost. For example, the cost of a gallon of gasoline sold cannot be identified with its original cost because a new delivery of gasoline mixes with the gallons already in the storage tank. Other examples include units of inventory that are identical, such as textbooks at the campus bookstore and hand tools at a hardware store. Therefore, an assumed flow of cost is necessary to implement the matching principle when prices are changing.

The flow of cost assumed does not have to conform to the actual physical movement of goods. A firm may rotate its stock so that the oldest units are sold first. However, in determining the cost of units sold, the cost of the most recent purchases may be assigned to cost of goods sold. All that generally accepted accounting principles require is that the method selected be used consistently and that the cost allocation be systematic and rational. Although a switch in cost-flow assumption may occur occasionally, such a change is infrequent in the life of most firms.

Four methods are commonly used to allocate cost: (1) specific identification; (2) first-in, first-out (FIFO); (3) last-in, first-out (LIFO); and (4) average cost. The average cost method is called the weighted average method when a periodic inventory system is used. It is called the moving average method when a perpetual system is used. All four methods are considered acceptable for accounting purposes, but when prices are changing, each will produce different ending inventory and cost of goods sold amounts. LIFO, FIFO, and average cost are the most commonly used methods, as shown by a survey of 600 companies, reported in Figure 12-1. As noted in Figure 12-1, a company does not have to use a single inventory method for each type of inventory item.

Costing Method	Number
FIFO	379
LIFO	396
Average cost	213
Other	50
Total	1,038

The total exceeds 600 companies because a company may adopt a different method for different types of inventory held.

Source: Accounting Trends and Techniques, 1989 edition (New York: AICPA, 1989).

FIGURE 12-1
INVENTORY COST METHODS USED BY 600 COMPANIES

To illustrate the effects of the four inventory costing methods on the allocation of the total cost of goods available for sale to ending inventory and cost of goods sold, the inventory record in Figure 12-2 of a computer game will be assumed for the fiscal period.

Date		Number of Units	Unit Cost	Total Costs
Jan. 1	Beginning merchandise inventory	20	$10	$200.00
	Purchases made during the current period:			
April 15	Purchase	24	11	$264.00
July 7	Purchase	30	12	360.00
	Total purchases	54		624.00
	Goods available for sale	74		824.00
Dec. 31	Ending merchandise inventory	38		?
	Sales made during the current period	36*		$?
? Dollar amount will be computed later				
*Sales made during the current period:		Units		
April 20 Sales		16		
August 12 Sales		20		
Total unit sales		36		

FIGURE 12-2
INVENTORY RECORD FOR A COMPUTER GAME

PERIODIC INVENTORY SYSTEM

With a periodic inventory system, the number of units on hand at the end of the period must be determined by taking a physical inventory. In this illustration, it is assumed that 38 units were counted on December 31. The total cost of these units must then be determined from invoices or other inventory records. When prices are changing, the cost assigned to the ending inventory depends on the cost flow assumption that the firm adopts. Once the cost of the ending inventory is determined, the cost of goods sold is computed by deducting the ending inventory cost from the cost of goods available for sale of $824.

SPECIFIC IDENTIFICATION METHOD

The **specific identification method** requires that the cost of each unit sold and each unit on hand be identified with a particular purchase invoice. To do this, the firm must use some form of identification such as serial numbers.

To illustrate, assume that the 38 units in the ending inventory can be separately identified as 20 units from the July 7 purchase and 18 units from the beginning inventory. Costs are assigned as follows:

Cost of goods available for sale --74 units $824.00
Less: Cost of 38 units in the ending merchandise inventory

Date	Unit	Unit Cost	Total Cost
1/1	18	$10	$180.00
7/7	20	12	240.00

Cost of ending merchandise inventory--38 units   420.00
Cost of goods sold--36 units $404.00

As can be seen, the cost of goods sold is a residual amount, but the $404 figure can be verified as follows:

Cost of goods sold -- 36 units
  2 units from the beginning inventory at $10 per unit $ 20.00
24 units from the April 15 purchase at $11 per unit   264.00
10 units from the July 7 purchase at $12 per unit   120.00
Total cost of goods sold $404.00

Using the amounts computed for the specific identification method, the cost allocation procedure is diagrammed as follows.

	Cost of beginning				Cost of ending	
$200	inventory				inventory	$420
			Cost of goods			
	+	=	available	=	+	
			for sale			
					Cost of goods	
					sold	
624	Cost of purchases					404
$824		=	$824	=		$824

Under a periodic inventory system, the ending inventory ($420) is reported as a current asset in the balance sheet and as a deduction from cost of goods available for sale in the income statement. As shown in Chapter 10, these amounts may be entered in the ledger accounts as part of the closing or adjusting process. Recall that Merchandise Inventory is credited for $200 to remove the beginning inventory balance from the account and Merchandise Inventory is debited for $420 to record the ending inventory. These procedures are the same for the three other costing methods, but the amounts will vary with the costing method used.

FIRST-IN, FIRST-OUT (FIFO) METHOD

The *FIFO method* of determining the cost of goods sold is based on the assumption that the first units acquired (first-in) are the first units sold (first-out). In other words, the cost of the oldest units in the inventory is charged to the cost of goods sold to be matched against revenue. Therefore, the cost of the units on hand is that of the most recent units purchased. Once again, this is a cost flow assumption and need not represent the actual physical movement of goods.

It should be emphasized that the name of the inventory method, for example, FIFO, refers to the flow of cost and the determination of cost of goods sold and not to the ending inventory. That is, under FIFO, the cost of goods sold is made up of the beginning inventory and the first units purchased, while the ending inventory is made up of the last units purchased.

In the periodic inventory system, the ending inventory is computed first and is subtracted from the cost of goods available for sale to compute the cost of goods sold as follows:

Cost of goods available for sale--74 units				$824.00
Less: Cost of 38 units in the ending merchandise inventory				
Date	**Unit**	**Unit Cost**	**Total Cost**	
7/7	30	$12	$360.00	
4/15	8	11	88.00	
Cost of ending merchandise inventory--38 units				448.00
Cost of goods sold--36 units				$376.00

Note that the 38 units in the ending inventory are associated with the last two purchases. In a periodic inventory system, the cost of goods sold is a residual amount, but in this example, it can be verified as follows.

Cost of goods sold -- 36 units	
20 units from the beginning inventory at $10 per unit	$200.00
16 units from the April 15 purchase at $11 per unit	176.00
Total cost of goods sold	$376.00

The cost of the 36 units sold this period consists of the 20 units from the beginning inventory and 16 units from the first purchase made on April 15. The other eight units from the April 15 purchase were assumed to be on hand as of December 31.

LAST-IN, FIRST-OUT (LIFO) METHOD

Under the *LIFO method*, the last units purchased (last-in) are assumed to be the first units sold (first-out). Consequently, the costs of the most recent purchases are matched with sales revenue in the income statement. The cost of the ending inventory consists of the costs of the beginning inventory and the earliest purchases. The cost allocation is:

Cost of goods available for sale--74 units				$824.00
Less: Cost of 38 units in the ending merchandise inventory				
Date	**Unit**	**Unit Cost**	**Total Cost**	
1/1	20	$10	$200.00	
4/15	18	11	198.00	
Cost of ending merchandise inventory--38 units				398.00
Cost of goods sold--36 units				$426.00

The cost of goods sold can be verified as follows:

Cost of goods sold -- 36 units	
30 units from the July 7 purchase at $12 per unit	$360.00
6 units from the April 15 purchase at $11 per unit	66.00
Total cost of goods sold	$426.00

Note that when the LIFO method is used with a periodic inventory system, no attempt is made to compare the dates of sales with those of purchases. Units on hand at the end of the period are assigned the cost of the beginning inventory and the earliest purchases. Thus, units sold during the period are assigned the cost of the most recent purchases. In other words, it is possible to expense the cost of units sold, even though they were not on hand at the time of sale. For example, in applying the LIFO method, if a purchase had been made after August 12 (the date of the last sale), those units would be considered sold first, when calculating cost of goods sold at the end of the period.

WEIGHTED AVERAGE METHOD

Under the **weighted average method**, an average cost per unit is computed by dividing the total cost of goods available for sale, including the cost of the beginning inventory and all purchases made during the accounting period, by the total number of units available for sale. This weighted average is then multiplied by the number of units on hand to determine the cost of the ending inventory as follows:

$$\frac{\text{Cost of goods available for sale}}{\text{Number of units available for sale}} = \frac{\$824.00}{74 \text{ units}} = \$11.14 \text{ per unit *}$$

*Rounded to the nearest cent.

Ending inventory = 38 units x $11.14 per unit = $423.32

The cost of goods sold is:

Cost of goods available for sale--74 units	$824.00
Less: Cost of ending merchandise inventory--38 units	423.32
Cost of goods sold--36 units	$400.68

The cost assigned to cost of goods sold is confirmed as follows:

36 units x $11.14 per unit = $401.04
(The difference is due to rounding the unit cost.)

The use of this method results in all units sold and on hand being priced at the average cost of $11.14 per unit.

PRACTICE ACTIVITY 12-2

The beginning inventory and the transactions related to the inventory of the Helmuth Company during March 19X2 are as follows:

		Units	Unit Cost	Total Cost
March 1	Beginning inventory	200	$10	$2,000
3	Purchase	300	14	4,200
8	Sale	220		
15	Purchase	100	18	1,800
22	Purchase	200	22	4,400
29	Sale	280		

The Helmuth Company uses the periodic inventory system.

Required:

Compute the cost of goods available for sale, the ending inventory, and the cost of goods sold for March 19X2, using each of the following inventory costing methods.
1. FIFO.
2. LIFO.
3. Weighted average.

4. Specific identification. The sale of March 8 was identified with the March 3 purchase, 100 units of the March 29 sales were identified with the beginning inventory, and the remainder was identified with the March 22 purchase.

	FIFO	LIFO	Weighted Average	Specific Identification

COMPARISON OF COSTING METHODS

The preceding sections examined the procedural aspects of each costing method. This section discusses the justifications, features, advantages, and disadvantages of each method. In doing so, the effects of each of the four methods on the firm's financial statements are compared, and the results are illustrated in Figure 12-3. It is assumed that the 36 units were sold for a total of $720, operating expenses totaled $180, and the average income tax rate was 30%. The sales and operating expenses are the same in all cases because the inventory method used does not affect those income statement items. The beginning inventory in each case was assumed to be 20 units costing a total of $200. In the next period, the beginning inventory value will vary, depending on the costing method selected, and it will be equal to the ending inventory computed in the current period.

Note that the computations in Figure 12-3 are based on the assumption that the unit cost increased steadily from $10 to $12 during the period. If the unit cost had not changed during the period, cost of goods sold, net income, and ending inventory values would be the same for all four methods. When costs change during a period, the costing method selected can have a significant effect on the firm's reported assets and net income figure. Even in this simple example, with increasing prices and only one inventory item held for sale, FIFO net income was almost 45% greater than the LIFO net income. However, keep in mind that all four methods are based on the cost concept. Although cost of goods sold and net income may vary between accounting periods (remember that sales revenue is unaffected by the cost method used), the total cost of goods sold and total net income reported over the life of the firm are the same using all four methods, because only the actual costs incurred for inventory can be expensed.

Periodic Inventory System

	Specific Identification		FIFO		LIFO		Weighted Average	
Sales--36 units		$720		$720		$720		$720
Beginning inventory	$200		$200		$200		$200	
Add: Purchases	624		624		624		624	
Goods available for sale	824		824		824		824	
Less: Ending inventory	420		448		398		423	
Cost of goods sold		404		376		426		401
Gross profit on sales		316		344		294		319
Less: Operating expenses		180		180		180		180
Income before taxes		136		164		114		139
Less: Income taxes--30%*		41		49		34		42
Net income		$ 95		$115		$ 80		$ 97
Ending inventory		$420		$448		$398		$423

*Income taxes are rounded to the nearest dollar.

FIGURE 12-3
COMPARISON OF FOUR COSTING METHODS

SPECIFIC IDENTIFICATION METHOD

Under the specific identification method, when a sale is made, the item sold is identified and the cost of that item is matched against revenues. Thus, the method is based on the actual physical flow of goods.

Use of this method is primarily limited to businesses that sell easily identified items with a high unit cost (e.g., automobile dealerships and jewelry stores). Most other firms find this method impractical because it is both costly and time-consuming. Another disadvantage of the method is that if the inventory units are identical and have different costs, it is possible for management to manipulate income by choosing to sell a unit with a low or a high cost.

FIRST-IN, FIRST-OUT METHOD

The FIFO method is widely used because it is easy to apply. When stock is rotated so that the oldest units are sold first, the method's cost flow assumption approximates the actual physical flow of goods. The method does not permit manipulation of income, since management is not free to pick the cost of a certain item to be matched with revenue. Instead, it must expense the oldest unit cost available for sale.

As can be seen in Figure 12-3, during periods of rising unit cost, this method results in reporting a lower cost of goods sold and higher net income than either the LIFO or the weighted average method. On the balance sheet, the ending inventory reflects the higher cost of the most recent purchases--a more realistic measure of the inventory's value than is provided by the other methods. However, during a period of declining unit cost, FIFO will produce the highest cost of goods sold, the lowest net income, and the lowest ending inventory values.

Many accountants argue that using FIFO during periods of rising prices results in an overstatement in real net income. To illustrate this point, consider the data used in our previous illustration.

January 1	Beginning inventory	20 units @ $10
April 15	Purchase	24 units @ $11
April 20	Sales	16 units @ $20
July 7	Purchase	30 units @ $12
August 12	Sales	20 units @ $20

On April 20, the firm sold 16 units for $20 per unit. Under FIFO, the company charged $10 per unit to cost of goods sold, which resulted in a gross profit of $10 per unit. However, these units were replaced on July 7 with units costing $12 each. Therefore, $2 of the gross profit per unit ($12 replacement cost less historical cost of $10) was used to replace the units sold, and only $8 per unit represents the distributable gross profit of the firm. Inclusion of the $2 in gross profit is considered misleading because it cannot be distributed to the owners or reinvested in other aspects of the business without reducing the firm's ability to replace units sold. For this reason, it is sometimes called "phantom profit" or "illusory profit." The same line of reasoning applies to the units sold on August 12, which, if prices continue to rise, must be replaced with higher cost units.

LAST-IN, FIRST-OUT METHOD

The basic assumption of the LIFO method is that the firm must maintain a certain level of inventory to operate. When inventory is sold, it must be replaced at its current replacement cost. Income is not considered earned unless the sales price exceeds the cost to replace the units sold. Although the cost of goods sold does not always equal the cost to replace the units sold, because of price changes after the sale, it is frequently argued that LIFO provides the best measure of net income because it matches the more recent costs with current revenues. Since prices have generally moved upward, the effect of this method is to produce (1) a higher cost of goods sold and (2) a lower net income than the other methods (see Figure 12-3).

However, balance sheet values soon become outdated under LIFO because the oldest unit costs remain in inventory. To illustrate, assume that during the next five years the unit cost increased to $20, and that in each year the firm sold the same number of units that were purchased. In this case, using the LIFO cost flow assumption, the cost of goods sold will be equal to the cost of the units purchased each year; the ending inventory each year will continue to be the 38 units at a total cost of $398. However, the cost to replace these units is now $760 (38 x $20). This understatement in the value of the inventory creates a problem in evaluating the working capital position of a firm. In addition, if the number of units on hand falls below the 38 units, there is a matching of old costs with current revenues, which distorts income in the year of the inventory decrease. To continue the illustration, assume that five years from now the sales price is $40 per unit and the unit cost is $20. If the number of units sold is greater than the number of units purchased in the fifth year, part of the beginning inventory is accounted for as sold. The gross profit per unit on current purchases and the beginning inventory purchased on April 15 are compared below:

	Current Purchases	Beginning Inventory
Sales price	$40	$40
Cost of goods sold	20	11
Gross profit	$20	$29

Inclusion of the $29 gross profit in the current period's income statement may distort comparison of the performance of the company to other periods. For this reason, a material effect on income from a reduction in the LIFO beginning inventory should be disclosed.

Another disadvantage of LIFO is that the possibility exists for management to manipulate net income by buying or not buying goods at the end of the period. If management wants to increase net income, for example, it could delay the purchase made on July 7 until the next fiscal period. In this case, the cost of the 36 units sold is:

24 units from the April 15 purchase at $11 per unit	$264.00
12 units from the beginning inventory at $10 per unit	120.00
Cost of goods sold	$384.00

Thus, under this assumption the cost of goods sold is $42 ($426 − $384) less than if the July 7 purchase is made. As a result, net income is $42 higher.

Note that in Figure 12-3 the income tax expense under LIFO is the lowest of the four methods ($34). Thus, although all four methods are acceptable for computing taxable income, using LIFO during periods of rising prices produces a tax benefit in the current period. The reduced cash outflow for taxes makes more cash available for use in the firm's operations. However, as noted earlier, only the actual cost incurred is deductible as an expense. Thus, if the beginning inventory is eventually sold or if prices decline, the total cost of goods sold will be lower and taxable income will be greater under LIFO. Over the life of the firm, however, these items will be the same for all four methods.

Despite the tax benefit, some firms have been reluctant to switch to LIFO because current tax law requires that if LIFO is used for tax purposes, it must also be used for financial reporting purposes.[1] This means that firms using LIFO must report lower earnings, and such a report may have an unfavorable effect on investors.

WEIGHTED AVERAGE METHOD

The weighted average cost method is usually justified because the method is simple to apply and is less subject to income manipulation. In applying this method, the average unit cost is affected by (1) the number of units and cost of units in the beginning inventory and (2) all purchases made during the year. As a result, the cost of goods sold, net income, and ending inventory amounts reported under the weighted average cost method fall between the extremes produced by FIFO and LIFO when prices are dropping or rising. Thus, the use of the weighted average cost method tends to smooth out net income and inventory values with neither the cost of goods sold nor the ending inventory reported at current values.

Since purchases made at the end of the year are included in the weighted average unit cost, it is possible for management to affect net income by making or delaying purchases at the end of the year. However, the impact is usually not significant because of the averaging effect. Although the average cost method is not used as frequently as FIFO and LIFO, it is sometimes employed when the inventory units involved are homogeneous in nature, and it is difficult to establish a physical-flow assumption. Examples of such inventory are grain in a grain elevator or gasoline in a storage tank. It is not possible to identify each unit with its original cost because a new delivery mixes with the units on hand. Remember, however, that although the physical flow is on an average basis, the owner may elect to use the FIFO or LIFO cost-flow assumption.

WHICH METHOD TO SELECT?

The selection of the cost method to use for a particular type of inventory depends upon many factors, including the effect on the firm's financial statements, income tax considerations, the information needs of management and statement users, and the clerical cost of applying the method. In practice, more than one of the methods may be considered appropriate in accounting for the same type of inventory. That is, generally accepted accounting principles do not prescribe the use of a specific costing method as being "best" for a particular set of inventory conditions. It is up to management and to the firm's accountant to decide which method both provides the most useful information to its statement users and best satisfies other needs as well.

---

[1] A company may use an inventory method other than LIFO in reports submitted as a supplement to, or as an explanation of, a primary presentation of financial income. For example, in a supplemental section of the annual report, management may discuss the effect of using the LIFO method instead of another accounting method. Prentice-Hall, Inc., Federal Taxes 2nd, 33, 264-33, 265.

CONSISTENCY IN USING A COSTING METHOD

Clearly, the inventory costing method selected can have a significant impact on the firm's reported net income and asset amounts. For this reason, the method used to assign cost to inventory and cost of goods sold should be disclosed in the financial statements.

Once a costing method has been selected, management cannot indiscriminately switch to another method. When alternative accounting methods or procedures are considered acceptable in a given situation, *the principle of consistency* requires that a firm apply the same method from one accounting period to the next. If switching accounting methods between periods were permitted, the accounting data produced in different accounting periods would be inconsistent and not comparable.

The consistency principle does not completely rule out changing to an acceptable alternative method, if the new method results in improved financial reporting. However, for tax purposes, a change in inventory costing methods, except a switch to LIFO, can only be made with the consent of the Internal Revenue Service. Generally, the approval to switch is automatic. A firm can switch to LIFO by merely using the method in the tax return and including a required form. Once a change is made, the nature of the change, the effect of the change on the financial statements, and the reasons the newly adopted method is preferred must be fully disclosed in the notes accompanying the financial statements. Such disclosure is illustrated in Figure 12-4. Without such disclosure, the statement reader may assume that no material changes in accounting methods were made during the period.

> Effective January 1, 19X0, the Company changed its method of determining the cost of its inventories from the first-in, first-out (FIFO) method to the last-in, first-out (LIFO) method. The Company believes the LIFO method will more fairly present results of operations by reducing the effect of inflationary cost increases in inventories and thus match current cost with current revenues. The 19X9 results of operations do not reflect this accounting change. Pro-forma effects of retroactive application of LIFO to prior years are not determinable, and thus there is no cumulative effect on retained earnings at the beginning of the year. Thus the December 31, 19X9, inventories valued at FIFO are the opening LIFO inventories. The effect of the change in 19X0 was to reduce inventory and net earnings by $1,262 000.

FIGURE 12-4
ILLUSTRATION OF REPORTING CHANGE IN INVENTORY COSTING METHOD

PRACTICE ACTIVITY 12-3

Complete the following statements by entering a word or words in the blank space(s) that will make the statement a valid statement.

1. When the _____ inventory system is used, no entry is made at the time of sale to record the cost of goods sold.

2. If unit costs are increasing, the _____ cost flow method produces the lowest net income of the four methods.

3. If unit costs are increasing , the _____ cost flow method will result in the highest ending inventory of the four methods.

4. A physical count of inventory on hand must be taken when the _____ inventory system is used.

5. Under the _____ cost flow method, the costs of the first items purchased are matched against revenue.

6. When using _____, ending inventory is assumed to consist of the first units purchased.

7. The weighted average cost per unit is computed by dividing the _____ ___ _____ _____ _____ _____ by the _____ __ ____ available for sale.

8. Of the four inventory methods, using the _____ method will result in the lowest income tax expense when prices are rising.

9. The _____ principle discourages changing accounting procedures and policies from one period to the next.

10. If prices are increasing, net income using the _____ method will be higher than that computed using LIFO.

11. When prices are increasing, cost of goods sold using the _____ _____ method will be between that produced by FIFO and LIFO.

12. When the _____ _____ costing method is used, the cost of units sold is traced to a specific purchase invoice.

THE LOWER OF COST OR MARKET RULE

Cost is the primary basis for recording and reporting most assets. The four inventory costing methods previously discussed are alternatives for arriving at the cost of inventory when the unit cost fluctuates during an accounting period. However, when the value of inventory or the cost to replace the inventory decreases, it is sometimes considered appropriate to report inventory at an amount below its cost. The decline in value could result from obsolescence, damage, deterioration, or a decline in unit costs caused by supply and demand factors. If, at the end of the period, the cost of replacing the inventory is less than its historical cost, the inventory is written down to the lower replacement cost and a loss is reported. This valuation approach is referred to as the *lower of cost or market (LCM) rule*. Market, as the term is used here, is ***the cost to replace*** the inventory in the quantities typically purchased through the usual sources of supply.

Using a valuation figure that is lower than cost is justified by the convention of conservatism. Under this convention, a decrease in value is recorded in the accounts in the period in which the decrease occurs. Thus, application of the LCM rule results in a loss in inventory value being recorded (matched against revenue) in the period in which the decline in value occurs, rather than in a subsequent period when the inventory is sold. Increases in the cost to replace inventory are not recorded because they have not yet been realized by a sale (revenue principle).

To illustrate, if the ending inventory has a cost of $140,000 and a replacement cost of $138,500, a loss of $1,500 is recognized in the current period. Under a periodic inventory system, the ending inventory amount to be subtracted from the cost of goods available for sale is $138,500. As a result, cost of goods sold is increased by the $1,500. This approach is acceptable if the loss is not material in relation to the cost of goods sold. If the loss is material, it should be reported as a separate item in the income statement, since it is not related to selling goods. On the other hand, if the inventory had a cost of $140,000 and the replacement cost was $142,000, the increase in value is not recognized.

METHODS OF APPLYING THE LCM RULE

The LCM rule may be applied using three alternative approaches. Any of these approaches is acceptable for accounting, but once selected, the method should be used consistently. The LCM rule may be applied as follows:

1. To each inventory item, such as a particular model of tape deck.
2. To each major inventory category, such as all tape decks or all electronics stocked by a department store.
3. To the total inventory.

Computing the ending inventory value using each of these approaches is illustrated in Figure 12-5. The three approaches result in an ending inventory value of $5,860 when applied to each inventory item, $6,070 when applied to major categories, and $6,280 when applied to the total inventory. Whichever approach is used, the ending inventory value computed is reported on the balance sheet and subtracted from the cost of goods available for sale in the income statement. Also, the approach used must be applied consistently.

Several modifications to the LCM rule as illustrated above are used in practice to determine the market value to be compared to historical cost. These modifications and other issues related to applying the LCM rule are discussed in Intermediate Accounting.

| | Unit Price | | | | | LCM | | |
Item	Quantity	Cost	Market Price	Total Cost	Total Market	Item	Major Category	Total Inventory
Computers:								
IT3	4	$400	$250	$1,600	$1,000	$1,000		
IT35	6	600	620	3,600	3,720	3,600		
				5,200	4,720		$4,720	
Printers:								
PRT5	3	150	120	450	360	360		
PRT18	4	225	300	900	1,200	900		
				1,350	1,560		1,350	
				$6,550	$6,280	$5,860	$6,070	$6,280

FIGURE 12-5
APPLYING LCM RULE

NET REALIZABLE VALUE

The inventory of a retail or wholesale business often contains units that have been used or that are obsolete, shop-worn, or damaged. Such inventory items are generally reported at *net realizable value*--the anticipated sales price in the normal course of business, less the estimated cost of selling and disposal. To illustrate, assume that a company is holding a tape deck that cost $340 and normally sells it for $415. Because the unit was used as a demonstrator, however, it is estimated that it could be sold for $310 after the unit is reconditioned for a cost of $45. A sales commission on the unit is expected to be $31. The value of the unit is computed for inventory purposes as follows:

Estimated sales value	$310
Estimated selling and reconditioning cost	76
Estimated net realizable value	$234

Since the estimated net realizable value is below the historical cost of $340, the unit should be carried in the ending inventory at $234. This results in a loss of $106 ($340 – $234) being reported in the period in which the decrease in value occurs, rather than in the period in which the unit is sold. Under a periodic inventory system, the loss becomes a part of the cost of goods sold. (If a perpetual inventory system is used, the inventory card is adjusted to reflect the lower value, and an entry is made to reduce the Merchandise Inventory account and recognize a loss.) If the net realizable value is greater than the historical cost, the inventory is not written up to reflect the higher value. Again, the historical cost of the unit is the upper value to be used in valuation. In addition, if inventory is written down to net realizable value or replacement cost, the new value substitutes for the original cost figure for computations in future periods.

PRACTICE ACTIVITY 12-4

Part 1. Lower of cost or market rule.

Ending inventory for Midtown Home Entertainment Sales is shown below.

Item	Quantity	Unit Cost	Unit Market
Televisions:			
T25	20	$100	$ 80
T55	5	175	190
VCR:			
V15	10	125	140
V75	8	240	230

Required:

Compute the value of the ending inventory applying the LCM rule to:

1. Individual inventory items
2. Major categories of televisions and VCRs
3. Total inventory

Part 2. Net realizable value.

Empire Computer Sales has a personal computer that has been used as a demonstration model. The computer cost $800 and would normally sell for $1,180. Empire estimates that repairs in the amount of $100 are needed, and then the computer could be sold for $900. Empire pays a 15% sales commission to all its salespeople. Compute the net realizable value of the computer.

PERPETUAL INVENTORY SYSTEMS

This part of the chapter illustrates the application of the four cost flow methods--specific identification, FIFO, LIFO, and weighted average--with a perpetual inventory system. Under the perpetual system, the inventory records are updated at the time of purchase or sale. This involves a great deal of time and, consequently, money. The availability of more versatile and less costly computers, however, has allowed more companies to adopt the perpetual inventory system and, thus, to achieve better inventory control.

In a perpetual inventory system, an inventory card is maintained for each item in stock, and an inventory control account is kept in the general ledger. To provide a continuous and current record of inventory transactions, the appropriate inventory card and the Merchandise Inventory account are adjusted as purchases and sales transactions occur. Inventory purchases are recorded at cost in the Merchandise Inventory account and in the individual inventory cards. Chapter 6 showed that the following two entries are made at the time of sale:

Mar.	15	Accounts Receivable (or Cash)	20	
		Sales		20
		Sold one unit of inventory for $20.		
	15	Cost of Goods Sold	10	
		Merchandise Inventory		10
		Transferred cost of unit sold to Cost of		
		Goods Sold account.		

The dollar amount of the first entry is based on the sales price. If the per-unit cost varies, the dollar amount recorded in the second entry depends on the cost flow method used.

SPECIFIC IDENTIFICATION METHOD

The computations for the specific identification method would be the same as those described earlier for a periodic inventory system. They will not be repeated here. The only difference between the two methods is that under the perpetual system an entry is made at the time of sale to record the transfer of cost from the Merchandise Inventory account to the Cost of Goods Sold account.

FIRST-IN, FIRST-OUT METHOD

A perpetual inventory card using the same data presented earlier for the periodic inventory system is shown in Figure 12-6. Note that the perpetual inventory record shows the units and dollar amounts on a continuous basis for goods on hand, goods purchased, and goods sold.

Under the FIFO method, the cost of units removed from inventory is assumed to be from the first units available for sale at the time of each sale. The cost of the units on hand is composed of the most recent purchases. Thus, in Figure 12-6, the cost of the 16 units sold ($160) on April 20 is computed from the unit cost of the earliest units available, which are those in the beginning inventory. The 28 remaining unsold units are identified as (1) four units from the beginning inventory and (2) 24 units from the April 15 purchase.

The identification of units from separate purchases results in what are frequently called "inventory cost layers." For the next sale, the cost of four units from the beginning inventory ($40) and 16 units from the first purchase ($176) is transferred to cost of goods sold. This leaves an ending inventory of 38 units valued at $448. Thus, at the end of the period, the Cost of Goods Sold account will show a balance of $376 ($160 + $216).

Item: Computer Software--Bridge for the Novice   Minimum Stock: 10
Code: CS115   Location: Store Display   Maximum Stock: 60

Date	Explanation	Purchases			Cost of Goods Sold			Balance		
		Unit	Unit Cost	Total Cost	Unit	Unit Cost	Total Cost	Units	Unit Cost	Total Cost
1/1	Beginning balance							20	10.00	200.00
4/15	Purchases	24	11.00	264.00				20	10.00	200.00
								24	11.00	264.00
4/20	Sales				16	10.00	160.00	4	10.00	40.00
								24	11.00	264.00
7/7	Purchases	30	12.00	360.00				4	10.00	40.00
								24	11.00	264.00
								30	12.00	360.00
8/12	Sales				4	10.00	40.00	8	11.00	88.00
					16	11.00	176.00	30	12.00	360.00

FIGURE 12-6
INVENTORY CARD PERPETUAL INVENTORY SYSTEM – FIFO COST FLOW METHOD

LAST-IN, FIRST-OUT METHOD

When the LIFO method (see Figure 12-7) is used in conjunction with a perpetual inventory system, the cost of goods sold is determined at the point of each sale, based on the assumption that the last units acquired are the first ones sold. Thus, the cost of the 16 units sold on April 20 consists of the cost of the most recent units purchased on April 15. The inventory balance of 28 units consists of two inventory cost layers--20 units from the beginning inventory and eight units from the April 15 purchase. Similarly, the 20 units sold on August 12 are identified with the most recent units acquired on July 7. The cost of goods sold for the period is $416 ($176 + $240). The ending inventory is $408 ($200 + $88 + $120).

Item: Computer Software--Bridge for the Novice
Code: CS115   Location: Store Display

Minimum Stock: 10
Maximum Stock: 60

Date	Explanation	Purchases Unit	Unit Cost	Total Cost	Cost of Goods Sold Unit	Unit Cost	Total Cost	Balance Units	Unit Cost	Total Cost
1/1	Beginning balance							20	10.00	200.00
4/15	Purchases	24	11.00	264.00				20	10.00	200.00
								24	11.00	264.00
4/20	Sales				16	11.00	176.00	20	10.00	200.00
								8	11.00	88.00
7/7	Purchases	30	12.00	360.00				20	10.00	200.00
								8	11.00	88.00
								30	12.00	360.00
8/12	Sales				20	12.00	240.00	20	10.00	200.00
								8	11.00	88.00
								10	12.00	120.00

FIGURE 12-7
INVENTORY CARD PERPETUAL INVENTORY SYSTEM – LIFO COST FLOW METHOD

MOVING AVERAGE METHOD

Under the moving average method (see Figure 12-8), a new average cost per unit is computed after each purchase, rather than simply computing a weighted average at year-end. The moving average cost is used to compute the cost of goods sold and inventory on hand until additional units are acquired at a different unit price. It is computed as follows:

$$\frac{\text{Cost of goods available for sales currently}}{\text{Total number of units available for sale currently}} = \text{Moving average cost}$$

In our illustration, the average cost per unit after the April 15 purchase is:

($200 + $264) ÷ (20 units + 24 units) = $10.55 per unit

Since there were no additional purchases made before the sale of the 16 units on April 20, the cost of the units sold is $168.80 (16 units x $10.55 per unit). The 28 units on hand are valued at $295.20 ($464.00 – $168.80). As a result of rounding, the cost of the units on hand is approximately equal to the 28 units times the $10.55 per unit. This average $10.55 cost would be used to cost additional units sold until another purchase is made, at which time a new moving average cost is computed, as shown in Figure 12-8.

Item: Computer Software--Bridge for the Novice   Minimum Stock: 10
Code: CS115   Location: Store Display   Maximum Stock: 60

		Purchases			Cost of Goods Sold			Balance		
Date	Explanation	Unit	Unit Cost	Total Cost	Unit	Unit Cost	Total Cost	Units	Unit Cost	Total Cost
1/1	Beginning balance							20	10.00	200.00
4/15	Purchases	24	11.00	264.00				44	10.55	464.00
4/20	Sales				16	10.55	168.80	28	10.55	295.20
7/7	Purchases	30	12.00	360.00				58	11.30	655.20
8/12	Sales				20	11.30	226.00	38	11.30	429.20

Computations
4/15 ($200.00 + $264.00) / (20 units + 24 units) = $10.55 per unit*
7/7 ($295.20 + $360.00) / (28 units + 30 units) = $11.30 per unit
     *Rounded to the nearest cent.

FIGURE 12-8
INVENTORY CARD PERPETUAL INVENTORY SYSTEM – MOVING AVERAGE COST FLOW METHOD

PRACTICE ACTIVITY 12-5

The Lucille Mitchell Corporation uses a perpetual inventory system. The inventory records for June 19X2, are shown below:

Transactions	Units	Unit Cost
Beginning inventory, June 1	200	$8.00
Purchase, June 10	500	8.60
Sale, June 12 (at $15 per unit)	330	
Purchase, June 18	400	9.20
Sale, June 30 (at $16 per unit)	540	

Required:

A. Prepare an inventory card for the month of June assuming a FIFO cost flow.
B. Prepare an inventory card for the month of June assuming a LIFO cost flow.
C. Prepare an inventory card for the month of June, assuming a moving average cost flow. (Round computations to the nearest cent.)

A. FIFO

Date	Explanation	Purchases			Cost of Goods Sold			Balance		
		Unit	Unit Cost	Total Cost	Unit	Unit Cost	Total Cost	Units	Unit Cost	Total Cost

B. LIFO

Date	Explanation	Purchases			Cost of Goods Sold			Balance		
		Unit	Unit Cost	Total Cost	Unit	Unit Cost	Total Cost	Units	Unit Cost	Total Cost

C. Moving average

Date	Explanation	Purchases			Cost of Goods Sold			Balance		
		Unit	Unit Cost	Total Cost	Unit	Unit Cost	Total Cost	Units	Unit Cost	Total Cost

COMPARISON OF COSTING METHODS

The justifications and disadvantages of using each method are the same as those discussed earlier for the periodic inventory system and will not be repeated here. The relative dollar amounts of cost of goods sold, net income, and ending inventory produced by the four methods would also be the same. That is, in periods of rising prices, LIFO will produce a higher cost of goods sold, a lower net income, and a lower ending inventory than the FIFO or average cost methods.

COMPARISON OF THE PERPETUAL AND PERIODIC INVENTORY SYSTEMS

Application of the four alternative cost flow assumptions has been illustrated using the same data for both the periodic and perpetual inventory systems. For comparison, the results obtained for both systems are presented in Figure 12-9. Figure 12-9 assumes that the 36 units are sold for a total of $720. Operating expenses are $180, and the average income tax rate is 30%.

Perpetual Inventory System

	Specific Identification	FIFO	LIFO	Moving Average
Sales--36 units	$720	$720	$720	$720
Less: Cost of goods sold	404	376	416	395
Gross profit on sales	316	344	304	325
Less: Operating expenses	180	180	180	180
Income before taxes	136	164	124	145
Less: Income taxes--30%*	41	49	37	44
Net income	$ 95	$115	$ 87	$101
Ending inventory	$420	$448	$408	$429

Periodic Inventory System
(From Figure 12-3)

	Specific Identification	FIFO	LIFO	Weighted Average
Sales--36 units	$720	$720	$720	$720
Beginning inventory	200	200	200	200
Add: Purchases	624	624	624	624
Goods available for sale	824	824	824	824
Less: Ending inventory	420	448	398	423
Cost of goods sold	404	376	426	401
Gross profit on sales	316	344	294	319
Less: Operating expenses	180	180	180	180
Income before taxes	136	164	114	139
Less: Income taxes--30%*	41	49	34	42
Net income	$ 95	$115	$ 80	$ 97
Ending inventory	$420	$448	$398	$423

*Income taxes are rounded to the nearest dollar.

FIGURE 12-9
COMPARISON OF INVENTORY SYSTEMS AND FOUR COSTING METHODS

Specific Identification and FIFO Methods

Using either inventory system, both the specific identification and FIFO methods assign the same amount of cost to the ending inventory and cost of goods sold. The values obtained with the specific identification method are the same because the units identified as sold are the same under both inventory systems. Using FIFO, the same amounts are obtained because the cost of goods sold is computed, assuming that the oldest units available for sale are always sold first.

LIFO Method

When the LIFO method is used, both the ending inventory and the cost of goods sold dollar amounts may vary between the perpetual and periodic systems (see Figure 12-10). The periodic system with LIFO produced a cost of goods sold of $426 and an ending inventory of $398. The amounts for a perpetual inventory system were $416 and $408, respectively. The two methods produce different results because of the timing of the computation of cost of goods sold.

Under the periodic system, the cost of goods sold is computed at the end of the period, and the dates of sale are ignored. Under the perpetual system, the cost of goods sold is computed at the time of each sale. The cost of goods sold and ending inventory computations for both inventory systems are as follows:

Under a periodic system with LIFO, the last units purchased with a higher unit cost were included in the cost of goods sold computation; the lower cost units in the beginning inventory and first purchase are considered to be on hand in the ending inventory.

When the perpetual system is used and prices are rising, units with a lower cost (i.e., the more recent purchases at the time of each sale) are charged to cost of goods sold. As a result, ten units of the last purchase on July 7 are included in the ending inventory.

Average Cost Method

Although the computation of average cost is essentially the same under both systems, each system produces different results when prices change during the reporting period. This difference occurs because under the periodic system, one weighted average cost is used to cost all goods sold during the entire period. When a periodic weighted average is computed (at the end of the period), it is affected by the higher unit cost of purchases made late in the period. Under the perpetual system, the cost transferred to cost of goods sold each time a sale is made is based on a moving average. The moving average is unaffected by price changes that occur after the sale. When prices increase, a moving average will yield a lower cost of goods sold and a higher ending inventory than a periodic weighted average.

When prices are changing, the periodic and perpetual systems will produce different net income figures under the LIFO and average costing methods. The extent of the variation is determined primarily by the rate of change in prices during the period and the frequency with which the inventory is purchased and sold.

Periodic Inventory System (LIFO)				Perpetual Inventory System (See Figure 12-7) (LIFO)			
COST OF GOODS SOLD							
Date Acquired	Units	Unit Cost	Total	Date Acquired	Units	Unit Cost	Total
4/15	6	$11	$ 66	4/15	16	$11	$176
7/7	30	12	360	7/7	20	12	240
Cost of goods sold			426	Cost of goods sold			416
ENDING INVENTORY							
1/1	20	$10	$200	1/1	20	$10	$200
4/15	18	11	198	4/15	8	11	88
--	--	--	--	7/7	10	12	120
Ending inventory			398	Ending inventory			408
Total cost of goods available for sale			$824	Total cost of goods available for sale			$824

FIGURE 12-10
COMPARISON OF LIFO METHOD

SOLUTIONS TO PRACTICE ACTIVITIES

PRACTICE ACTIVITY 12-1

1. buyer
2. Evans, consignor
3. FOB destination
4. seller

PRACTICE ACTIVITY 12-2

	FIFO	LIFO	Weighted Average	Specific Identification
Beginning inventory	$ 2,000	$ 2,000	$ 2,000	$ 2,000
Add: Purchases	10,400	10,400	10,400	10,400
Goods available for sale	12,400	12,400	12,400	12,400
Less: Ending inventory	6,200	3,400	4,650	4,360
Cost of goods sold	$ 6,200	$ 9,000	$ 7,750	$ 8,040

Ending inventory computations
FIFO

March 22	purchase	200 X $22 =	$4,400
March 15	purchase	100 X $18 =	1,800
			$6,200

LIFO

Beginning inventory		200 X $10=	$2,000
March 3	purchase	100 X $14 =	1,400
			$3,400

Weighted average
Cost of goods available for sale ÷ units available for sale
$12,400 ÷ 800 = $15.50
Ending inventory = 300 units X $15.50 = $4,650

Specific identification

Beginning inventory		100 X $10=	$1,000
March 3	purchase	80 X $14=	1,120
March 15	purchase	100 X $18=	1,800
March 22	purchase	20 X $22 =	440
			$4,360

PRACTICE ACTIVITY 12-3

1. periodic
2. LIFO
3. FIFO
4. periodic
5. FIFO
6. LIFO
7. cost of goods available for sale, number of units
8. LIFO
9. consistency
10. FIFO
11. weighted average
12. specific identification

PRACTICE ACTIVITY 12-4
Part 1

Item	Quantity	Cost	Market	Cost	Market	LCM by Item	LCM by Category
Televisions:							
T25	20	$100	$ 80	$2,000	$1,600	$1,600	
T55	5	$175	$190	875	950	875	
Totals				2,875	2,550		$2,550
VCR:							
V15	10	$125	$140	1,250	1,400	$1,250	
V75	8	$240	$230	1,920	1,840	1,840	
Totals				3,170	3,240		3,170
Total inventory				$6,045	$5,790		
Totals						$5,565	$5,720

LCM based on total inventory $5,790

Part 2

Estimated sales value		$900
Estimated selling and disposal cost:		
Repairs	$100	
Sales commissions (15% X $900)	135	235
Net realizable value		$665

PRACTICE ACTIVITY 12-5

A.   FIFO

Date	Explanation	Purchases Unit	Purchases Unit Cost	Purchases Total Cost	Cost of Goods Sold Unit	Cost of Goods Sold Unit Cost	Cost of Goods Sold Total Cost	Balance Units	Balance Unit Cost	Balance Total Cost
6/1	Beginning balance							200	8.00	1,60
6/10	Purchases	500	8.60	4.30				200	8.00	1,60
								500	8.60	4,30
6/12	Sales				200	8.00	1,60			
					130	8.60	1,11	370	8.60	3,18
6/18	Purchases	400	9.20	3,68				370	8.60	3,18
								400	9.20	3,68
6/30	Sales				370	8.60	3,18			
					170	9.20	1,56	230	9.20	2,11

B.   LIFO

Date	Explanation	Purchases Unit	Purchases Unit Cost	Purchases Total Cost	Cost of Goods Sold Unit	Cost of Goods Sold Unit Cost	Cost of Goods Sold Total Cost	Balance Units	Balance Unit Cost	Balance Total Cost
6/1	Beginning balance							200	8.00	1,60
6/10	Purchases	500	8.60	4.30				200	8.00	1,60
								500	8.60	4,30
6/12	Sales				330	8.60	2,83	200	8.00	1,60
								170	8.60	1,46
6/18	Purchases	400	9.20	3,68				200	8.00	1,60
								170	8.60	1,46
								400	9.20	3,68
6/30	Sales				400	9.20	3,68	200	8.00	1,60
					140	8.60	1,20	30	8.60	25

C.   Moving average

Date	Explanation	Purchases Unit	Purchases Unit Cost	Purchases Total Cost	Cost of Goods Sold Unit	Cost of Goods Sold Unit Cost	Cost of Goods Sold Total Cost	Balance Units	Balance Unit Cost	Balance Total Cost
6/1	Beginning balance							200	8.00	1,600.0
6/10	Purchases	500	8.60	4.300.0				700	8.43	5,900.0
6/12	Sales				330	8.43	2,781.9	370	8.43	3,118.1
6/18	Purchases	400	9.20	3,680.0				770	8.83	6,798.1
6/30	Sales				540	8.83	4768.2	230	8.83	2,029.9

Moving average unit cost:

After June 10 purchase   ($1,600.00 + $4,300.00) ÷ (200 + 500) = $8.43 per unit

After June 18 purchase   ($3,118.10 + $3,680.00) ÷ (370 + 400) = $8.83 per unit